2"

To Shirley.

Enjoy this "Dance"
May your own dance
be long and very
blessed.

M.M. Rhom

Dancing through Time

and other essays

Dancing through Time

and other essays

Y. Y. RUBINSTEIN

TARGUM/FELDHEIM

First published 2002
Copyright © 2002 by Y. Y. Rubinstein
ISBN 1-56871-208-1

All rights reserved

No part of this publication may be translated, reproduced, stored in a retrieval system, or transmitted in any form or by any means, electronic, mechanical, photocopying, recording, or otherwise, without prior permission in writing from both the copyright holder and the publisher.

Published by:
TARGUM PRESS, INC.
22700 W. Eleven Mile Rd.
Southfield, MI 48034
E-mail: targum@netvision.net.il
Fax: 888-298-9992
www.targum.com

Distributed by:
FELDHEIM PUBLISHERS
202 Airport Executive Park
Nanuet, NY 10954

Printed in Israel

HAGAON HARAV MATISYAHU SALOMON, *shlita*
Mashgiach Ruchani of Beth Medrash Govoha
Lakewood, New Jersey

I have read the essays prepared for a book called *Dancing through Time* written by Rabbi Yehudah Yonah Rubinstein, *shlita*.

These essays are both rich in content and style. They will surely inspire the reader to a greater awareness of Divine Providence and the destiny of a Jew in our world.

I have known Rabbi Rubinstein, *shlita*, for many years, and his success in bringing the Torah message to the broader public is already legendary.

This book will serve as another leap in his ever expanding service to *Klal Yisrael*.

            Rabbi Matisyahu Salomon

RABBI B. RAKOW
Rav of Gateshead
138 Whitehall Road, Gateshead NE8 1TP, Tyne & Wear

ב"ה חודש מרחשוון תשס"ב לפ"ק

ידידי הרב יהודה יונה רובינשטיין שליט"א הראה לי קובץ של מאמרים בעניני השקפה שכבר פרסם בעתונות המודיע ועוד.

הרב הנ"ל מפורסם כבר לנאה דורש ונאה מקרב צעירים לתורה ותעודה. ומאד מצליח בשיעוריו שנאמרו ברבים שהם מלאי תוכן של יראת שמים והשקפת התורה.

ועכשיו הוא נדרש ע"י אחרים לפרסם המאמרים בצורת ספר, ובזה יהיה תועלת לרבים גם מי שאינו קורא בעיתונות

וודאי הוא עניין טוב ומועיל וגם ידי תחזקנה ומאחל לידידי בזה הצלחה לברך על המוגמר ויצלח בזה לזכות את הרבים המבקשים דרך האמת להשקפת התורה.

ידידו מברכו
הק' בצלאל ראקאוו

In memory of

KATIE MANSON ע״ה
ביילא בת יונתן לייב

An adored and treasured daughter and sister
who gave love, laughter,
and smiles to all who met her

In loving memory of

MOISHE YOUNGER ז״ל
משה יואל בן מנחם דב

Satmar, Glasgow, Manchester

Who was respected by all who knew him
and is sorely missed by his wife and sons

In memory of

RUTH ZAIRE
BAS AVROHOM ע״ה
December 23, 1964
18 Teves 5725

A true *eishes chayil* who inspired many
and is remembered by all
who came in contact with her

Gita and Abe Wagschal

In loving memory of

DOV (BERNARD) KAHN ז״ל
London, England

Who loved and supported Torah
in England and Israel
and helped in founding the
yishuv in Eretz Yisrael

His grandchildren and great-grandchildren

Contents

Foreword 13
Preface 17
A Tale of Two Cities 21
Keep Looking Up 25
Dancing through Time 29
Finding the Very, Very Best 35
Put in the Big Rocks First 40
From Cardboard to Concrete 45
The Violinist and the Artist 50
Beware Empty Black Taxis 55
New York, Lockerbie, and Sedom 60
Lost in Glasgow 67
If You'll Take My Advice 73
Counted In and Counted Out 78
Teaching…or Teaching Talmidim 83
Avraham's Gift 89
Smile 93
Chinese Whispers 98
The Hand, Not the Foot 103
Virtual Chesed 109
A Very Stubborn People 114
When the Cub Becomes a Lion 119
Not Seeing the End 127
Seeing through the Satan 133

Please...Help Yourself 137
Flight AA 176 Los Angeles to London 141
The Chesed Bank 148
Have a Safe Journey Home 154
There Are No Prophets — Not Even You 160
The Flight to Teshuvah 166
Hidden Fruit 170
Happy Families 174
Avoiding Mistakes 179
Judaism and Magic 184
The Stamp of Approval 192
The Further Away You Are, the Louder the Call 198
The Torah Is a Minimum 207
The Greatness of a Little Yud 214

SELECTIONS ON THE YAMIM TOVIM
A Door That's Never Closed 223
Hearing the Shofar's True Call 228
Forgiving the Unforgivable 232
Winning the War 237
Building with Mesiras Nefesh 241
When "They" Become "Us" 246
Peering behind the Veil 251
Saintly Women B'Chol Dor VaDor 256
Struggling with Memory 261
Sorry, No Change 266
Putting Someone in Your Pocket 271
Finding the Right Place 275
Even Still 281
  Glossary 287

Foreword

BY RAV SHLOMO ASCHKENASY
Rosh Kollel of Boston in Jerusalem and Hamodia Torah editor

Years ago a famous *maggid* from Yerushalayim came to America and told the following story.

There was a man who was addicted to alcohol. Every day his family found him lying in a stupor in a corner of their home. Trying to find a means to help the head of their household out of this unpleasant state, some family members came up with a brilliant idea. "Surely he's not aware of what he looks like when he's drunk. If he would only know, he would take himself in hand and change."

They decided that in one of his sober moments they would take him to a place where there were many drunkards lying in the street. They were certain that he would find the sordid sight repugnant and be motivated to make a change.

They did as planned, and at the right moment they took their father to a yard in front of a bar. There was one drunkard lying in the gutter who was a most disgusting sight. He was tossing from side to side, filthy from head to toe, covered with mud from the street. In this semiconscious state, he was really a pitiful sight.

As they approached the man, their father emitted a sound. They thought he must be expressing sympathy for the poor fellow. But when they got close enough, they couldn't believe what happened next. Their father let out a broad smile, bent over the drunkard, and asked, "Brother, tell me, what wine did you drink to get into such a state? How did you do it? It must have been really great stuff!"

Mussar greats and chassidic masters taught that although different people may see the same thing, each one has his interpretation of what he is looking at. Rabbi Yehudah Yonah Rubinstein has a very perceptive eye. He moves through the myriad events that constitute the story of our lives, takes a snapshot, studies it, and learns a lesson. Others might barely notice the incident, and if they do, it's only for its trivial details. Not so Rabbi Rubinstein. He sees the world with Torah eyes, envisioning a stage upon which the timeless lessons of the Torah are played.

My rebbe, Rav Gedalya Schorr, *zt"l*, used to interpret David HaMelech's prayer, *"Gal einai v'abitah* — Open my eyes so that I may see wonders from your Torah" (*Tehillim* 119:18) in this vein. David was beseeching Hashem not just to see and descend into the depths and wonders of the Torah. He was asking Hashem to open his eyes and clarify his views through Torah so he would see everything in the appropriate light.

Every morning we daven to Hashem and make a very heartfelt plea for compassion concerning our Torah study. We beg, *"Avinu av harachaman...* — Our Father, merciful Father, Who is so merciful, have pity upon us and imbue our heart with insight to understand and comprehend, to listen, to learn and to teach, to keep, adhere, and fulfill all the words of your Torah." A most detailed and elaborate request that seems to cover every aspect of Torah study and observance.

Yet immediately thereafter comes another request: *"V'ha'er*

Foreword

eineinu b'Torasecha... — Enlighten our eyes in Torah, attach our hearts to your mitzvos, and unify our hearts to love and fear Your Name." What is the meaning of this additional request?

It is not enough to learn, study, know, understand, and keep the Torah. One must also strive to be enlightened by the Torah, to open the eyes and the soul and see the world in a different light, with the bright, crystal-clear view of Torah. With Torah eyes the world becomes a different place, one which is a source of inspiration for *deveikus*, attachment to Hashem out of love and fear.

For a long time, readers of *Hamodia* newspaper have been privileged to be exposed to the visions of Rabbi Rubinstein's Torah glasses. Sometimes he uses a telescope to make closer things look far away so that we can see the big picture. Sometimes he uses a microscope to study minute details and reveal fascinating insights. Sometimes he teaches us to use a periscope, showing us that we are in deep water and how we must raise ourselves up out of the murkiness to get a true view of things. At all times, whenever we read an article from Rabbi Rubinstein, we find ourselves dancing — whether through the various places he visits or through the different ideas he expounds upon or simply out of joy at his enlightening insight. Most important, though, whatever time we spend reading his articles is good time, well invested and with very lucrative returns.

I am sure that just as thousands of readers of *Hamodia* have benefited from and enjoyed reading Rabbi Rubinstein's articles, this book will provide its readers with revelations that will make life's dance more comprehensible and joyously in tune with the song of the Torah.

My personal wishes to Rabbi Yehudah Yonah for continued Heaven-sent success in his dissemination of Torah throughout the world in oratory and in writing.

Preface

One of my teachers told me that his rabbi went to see the saintly Chafetz Chaim before taking up a rabbinical position. After giving various pieces of advice, the Chafetz Chaim sent him on his way with the words "*Alleh mohl mit a ma'aseh* — Always with a story." The Chafetz Chaim was saying that the Torah's teachings should be illuminated by the use of stories.

I have been privileged to be close to some of the greatest *rabbanim* and teachers of our time. And while traveling to speak to Jewish audiences all over the world, I have known many simple, ordinary Jews from every part of the globe. If truth be told, there is no such thing as an "ordinary" Jew. Every Jew is a story — often many stories. Some of these people you will meet in the pages of *Dancing through Time*. All are inspirational, and all deserve their own book. Their stories have enormously enhanced the Torah contained in these pages.

The Mishnah often begins with the words "*Hu hayah omer* — He used to say." I heard a different translation from the head of Manchester's famous Bais Yaakov Seminary, where I sometimes teach: "He was and he said." The essential prerequisite to any Jewish book is that its author exemplify the ideas he is writing about. Aristotle is said to have proclaimed to his students, "Learn from what I say, not from what I do." Someone with that attitude could never have written a book worthy of a place on a Jewish bookshelf.

Dancing through Time

The most I can claim is that I try to adhere to the ideas of the Torah giants whose teachings I quote in these pages. Certainly I can promise you that every story you will find here is true, although the details have often been changed to protect the privacy of the people whose stories they are.

There are so many people that I should give thanks to, but I believe that introductions should be as short as possible, and anyway you will meet most of them in the pages of *Dancing through Time*. I would be remiss, though, not to mention those who have the most claim on my time but were willing to let me travel all over the world to meet the people who appear in these pages — my children, Binyomin Zev and Esther, Aryeh Leib and Rivka, Eliyahu Eliezer, Moshe Dovid, Rivka Leah, and Rochel Miriam. I would also like to extend my sincere thanks to everyone at Targum Press. They have been a pleasure to get to know and to work with. There is someone, though, who has to be mentioned specially, so let me tell you a story.

Many years ago I worked for the well-known women's seminary, Neve Yerushalayim. Often young women would come into our home and mention to my wife that they were hoping to meet the person who would be their perfect match, their *bashert*. My wife would ask them what sort of person they were looking for. One young lady unhesitatingly replied, "Oh! Someone just like your husband."

This young woman was young and idealistic and hoped to have a life involved in reaching out to Jews who, like her, had never had the chance to discover what their religion and people were all about. At that time I was exclusively involved in *kiruv* (outreach). I conformed exactly to the sort of person she saw herself marrying.

When my wife heard this, she smiled and replied wisely, "You know, he wasn't like this when I married him!"

Nor was I.

Preface

She was trying to convey the Torah's teaching that everything goes after the woman. She was telling this young woman that her role was to marry some young man and guide him and help him to fulfill his potential. And so, I would like to thank the true author of *Dancing through Time*, my wife.

A Tale of Two Cities

(Hamodia, October 1999)

New York and Gibraltar are two places that don't immediately invite comparison. You look up at the buildings in New York, and you look up and up and...well, up! You look up at the buildings in Gibraltar, and you find you don't have to lift your head very high.

New York is a huge place with a population of about eight and a half million. Gibraltar has a population of about thirty-five thousand. Economically, culturally, artistically, academically, and by almost every other measure, New York reflects its giant status. Gibraltar is, well, small. You would have to try very hard, indeed, to find any comparison beyond those made in the most general sense. Except in one area: their Jews.

A few weeks ago I was lecturing in New York. One of my closest friends, Rabbi Dovid Gottlieb of Yerushalayim, also spends much of his time speaking abroad. I recall him once telling me that one of the compensations for being away from your family is that you invariably find yourself staying with the nicest people. On this New York trip I struck gold.

My hosts were a chassidic couple whose children have already grown up and married. The *ba'al habayis* found a few days off from work during which he treated me to a tour of Boro Park. He showed me scores of shuls, yeshivos, and the splendor of the institutions of Bobov. He worried about whether I had phoned home and had enough food. When he was satisfied that I had everything I needed, he would go off to one of the several *shiurim* he attended each day. We would rendezvous at *ma'ariv* and return to his home for supper.

At one meal his wife mentioned the difficulties involved in maintaining a true Jewish perspective when surrounded by the wealth and opulence of America. "While we are busy trying to live it down," she commented, "others are busy trying to live it up!"

For this couple and their family and friends there was Torah, davening, and helping other people, in keeping with the dictum "*Al sheloshah devarim ha'olam omeid...* — On three things the world stands: on Torah, on prayer, and on acts of kindness."

The week before I had spoken in Gibraltar. The tiny Jewish community manages to maintain a Jewish school system, with primary grades and separate boys' and girls' secondary schools, four synagogues, a kosher restaurant, and a *kollel*. Here, overlooking the narrowest bit of the Mediterranean, where you can see across the sea to Morocco, can be heard the sounds of Torah being learned and taught.

One of the synagogues, which must be the most beautiful shul I have ever seen, is called "Nefutzot Yehudah." Its patterned, ornate plasterwork and hanging silver candleholders complement a stunning *aron kodesh* of absolutely unique design. The chazzan is an elderly man whose voice still carries a gentle beauty and whose passion for Sefardic melodies has only grown in his seventy-seven years.

He found me in the shul one night. I had arrived well before my lecture, and he approached me with a concerned expression. "You look as though you are worried about something," he said. Indeed, I had been thinking over a problem or two. He looked up into my eyes and put his arms on my shoulders and started to sing

A Tale of Two Cities

to me. The tune was one I had never heard before, and the words he sang so quietly were words of *Tehillim*: "He will not allow your foot to stumble. Your Guardian will not slumber" (*Tehillim* 121:3).

This was his *berachah* to me, expressed so sincerely in the way he knew best. Someone told me he often does this if he likes someone or sees him looking worried.

Another town, another place, but here, too, Torah, prayer, and tremendous *chesed*.

At the end of *Mishpatim*, Moshe, Aharon, Nadav, Avihu, and the Elders ascend Har Sinai. The Torah reports that they saw a vision of Hashem. Under His "feet" was a floor made of sapphire bricks. Rashi comments that the flooring in Heaven was like this throughout the enslavement of the Jews in Egypt to act as a constant reminder of their bitter situation, that they had to build with bricks. The obvious difficulty with this *Rashi* is that Hashem doesn't need a reminder. He is constantly aware of everything.

Reb Simchah Zissel, *zt"l*, explains that if you are going to be able to be concerned about people and want to help them, you must picture their situation clearly in your mind. After that, you must take it a stage further — imagine the same picture, only with you in it. That was the message Hashem was giving to Moshe with this vision.

Earlier in the parashah, the Torah demands, "If you lend my people money, the poor man with you, do not press him for repayment and do not charge interest." Rashi questions why the verse says "the poor man with you," and he makes the same point: "Picture yourself as though you were the poor man."

There is a famous *gemara* that states, "Rav Acha bar Chaninah says: Someone who visits an ill person takes away one-sixtieth of his illness" (*Nedarim* 39b). The Gemara exclaims, "Then let sixty people visit a sick person to cure him!" The statement of Rav Acha bar Chaninah is then qualified. The first visitor takes away one-sixtieth of the person's suffering. The second visitor takes away one-sixtieth of the remainder, and the next takes away one-sixtieth of the remaining fraction. Sixty visitors will not be enough. Then the Gemara makes a further qualification. Only if the visitor is *"ben gilo"* will he be able to alleviate the person's condition.

Rashi says *"ben gilo"* refers to a young man visiting a young man or an old man visiting an old man. The Ran says *"ben gilo"* means the visitor has to have been born with the same *mazal*, under the same constellation, as the ill person. Both are saying the same thing. The visitor needs to be able to picture himself as though he were the one who is ill. In Heaven they have decided that the invalid should have a certain amount of suffering, no more and no less. If someone feels so much empathy with the sufferer that he sees himself as though he were lying there, he will take some of the suffering that was intended for the person he is visiting. That amount of pain is no longer available to give to the patient.

While I was in New York, I went into the Lakewood Beis Midrash on Sixteenth Avenue to daven *minchah*. There sat scores of partners learning together, most well over sixty years old. Chairs scraped the floor as people stood up and started to daven. When they did so, it was with the sincerity and concentration that a lifetime of davening produces. There was total concentration and sincerity. I turned my mind back to the elderly chazzan who had sang to me a few days before in Gibraltar.

Here, too, was *Klal Yisrael*. Whether young or old, in one city or another you will find them learning Hashem's Torah or davening with complete devotion. If you are a guest from out of town, you'll find them bombarding you with the most unbelievable *chesed*. Just before they approach you, they will have pictured themselves as the stranger in town and wondered, *If I were in that situation, what would I like people to do for me?* Then they will be asking if you have a place to stay or would you join them for a meal and worrying about whether you've had a chance to phone home.

Keep Looking Up

(The Jewish Tribune, November, 26, 1998)

A while ago I was standing in a train station in London. Together with hundreds of others, I gazed up at the screens that show the times and locations of departing trains. The board announced that the train to Manchester was being prepared. It was taking so long. I pictured them finishing off the welding on the undercarriage and giving it its final coat of paint.

Beside the screen, there was another, bigger and brighter one. This one flashed that week's television programs on a certain channel. Commuters standing around bored, waiting for other "unprepared" trains, were meant to comfort themselves with the prospect of what they could spend the evening watching.

The TV screen also advertised for contributors to forthcoming documentaries that they had in the "pipeline." One gem was a search for volunteers to tell of their bizarre past. "Would you be willing to come onto a new talk show and share your story with the nation?" They also tempted the train travelers with their breakfast program, in which the hosts would "as usual" be looking through the morning papers for the "strangest" stories.

Neither I nor anyone reading this will feel deprived that we will not be seeing any of these works of art. The clash between our values and those portrayed on television was transparent to the *gedolim* as soon as the "box" arrived on the scene. That clash would now be more of a full-scale war as programming spins farther and farther away from a moral orbit. There is hardly any necessity to state the obvious — that Torah and TV don't mix.

But the damage tabloid television inflicts on society at large does affect us, if only because it affects those who watch it. The effect is subtle but present nevertheless as we enter an office, go shopping, or walk down the street. How people see themselves affects how we see ourselves.

In the Torah we read that Noach was a complete tzaddik in his generation. Every tzaddik uses a unique approach in his *avodas Hashem*. Avraham used *chesed* (kindness), Yitzchak used *yiras Hashem* (fear of God), and Yaakov used *emes* (truth).

Several years ago I was lecturing at the Normandy Hotel in Bournemouth. The hotel's minyan was honored by the presence of the late Manchester *rosh yeshivah*, who was staying in a nearby flat. Numbers were a bit tight, and after the Friday night davening, he turned to me and asked, "Yehudah Yonah, will you be davening with us tomorrow?"

"*Im yirtzeh Hashem*," I replied.

The *rosh yeshivah* nodded and turned to go, but then he turned back and with a smile and a sparkle in his eyes added that his attendance was also *"im yirtzeh Hashem."*

To see his davening was to be inspired and the tears that required so many tissues during *Shemoneh Esreh* showed exactly what true *tefillah* should be. Prayer is also a path to *tzidkus* (righteousness).

Moshe Rabbeinu was *"anav me'od mikol adam* — humbler than any other man." The Satmar Rebbe, *zt"l*, asks, how would a student of physics feel in the presence of Einstein or a music student meeting with Beethoven? Naturally they would be awed and humbled. But it wasn't the fact that Moshe so frequently came face to face with Hashem that sparked his humility. Moshe would feel humble

Keep Looking Up

even in the presence of you or me! Chazal say that Moshe knew exactly what his greatness was and where his *tzidkus* lay. By looking at others and seeing qualities and talents he did not have, he maintained his humility.

Rav Shlomo Wolbe, *shlita*, suggests a way of discovering what we are really like. Imagine a slide projector. The image we are looking at on the screen is exactly the picture that is inside the machine. What is inside us is what we see in other people! A tzaddik like Moshe Rabbeinu will always be worrying that his own *avodas Hashem* is deficient, but what he projects onto other people is what is inside him. Moshe would see his own greatness in others. Achieving humility requires other people.

Noach's path to *tzidkus* was also through humility, as Rashi reveals in tractate *Avodah Zarah*. But he did not have other people to look to in order to become a perfect *anav*. Hashem had already told him that the people in his generation were so wicked that they were to be destroyed. He would be unable to see their good qualities — they had none. He would be unable to project his *tzidkus* onto them, because he was told that they were evil. The Satmar Rebbe makes a brilliant observation. The last verse in *Bereishis* says, "And Noach found favor in the eyes of Hashem." The Midrash explains that how he did so is found in the first verse of *Noach*: "These are the generations of Noach." When Noach could no longer look "horizontally," to the people of his own generation, he looked up "vertically," toward the future generations that would come from him. He saw the qualities in Avraham and his sons that would allow him to remain a perfect *anav*.

The Satmar Rebbe's insight reveals an essential truth. How we see ourselves and the level we may reach is dependent on those we see around us. Society in general defines its mores through the people and values they are exposed to. Commuters return from work night after night to spend their evenings "glued to the box," watching programs that are morally corrosive. That defines how they see themselves. In our inevitable interactions among society, it becomes harder and harder to maintain that crucial Jewish trait of humility.

The Satmar Rebbe's explanation of how Noach solved his problem becomes an essential prescription. When it is hard to look horizontally, we must look vertically, up to those individuals who can inspire — *gedolim*, of course, but others, too, average Jews, if there is such a thing.

I knew a man who lived in Prestwich who always arrived at *simchah*s before they were due to start. He told me he did this so that no one should feel embarrassed for coming too early. He had learned the practice from his mother. A few years ago, when I started a new *shiur* in Prestwich, he used to attend. This man was a *talmid chacham* and certainly didn't need to listen to me, but he wanted to help establish another *shiur* in his beloved community and give a rabbi encouragement, so every week he came.

Once I stayed in New York with a Jew who was suffering great pain from an incurable illness. Even if he wasn't feeling well when he awoke, he would get dressed and with tallis and tefillin walk down to the pavement below. Only then would he go back to bed. He had to be sure that it was genuine illness that was keeping him in bed and not the *yetzer hara* fooling him. It is exactly this sort of "average Jew" who can keep us looking up. *Klal Yisrael* is full of them.

Dancing through Time

(Hamodia, May 4, 2001)

I once heard a *rav* comment that watches that tell the time by displaying hands that go around a clock face have a distinct advantage over the digital type. A watch with hands shows you not only what the time is now, but also how much time has gone by and how much time is left — the past, the present, and the future.

Acharei Mos begins with the words "Hashem spoke to Moshe after the death of the two sons of Aharon." Moshe Rabbeinu was instructed to warn Aharon not to make the same mistake his sons made when he performs his duties in the Mishkan. Aharon was also being told that he was expected to carry on and move forward from the present and the loss of his two sons, toward the future. He was still expected to perform his duties flawlessly.

The Ramban says these words were spoken immediately after the deaths of Nadav and Avihu, at the same time Moshe offered his brother the words of comfort recorded in *Shemini*.

Chazal are at pains to point out the greatness of Nadav and Avihu and the repercussions of the loss of these two giants. They possessed aspects of greatness denied even to Moshe and Aharon, and this was now lost to the Jewish people. In addition, Rashi emphasizes that Chazal deduce from their deaths the principle that the death of tzaddikim causes the rest of the Jewish people to repent. There was, though, a far more simple aspect to this tragedy that is sometimes overlooked.

Rav Eliyahu Dessler talks about a *rosh yeshivah* who identifies a young man in the yeshivah as someone with the potential to be the next *gadol hador*. He invites him to stay in his home so he can personally groom him for greatness. The young man never leaves his rebbe's side, and the *rosh yeshivah* loves him like a son. The *rosh yeshivah*'s own son is an average young man and may even be a disappointment to his father. One night a fire breaks out, and the *rosh yeshivah* has only enough time to save one of the two. Which one does he save? The answer is obvious: he saves his son. Aharon was still a father who had lost his children.

The Torah reports Aharon's reaction when Moshe told his brother, "This is what Hashem meant when He said, 'With those who are close to Me I shall be made holy, and before all the people I will be honored,' and Aharon was silent." Aharon's silence shouted his acceptance of the Heavenly decree. His silence shouted that he would move forward from the tragedy of the present and embrace the future.

A few months ago I was in Antwerp. I had gone to deliver *shiurim* and in particular to attend the wedding of a young lady whom I had taught in Manchester's famous Bais Yaakov Seminary. This was a wedding of two chassidic families, and the dancing went on until four in the morning. My wife and I know the parents of the *kallah* very well, but I had to wait until this *simchah* to meet her grandfather.

A band began to play, and the *kallah*'s father and his new son-in-law danced back and forth on the floor. In an instant they were surrounded by a circle of men dancing around them. The dancing, though, wasn't up to the standard of one old chassid, who appeared to be a man in his seventies. As the circle turned in a clockwise direction, he danced around inside in a counterclockwise direction. As he danced, his arms waved frantically, signaling to the young men to dance more quickly or motioning to them to sing. His efforts had an immediate effect, and soon the dancing was infused with a far greater enthusiasm. This was the grandfather of the *kallah*.

He is something of a legend in the Antwerp community. During the war he had been taken to Auschwitz. As Russian forces approached the camp, those prisoners who could walk were forced on what was known as the Death March. This old Jew, then a young man, went on that march. From Poland to Bergen-Belsen, hundreds of Jews began a trek that in their weakened state would mean death for many of them. Large numbers were suffering from dysentery and collapsed, sometimes wandering in circles before falling and dying.

Somehow this chassid had heard that charcoal was a cure for dysentery. At night, when the Jews slept in fields and anyone who dared to move risked being shot, he gathered wood and, by hiding a small fire behind people's bodies, managed to produce charcoal, which he administered to dysentery sufferers. Many who would not have survived the march did so due to this young chassid and his charcoal.

As I danced, watching this man fly past in the opposite direction, I wondered what must be going through his mind. He had watched Jewish feet tramp from one death camp to another. He had watched Jewish feet stumble and fall, never to rise. Now scores of Jewish feet flew past him in *simchah*, joy.

I found out what he had been thinking two days later. When I phoned the *kallah*'s parents to tell them how much I had enjoyed the wedding and how privileged I had felt to meet the grandfather, I heard that someone had asked him, as he danced, seemingly in a different world, "Tell me, Zeidy, where are you now?"

Dancing through Time

The grandfather didn't hesitate. "I am in Auschwitz!"

As we danced in a clockwise direction, he literally was dancing in a counterclockwise direction. The hands of the clock displayed the present, but he could see the past. Despite everything he had lost, he had still moved forward. He could be in two places at the same time, one Heaven and one hell, and be dancing in both!

Six years ago, on Purim, Jewish students at Manchester University arranged for their annual reading of the megillah on campus. The day before the Jewish world had been plunged into terrible despair. A Palestinian suicide bomber had walked into a group of Jewish children in Tel Aviv, blowing himself up and killing the children. One of the students phoned me to ask if they should cancel the megillah reading. I told him that under no circumstances would the event be canceled.

Holding a megillah, I walked into the room where a hundred students had gathered. I was confronted by a group of young Jews who clearly felt upset and uncomfortable that the reading was going ahead. The megillah was listened to with almost none of the enthusiasm of a normal reading. Haman made his appearance with very little verbal opposition.

After the reading was finished, I was asked to speak. I paused for a moment and sincerely prayed for help in finding the right words that would lift the gloom.

I recalled a story I once heard that occurred during the Second World War. A group of Jews was marched out of the Lublin Ghetto. An area had been fenced off with barbed wire, and the Jews were corralled into this tight space. The Nazis started to beat the Jews with clubs, forcing them onto the barbed wire. As the SS major watched, one of the Jews stumbled and tripped. He struggled to stop his fall, and while doing so he seemed to do a jig. This inspired the SS major. He ordered his club-wielding thugs back and called out, "Dance, Jews! Dance!" The Jews could see the machine guns pointed at them and knew quite well how this would end. Why dance for the amusement of this sadistic fiend?

One Jew, though, did dance, and as he danced he sang a well-known Jewish tune, but he substituted the usual words with ones that he thought up on the spot. *"Mir vellen zei iberleben Avinu shebaShamayim* — We will outlive them, Our Father in Heaven."

The major laughed at the stupid Jews who were actually entertaining him moments before he would order their deaths. Then others started to sing the new song, and they, too, danced. When the major realized what they were singing, he screamed hysterically at them to stop, but the Jews carried on dancing and singing, even as the guns opened fire.

I pointed out that if we were to cancel our festivals because of disasters that had occurred on that day, given our history we would never be able to celebrate a *yom tov*. In the last two thousand years of exile there is no day in the year that did not witness some massive Jewish tragedy.

The students were considering my words when I quoted to them the words of the Bartenura on the first *mishnah* in *Megillah*.

The Mishnah says: "The megillah is to be read on the fourteenth of Adar except in cities that were walled from the times of Yehoshua's conquest of the Land of Israel." Why not make it "if a city was walled from the time of Mordechai and Esther"? The Bartenura says that the Rabbis ordained that cities that were walled from the times of Yehoshua, even though they were not walled during the miracle, should read the megillah on the fifteenth like Shushan itself in order to give honor to Eretz Yisrael, which at that time was destroyed and desolate, so that it would be as if Eretz Yisrael's cities were rebuilt once again.

The students' faces were unreadable. I couldn't tell if my words were penetrating, but I went on.

"The Rabbis foresaw a time when the hands of the clock would move forward, and again children's voices would be heard playing and laughing in the streets of Yerushalayim. We are gathered here, on our festival of Purim, despite tragedy and horror, to attest that we, too, can see another time when the hands have moved forward and to show that we will move forward, too."

After I finished, one of the students started to sing "*Am Yisrael Chai,*" and others took up the song. Soon everyone was singing. Then they started dancing, and they danced out of the room and onto the university campus.

A young Jewish student was at that moment giving a verbal presentation in front of a group of examiners for his final exam on the subject of human ecology. Through an open window came the voices of the dancing students. He stopped in the middle of his presentation and said, "Ladies and gentlemen, you can hear the voices of Jewish students singing '*Am Yisrael Chai,*' which means, 'The Jewish people live.' The reason they are singing it is because today is the festival of Purim," and he went on to explain the Purim story. He passed his exam, receiving the top mark in his year.

Last night, before writing this article, I picked up my son from the airport in London. He was returning from yeshivah in Yerushalayim. This morning he came into my room holding a piece of jagged metal. The car bomb that had exploded a few months ago in Meah Shearim, miraculously injuring no one, had been only a few yards from his apartment. This was one of the pieces of the car, which had flown though his open window.

I held this piece of shrapnel and thought of Aharon HaKohen and the grandfather in Antwerp and the times in their lives that they had experienced human anguish and suffering. As I turned the metal between my fingers, I could envision another time as the clock's hands move forward: Jewish children singing and dancing in the streets of Eretz Yisrael. We just have to be determined that we will look ahead to that time and move forward to meet it like Aharon, attempting not to repeat the mistakes of the past.

Finding the Very, Very Best

(Unpublished)

The other day I was sitting at a bris. Nearby sat a well-known local businessman who was talking about lawyers and a recent case he had been involved in. He turned to a friend and said that his lawyer charged five hundred pounds an hour and in his opinion that was cheap. The rest of us sitting at the table, all *rabbanim*, were astonished. "Oh yes," he continued. "The very top lawyers charge fifteen hundred pounds an hour!" We all stared at him, incredulous.

A little while ago my oldest son and his new wife came out to the garden to say goodbye. They were going to live in Eretz Yisrael, and now that their *sheva berachos* week had passed, they were getting ready to fly the next day.

I had thought long and hard about this moment. I wanted to find the right words, not any old words, but words that would be significant and remain with them throughout their married life.

They sat down beside me, and I asked them an unusual question. "Suppose you needed to see a doctor. What sort of doctor would you want to see?"

They looked baffled, and I realized that I was not doing a very

Dancing through Time

good job despite my best intentions. I started again.

"All right, suppose you need to see a lawyer. What sort of lawyer would you want to see?"

This time I was making myself clearer, and they replied, "The best lawyer!"

That was the answer I was looking for, so I continued, "You would want the best lawyer, the best doctor, the best financial adviser you could possibly get." They agreed. "The problem with the best, in any field," I pointed out, "is that they charge the earth!" My son and daughter-in-law nodded. "Well, the very, very best doctor, financial adviser, and lawyer charges only 613. All you have to do is make sure you are keeping up your payments, and you'll have every assurance that if you ever need help you'll get the very, very best."

After the attacks of September 11, many in the religious Jewish world became acquainted with the words of one of our most famous sages. David HaMelech says the following: "If Hashem had not been with us, let Israel say it now. If Hashem had not been with us when a man rose up against us" (*Tehillim* 124:1–2).

Rabbi Chaim Vital says on this verse, "It is well known that there were meant to be four exiles — Babylonia, Persia, Greece, and Rome. In the future, though, there will be a fifth exile, the exile of Yishmael. The name Yishmael, which means 'Hashem will hear,' refers to the bitter cry of the Jewish people that will reach Heaven at that time. The Torah says that Yishmael will be a '*pere adam*,' a wild man, and his hand will be against everyone and everyone's hand against him. Later, at the time of the fifth exile, Yishmael will rule over the world as well as the Jewish people. It will be an exile where Yishmael aspires to nothing less than the total destruction of the Jewish people."

I read these words with dread.

Three years ago a friend gave me a tour of New York, and I found myself aboard the Staten Island Ferry, sailing toward the

Statue of Liberty. I took my camera and photographed Manhattan as we left it behind.

One of my sons had been in New York just three weeks after the terrorist attacks. He found himself standing on the same ferry, and, by coincidence, at almost the same moment as I had he pointed his camera at the shrinking skyline and returned with an almost identical picture. As my family compared the two and wondered at the strange coincidence of a father and son snapping an almost identical photograph, we noticed one glaring difference. My photo showed the Twin Towers. In his they were gone.

Recently a friend showed me a cutting from a news magazine. It was an article about Islamic extremism. A photograph accompanied the article. It was of a demonstration in London by British Muslims. One demonstrator was holding a banner that read, "Islam will dominate the world." Here we see the fulfillment of Rabbi Chaim Vital's prediction.

There are ample grounds for reading Rabbi Chaim Vital's words with worry and dread as they seem to come to life in front of our eyes. Perhaps before we become too despondent, we should remind ourselves of what the Rambam says when he explains how prophecy works.

"When a prophet utters words predicting suffering — for example, when he says someone will die or the year will bring a famine or war or other such things — if they do not come true, that does not mean that he is not a true prophet, and we do not say he made a prediction that failed to materialize. The reason [it did not come true] is that HaKadosh Baruch Hu is slow to anger and full of compassion, and He regrets bringing such events. In addition, it is possible that the subjects of the predictions have repented and Hashem has forgiven them, like the inhabitants of the city of Ninveh..." (*Hilchos Yesodei HaTorah* 10:4).

Even if Rabbi Chaim Vital had been a prophet (and since prophecy ceased around two thousand years before he was born, he certainly was not), the future he predicted can still be avoided by the actions of the Jewish people.

In his commentary on the words of *Tehillim*, Rabbi Chaim reveals an insight into the nature of Yishmael that is the key to guaranteeing that his descendants' ambitions are never realized: "Yishmael, as a son of Avraham, had a bris milah, circumcision. The Torah calls him a *'pere adam,'* wild man. The word *pere*, though, has another meaning. *Periah* is the procedure that completes a bris milah. Yishmael had a bris milah without *periah*."

He is a *pere adam* — his circumcision was never complete. Yishmael's descendants copied many ideas from Judaism. They have a form of Shabbos, but it is not a complete Shabbos — they celebrate it only on Friday night. They have a form of *taharas hamishpachah*, but not a complete form. They copied the laws of *shechitah*, but again not completely. They copied the Jewish calendar but, once more, not completely.

Rabbi Tzadok HaKohen, in his *Likutei Ma'amarim* (p. 95), discusses Yishmael and his descendants' beliefs. He says that the Torah demands that Pesach, the festival that attests to Hashem's relationship with the Jewish people, must fall out in the spring. The lunar calendar has to be "tied" to the solar calendar; otherwise, the shorter lunar months would cause our festivals to drift through the solar year, and we would find ourselves celebrating Pesach in the winter.

The sun and moon symbolize the relationship between the Jewish people and Hashem. Just as the moon reflects the light that comes from the sun, the Jewish people's task is to reflect God's holiness to the world. The cycles of the moon have to be tied to the seasons of the sun. (We guarantee this by inserting an extra month of Adar every few years.) This symbolizes that the Jewish people must remain tied to Hashem.

The non-Jewish nations chose a purely solar calendar. The seeds that gave birth to this approach were planted in the generation of Enosh. It was then that people first claimed that Hashem concerns Himself solely with Heavenly matters and leaves the earth entirely

Finding the Very, Very Best

to man to control. They rejected the idea contained in the symbolism of the relationship between the sun and the moon. This idea was given expression in a completely solar calendar.

Yishmael's children chose a purely lunar calendar. This is why their Ramadan (the ninth month of the Islamic year, observed with daily fasting from dawn to sunset) travels through the solar year, sometimes appearing in the winter, sometimes in the fall, and sometimes in the summer or spring. This choice reflects their acceptance that Hashem does control this world. Both the Rambam and the *Shulchan Aruch* (*Yoreh Deah* 123) state that they believe in one God, as well as other Jewish concepts that their prophet took from our Torah. But they refuse to follow this path all the way to the end and accept the Torah completely.

Rabbi Tzadok concludes that Yishmael is really no better than the other nations of the world. Ultimately, they are worse! They fall into the category of those "Who know their God and intend to rebel against Him."

Bnei Yisrael did not limit their commitment to Hashem. Their Shabbos is a complete Shabbos. Their adherence to *taharas hamishpachah* is complete, as is their observance of the laws of *shechitah*. And the Jewish calendar attests to the Jewish people's willingness to reflect every aspect of Torah.

Chapter 124 of *Tehillim* concludes with the words "Our help is through the Name of Hashem, Maker of heaven and earth." Rabbi Chaim Vital says that these words point to the time in the fifth exile when the Jewish people will finally realize that neither foreign ideologies nor the hope of "the strength and might of our hand" can help us. Our only hope is faith in HaKadosh Baruch Hu.

After all, if we want the very, very best doctor or financial consultant or lawyer — or savior — all we need to realize is that He takes only 613 as payment. As long as we make sure that they are a complete 613, with no half measures, even the most worrying of prophecies will not come true.

Put in the Big Rocks First

(The Jewish Tribune, December 23, 1999)

A friend of mine from Gateshead once told me something his father used to say. When I first heard it, I was confused. He said, "Two is bad." Only when I heard the complete adage did I understand that I had misunderstood. He didn't mean "two" is bad, but "too" is bad. Too tall is bad; too small is bad. Too fat is bad; too thin is bad. Even too clever is bad — after all, everyone needs to have someone to talk to and eventually marry. If a person is too clever, basic human relationships become problematic. In short, any "too" is bad, except one: too wise. A person can never have enough wisdom, which is why Shlomo HaMelech asked Hashem to give him that quality in abundance.

Recently the issue of teenagers from observant families going astray has moved from the sphere of something not to be mentioned to the sphere of open debate. The recent seventy-seventh annual convention of Agudath Israel devoted an entire session to this problem. *The Jewish Observer* dedicated an issue exclusively to the subject. The famous psychiatrist Rabbi Twerski is at the time this article is being written touring the UK, alerting our commu-

Put in the Big Rocks First

nity to the nature and scope of the phenomenon. Yet I heard someone say that although he had read all the articles on the subject he still did not know what practical steps to take to combat it.

This development requires as much unlimited wisdom as we can muster to find solutions. A friend of mine, who is a *mashgiach* in a prestigious yeshivah, told me something he heard from a *rav* in Yerushalayim. This *rav* claimed that adolescents going astray was always the norm in *Klal Yisrael*. "After the Second World War," he said, "Hashem had mercy on the remnant that survived, and this phenomenon was removed." He claimed that things are simply back to the way they have always been.

This is a moot point. Rav Yerucham Levovitz, *zt"l*, points out that the *satan* is always reinventing himself. In every age an ism comes along, like Hellenism or nationalism or socialism, and this *Zeitgeist* draws Jews away from the Torah, sometimes in the millions. Today, though, there is no "big idea" that young Jews find irresistible, no new *Haskalah* masquerading as a solution to the problems of the Jewish people. So if young souls are not leaving for a better tomorrow, they must be leaving because there is something wrong with today.

To find wisdom on the subject, we must turn to our sages. Rav Matisyahu Salomon, *shlita*, recently addressed a group of *mechanchim* on this very subject. He startled them with a very strong statement. "There is no such thing as a dropout. There is only a push-out!"

He went on to say (as difficult as it is to say and certainly to hear) that there is something wrong at the very basic foundation of religious homes that is allowing this problem to take hold.

I should add that all the *rabbanim* who are discussing this problem are identifying a general trend. There will, of course, be individual cases that do not fall within this general pattern and require specialized help. This caveat, however, merely confirms that a general pattern exists.

Rav Matisyahu identified the family as the place where this

problem was cultivated. Our natural reaction and instinctive desire would be to reject the finger-pointing here. We might be willing to accept it, though, if we could feel that what is going on is due to a mistake. It might be a mistake that is being made for the very best of Torah motives. We would certainly be more receptive to considering the family as being the originator of the trend if we could be assured that with a slight adjustment it could be put right.

If every character trait apart from wisdom is bad in excess, what about *chesed*? Rabbi Dessler, *zt"l*, identifies it in several places as being a *middah* that could become corrupted. At the beginning of his *Michtav MeEliyahu* (p. 10), he writes something I often try to say in my *shiurim*. This is not so much for the benefit of my audience as it is to remind myself of the lesson it contains. Rav Dessler writes: "It is very common to find the children even of tzaddikim going astray."

I mention this so often because of a warning I once received from one of my rebbes: "If you are going to be a rabbi, remember that it is not unusual for rabbis' children to feel that their father deserted them. They are so busy devoting their energies to other people and their problems that they don't see the problems that may be developing in their own children."

Chesed can be misplaced and misdirected. For a people who are *rachmanim bnei rachmanim*, merciful and the children of those who are merciful, *chesed* is their constant preoccupation. But that reality may also provide fertile ground for it to become corrupted and misplaced.

My *rosh yeshivah* Rav Leib Lopian, *zt"l*, often told *talmidim* that a man's first duty is to himself. After that, his duty is toward his family. After that, it is toward his street, and, finally, after all that, to *Klal Yisrael*. Rav Leib, despite being the *rosh yeshivah* of Gateshead, would conclude, "I find that I only have enough strength for my family and myself!"

Rav Shamshon Refael Hirsch points out that when Sarah was

Put in the Big Rocks First

expecting Yitzchak, Avraham moved to the south of Eretz Yisrael. Avraham's whole life was *chesed*. He dedicated himself to bringing people close to Hashem. Now, though, he was awaiting the arrival of the one who would be the next link in the Jewish people. So he moved from the main thoroughfares of Canaan to a place that was remote and quiet. The emphasis and purpose of his life had changed. Now he had to focus his *chesed* in a new and more important direction, the bringing up of his son. Everything else was a smaller project by comparison.

So much of what we do is external to the home. A doctor who is himself a *talmid chacham* was discussing communal problems with me recently. He said, "We tell tales of great people who went out and built this or did that. We rarely tell stories about people who stayed at home and put effort into their children's upbringing!" The same point was made to my wife by Rebbetzin Tziporah Heller when she stayed with us last year. This caused my wife to reflect that she had recently had to force herself to go out to a *shiur*. "Perhaps," she said, "the same way we often have to push ourselves to go out to a *shiur*, we should sometimes push ourselves to stay at home."

Getting the right balance between concentrating on our family and helping others is certainly something that requires wisdom. When I first found myself involved in community work, we turned to the Gateshead *rav* for advice in bringing up our own family. There are tactics to be applied. *Klal Yisrael* is fortunate that we have sages who can explain what they are.

A friend of mine sent me an interesting e-mail whose author was anonymous. It told a tale of a lecturer in one of America's elite business schools. One day during a lesson he produced a large glass jar, and he began to fill it with rocks. When he could no longer get in even one more, he turned to the class and asked, "Is the jar full?" They replied that it was. "Watch," he said. He took out a bag of pebbles and poured them into the jar. They fell between the spaces left by the rocks, and again he asked if the jar was full. When he received another yes, he produced a bag of sand and poured that into the jar, filling the gaps left by the pebbles. By now his bright students had the idea.

"Why do you think I showed you this?" the teacher asked. One student replied that he thought the professor was trying to illustrate that you can always push yourself just that little bit further. The professor frowned and shook his head. He explained that he was trying to show them that if he had started filling the jar the other way around, he would never have gotten everything into it.

"One day you are all going to be very wealthy and successful businesspeople. You will find yourselves very busy, and the demands on your time will be urgent and continual. Prioritize the important things — your wives and husbands and children," he demanded. "Make sure the really important things are attended to first, and you'll probably manage to get in the smaller things, too!"

It might be that in our frantic efforts to rebuild a *Klal Yisrael* that lay in tatters just two generations ago, we naturally focused our *chesed* on big projects that lay outside the home. Now, though, we are very fortunate to have been made aware of a problem before it becomes too big to solve. Its solution lies in refocusing our priorities. We still have time to remember the message of the professor and his jar. As we focus on the big things first — our own children — we'll probably find we still have time to fit in the other *chesed*, too.

From Cardboard to Concrete

(Unpublished)

I hadn't been back to Los Angeles for fifteen years. As the 747 circled the city on its approach for landing, I was looking out below, reminding myself how beautiful the landscape was. I was not the only one.

A young Irishman had been my neighbor on the long twelve-hour flight from London. He had never flown before, and I showed him how to summon the stewardess by pressing the button on the armrest rather than waving his arm in the air and shouting, "Miss!" He was very friendly and very excited. His first flight was bringing him to a new home. Like so many of his fellow countrymen, he was immigrating to the United States. Not just the United States, but Los Angeles!

As the plane banked right, I caught sight of a famous sign displayed on a hill. Huge white letters — tiny from the air — spelled out *Hollywood*. When my new friend saw it, he could hardly contain himself. "This is incredible! Imagine me, living here, in Hollywood!" He pronounced the word *Hollywood* in a whisper, with an almost mystical reverence. I parted from him at the luggage carousel, wishing him luck and success in his new country. Then I walked off to a very different Los Angeles from the one he was going to.

The *rav* I was staying with collected me and took me to his home. Over supper we shmoozed. His wife said, "In the twenty years since we moved here from New York, the Jewish growth of this city has been unbelievable."

She listed its achievements — the schools, the *kollels*, and the various communities — and commented, "It's strange that in this place, which has so much *tumah*, there has been such growth of Torah."

Rav Yisrael Salanter, *zt"l*, used to say that the *satan*'s headquarters is in Paris. Last century it moved to Hollywood, home of the film industry. The very same reasons that had caused that young Irishman on the plane to become excited at the thought of living in LA would cause any religious Jew worry and concern. Strangely, though, a Jewish community has grown up and prospered despite all that.

The next morning I arrived in shul fifteen minutes early, and this gave me the opportunity to open a *sefer*. I looked in *Sefas Emes* on *parashas Shemos*, and there I saw words that explained how LA's Jews could prosper.

Chazal say, "A good name is greater than good oil." The Midrash comments, "Chananiah, Mishael, and Azariah [who were willing to give up their lives and die by fire to sanctify God's Name] were greater than Nadav and Avihu, who died by fire, even though they were anointed with the anointing oil of the priesthood."

The Sefas Emes says that "good oil" refers, therefore, to those who have greatness given to them at birth, like the *kohanim*. Those who come to greatness through their own efforts are far greater. Chazal refer to the latter as possessing a "good name." That, he explains, is what the Torah refers to at the beginning of *Shemos* with the words "And these are the names of the children of Israel who came to Egypt."

From Cardboard to Concrete

The children of Israel maintained their spiritual level in Egypt despite living in the most adverse of societies. In a very real sense, their challenge would demand more of them than the *Avos*, who did not have to interact with the world under the pressure of a society like Egypt. The Jewish people's role differed from that of the *Avos*. They would have to awaken and spread holiness throughout the world even in a society like Egypt. Thus the Hebrew word for the Jewish tribes, *shevatim*, is related to the word *hispashtus*, which means "dissemination" or "spreading."

In *Vayigash* the Sefas Emes explains the contrast between the approach the *shevatim* would have to develop and that of the *Avos*. When Yaakov meets his beloved Yosef, after two decades of separation, he does not embrace him immediately. As Rashi explains, he stops first and recites the Shema. The Sefas Emes comments, "Yaakov feared that his love for Yosef at this meeting would momentarily eclipse his love for Hashem. He therefore prioritized his love for HaKadosh Baruch Hu and only then gave expression to his love for his son."

Rav Dessler elaborates on this: "Until now Yaakov clearly demonstrated his love for Yosef, as when he made him the famous special coat. The feelings of love for his son that he indulged conjured recognition of the source of that son, Hashem. That in turn magnified his love for Hashem."

Chazal mean exactly that when they say, "Someone who does not allow himself to take pleasure from this world is called a sinner." The pleasures of this world can be used as a vehicle to come closer to Hashem.

The reason Yaakov changed his approach now was that he was meeting Yosef in Egypt, not Eretz Yisrael. He was afraid that the approach he had adopted until now would fail in Egypt. A new approach was vital.

Some of the essential elements of this approach are spelled out in the Torah by the preparations Yaakov's children made before they went down to Egypt. Yehudah was dispatched ahead of the rest to locate a place where a yeshivah could be established. The Jewish people would live in their own city in Egypt, separate from the Egyptians. They would maintain a different language and dress and would keep their Jewish names. It would be essential that the way the Jews thought and talked remain solely Jewish, which would be reinforced by their appearance. Despite the seductive atmosphere of Egypt, the Jewish people's philosophy would be Torah driven and Torah based. Only when this carefully crafted approach started to be ignored by some could the corruption of Egypt work its evil among the Jewish people.

Chazal say that Egypt was the prototype of all future exiles. There would be a little bit of the Mitzrayim experience in every other *galus*. There would also be the antidote to those other exiles within the Mitzrayim experience, too.

The *rav* and his wife continued to tell me of the achievements of the Los Angeles community. The next morning, when both were out, I sat at the dining room table preparing the *shiurim* I would be giving during my stay.

As I wrote, I noticed sitting beside me a cardboard box, about twice the size of a shoe box. I peered in and saw that it contained little Lego figures. But these Lego men were different. The box had been transformed into a shul! A little piece of cloth split the box in two sections; that was the *mechitzah*. A cardboard *bimah* sat in the middle of the men's section, and a cardboard *aron kodesh* was lit by a tiny bulb. Cardboard shelves contained scores of tiny prayer books made from colored paper, and the word *siddur* had been written carefully down their spines. The Lego men wore carefully made *talleisim*, and on the ladies' side of the *mechitzah* (although, strictly speaking, I should not have looked), Lego women wore little *tichels* and had been given dresses that conformed to every halachah of *tznius*.

The children who had spent so many hours making this beautiful model shul made it clear where their thoughts and imaginations took them — to Torah and mitzvos. It was obvious how real shuls and real *frum* Jews were prospering here. These were Jews whose philosophy was Torah driven and Torah based, and they would pass that on to the next generation.

On my way to give one of those *shiurim* later in the day, I walked down a road that I remembered from fifteen years before. Today there are new shuls, a *kollel*, kosher restaurants, and grocery stores. An entire area proudly displays the fact that this is a Jewish place. Most interesting of all is a building that had been originally built as a temple to the products of Hollywood's film industry. Now, instead of a cinema, it is the center of one of the most successful outreach organizations in the city.

My young Irish friend would not have been able to understand it, but fifteen years since my last visit LA has rightly become famous, not for its film industry, but for its Torah.

The Violinist and the Artist

(Unpublished)

Despite the dominance of the Reform in Cincinnati, Ohio, which has its largest training school in the town, there are also Orthodox schools, a *kollel*, two Orthodox synagogues, and Chabad. When I speak there, I am always hosted by the largest Orthodox shul, which is called Agudas Yisrael. The other shul, Knesses Yisrael, is smaller, and on my last trip I met its *rav*. We sat together at a bris, and he told me an astonishing tale. He had learned in Lakewood Yeshivah, and his story came from its great founder and *rosh yeshivah*, Rav Aharon Kotler, *zt"l*.

Rav Kotler told him about a child protégé. The boy was an amazing violinist. His abilities on the instrument meant that his father could earn much needed money by letting his son perform in public. On one such occasion, the fund-raiser of the Slabodka Yeshivah heard the young boy play and afterward engaged him in conversation. It became immediately apparent that his genius with the violin was nothing compared to his genius in Torah. The fund-raiser approached the boy's father, whose name was Pines, and asked him to allow his son to come and learn in the yeshivah. The father explained that the family could not survive without the

The Violinist and the Artist

extra income generated by his son's performances. The man didn't hesitate. He offered to pay the father the same amount that his son's playing would earn. The agreement was made, and the boy went on to learn, and eventually he became a *rav*.

Rav Aharon's original family name was not Kotler. It was Pines. He had been that little boy.

It would be impossible to underestimate the contribution made to American Jewry by Lakewood Yeshivah. Generations of *talmidei chachomim* and *rabbanim* have sprung from there. Scores of *kollels* have sprouted from Lakewood and have been established all over America. They have brought Torah to places as far as Mexico. All this because someone saw the seeds of greatness in a little boy with a fiddle and was determined to allow those seeds to grow.

When I heard this story about Rav Aharon, I recalled a question that I once heard from another American *rosh yeshivah*. When Rav Matisyahu Salomon was still the *mashgiach* of Gateshead, he would give a *shiur* in his home every Thursday night to young *rabbanim*. On one occasion he invited a *rosh yeshivah* from the States who was staying with him to give the *shiur*. In the course of his *shiur*, this *rosh yeshivah* told us that he had been at school with someone who also went on to become a *rosh yeshivah*. While at school the boy displayed a phenomenal talent for art. He was astonishingly gifted. "I once plucked up courage and asked him, 'If Hashem has given you such a gift, isn't it a pity that you don't use it anymore?' "

It was an interesting thought, and it occurred to me that one could have asked the same of Rav Aharon and the musical gift that Hashem had given him.

One of my own rebbes was offered a place at Cambridge University because he was such a gifted mathematician, and a well-known *rosh yeshivah* in Eretz Yisrael displayed a tremendous talent for chess as a child, so great that he could easily have played the game at an international level.

At the end of the fifth chapter of *Avos*, Ben Bag Bag says,

Dancing through Time

"*Hafoch bah vahafoch bah d'cholah bah* — Turn the Torah over and turn it over again because everything is in it." The Ben Ish Chai tells a story that explains exactly what the *mishnah* means.

A father had two sons, and, in accordance with the Talmud's requirement that one equip his children with a profession, he apprenticed one to a tailor and the other to a carpenter. Apprentices were expected to be utterly dedicated to their craft, and often they would come in to help on their days off. These two boys were swept away with enthusiasm for their professions, and every Shabbos, after lunch, they would go and watch the master craftsmen at their work. The boys' father was extremely distressed and sought the counsel of his *rav*. He told the father to bring the boys to see him the next Shabbos.

The following week the *rav* greeted the boys with "*Shalom aleichem*" instead of the usual greeting of the holy day, "Good Shabbos." Then the *rav* said, "I greet you this way because you are turning Shabbos into a weekday, so that is the appropriate greeting to give you." The young men protested that they attended shul on Shabbos, and even if they did spend their afternoons at their places of work, they were not expected to violate Shabbos, nor did they. They only sat and observed. One of them recalled hearing the *rav* himself once explain in a *shiur* that it is not forbidden to think about work on Shabbos, and that was all they were doing.

The *rav* replied that they had not understood him properly. To think about work when the thought enters your mind by accident is not a sin. To actively spend time thinking about work is definitely forbidden. Apart from that, being seen entering a workplace on Shabbos inevitably invites people to assume the worst, and that, too, is forbidden.

The *rav* asked the boys what was it that so attracted them to their workplaces on Shabbos anyway. The boys began to enthuse about the wondrous talents of the craftsmen they were apprenticed to. The apprentice tailor described how the tailors took a simple piece of cloth and, seemingly without effort, cut it and shaped

The Violinist and the Artist

it. By the time the precise and almost invisible stitches were added, a perfect garment appeared that was an ideal fit for the customer.

His brother's enthusiasm for his trade was just as great. "The carpenter selects some wood and carefully measures and cuts it. Then he expertly carves dovetail joints, and soon all the pieces join together to produce a beautiful table or chair."

The *rav* listened and shook his head as if puzzled. "I don't understand. If that's what you enjoy, why don't you come and watch me on Shabbos. That's exactly what I do!"

The young men were baffled.

"Open that Gemara over there on the table and read out loud from whatever page you come to." One of the boys did this. The Gemara was opened to the tenth page of *Bava Basra*. He began to read aloud.

"Ten hard things were created in the world. A mountain is hard, but iron cuts it. Iron is hard, but fire melts it. Fire is hard, but water extinguishes it...."

The boy finished reading all ten things, and then the rabbi said, "There is a chapter in *Avodah Zarah* that deals with the laws concerning a mountain that was worshiped as a god. In the Talmud's discussion a question is raised." The *rav* carefully explained the complicated question to the boys and then continued, "The answer to this question is found in another tractate of the Talmud, in *Yevamos*. It is in a section called 'Iron Sheep.' "Again the *rav* explained the Talmud's argument there and how it solved the previous problem. "This piece of Gemara, though, contains a problem of its own, and the answer to it is contained in another tractate, in *Bava Kama*, in a section dealing with someone's liability if a fire he kindled damaged someone else."

And so the *rav* went on, stitching the *gemara* together and fitting them perfectly to the "ten hard things" spoken of in *Bava Basra*. The boys realized that the skill of their trades was more than matched within the Torah, and subsequently they attended the

Dancing through Time

rav's "workshop" on Shabbos instead.

The answer the *rosh yeshivah* received from his friend when he challenged him about neglecting the artistic gift of Hashem was that he hadn't abandoned it at all. "I see symmetry in the Gemara's argument," he replied.

No doubt Rav Aharon Kotler would have said that he heard harmony between the *gemaras*. My old rebbe would see logic and structure in the Torah, and the *rosh yeshivah* in Eretz Yisrael would anticipate the "next move" of a *talmid* challenging his argument in his *shiur* as he and the *talmid* struggled to check and then checkmate each other.

One of my very closest friends is a *maggid shiur* in Yerushalayim. Once, a lifetime ago, he played the flute in the Boston Symphony Orchestra. When I last visited, I notice a small black case lying in a corner beside his bookshelves, gathering dust. I asked him if that was his flute. He confirmed that it was. I asked him if he ever found time to play anymore, and he said that sometimes he'd take out the instrument for relaxation. In his *shiurim*, though, he often used music to illustrate a point and take a difficult idea from obscurity to comprehension.

Most of us have been given some unique skill as a gift from Hashem. It may lie in artistic talent or intellectual ability. It may lie in a natural gift for a certain *middah* so that Avraham's *chesed* or Moshe's humility finds a special resonance within one person that another person may miss. The true significance of such gifts lies beyond their usual boundaries. They can serve as a key and an approach in Torah.

The violinist can create a symphony with Torah, and the artist can paint the Talmud's pictures so that thousands can see and appreciate them for the first time.

Beware Empty Black Taxis

(The Jewish Tribune, November 25, 1999)

Winston Churchill was renowned for his quick wit. He was also well known for his opposition to the appeasement policies of Neville Chamberlain, which he saw as encouragement to the Nazis to launch the Second World War. He is once reputed to have quipped, "One day an empty black taxi pulled up outside the palace of Westminster, and out came Neville Chamberlain."

Churchill was observing that the man was as empty as the useless words he waved on his infamous bit of paper when he stepped from his aircraft after his "historic" return from Berlin. He announced that he had reached an understanding with the Germans. "Peace in our time," he declared. Empty words from an empty man.

When Avraham Avinu was forced to go to Egypt to escape the famine that raged in Canaan, he pretended that his wife, Sarah, was his sister. When Pharaoh's servants kidnapped her and brought her as a bride to their master, the Torah reports that Pharaoh and his household were stricken with a terrible disease *"al devar Sarah eishes Avraham* — because of the matter involving Sarah, Avraham's wife." Pharaoh immediately summoned Avraham and rebuked him. "What is this you have done to me? Why didn't you tell me she was your wife?"

The story seems to portray Avraham as the scoundrel and Pharaoh as the wounded and wronged innocent. A careful examination of the evidence shows the roles were in reality the reverse. The Alshich asks how Pharaoh knew to send for Avraham. He and his palace were taken ill. He should have sent for a doctor.

The answer lies in the phrase *"al devar Sarah eishes Avraham."* The true translation is "because of the words of Sarah, Avraham's wife." What were the words of Sarah? As soon as she was taken before Pharaoh she revealed the truth; indeed, she shouted the truth so that even his servants would know. "I'm a married woman!" Pharaoh didn't care, nor did his servants. When Hashem punished them they knew immediately who should be contacted — her husband, Avraham.

Pharaoh's complaint would have to be pronounced by an actor to make it sound plausible. He cried with pathos and anguish, "How could you have wronged me in this way?" Empty words from an empty man.

History repeats itself, and Sarah is kidnapped again, this time by Avimelech. Once more Avraham appears in the wrong. But when Avimelech appeals to him to pray that his illness be removed, the Torah reports that Hashem had brought a plague to Avimelech's household *"al devar Sarah eishes Avraham."* Sarah told him, too, that she was married, yet he soliloquizes, "How could you do this to us? What sin did I do to you that you brought such great guilt upon my people and me? The thing you did to me is simply not done!"

Another empty man with empty words.

The Rambam explains the essential components that a prophet must possess: "He must have great wisdom. He must have superb *middos* and never allow his inclination to conquer him.

Beware Empty Black Taxis

Rather, he must consciously and actively defeat his inclination. He must have broad knowledge. Someone possessed of all this and who is physically perfect..." (*Hilchos Yesodei HaTorah*, ch. 7).

The last qualification requires elucidation. Since a prophet represents Hashem, he must represent him well. Even his appearance must inspire respect.

Imagine the Queen riding in her carriage to the state opening of Parliament. She is flanked by the majestic spectacle of the soldiers of the Life Guards Regiment, with their gleaming breastplates, helmets, and sabers. Behind the carriage perch two footmen in extravagant costume — knickerbockers with white knee-length socks. Imagine, though, that one of these two footmen is a foot shorter than the other and rather scrawny-looking. It would destroy the splendor and excellence of the visual effect. A prophet, too, must be physically perfect. He is, after all, a representative of the King of kings.

These words of the Rambam provoke the Ran to ask an obvious question: "How, then, could Moshe be a prophet? He was not physically perfect — he could not speak properly." Surely, of all impediments, this should be the worst. A prophet, after all, is the mouthpiece, so to speak, of Hashem.

The Ran's answer is inspiring. It was essential that Moshe be the exception to the rule. Moshe had to be unable to speak well. History is full of people whose power of speech was renowned and who could move human hearts and minds. There must be no doubt that the Jewish nation followed Moshe Rabbeinu not because he was an inspiring speaker but because the message was carefully examined and found to be true.

My *rosh yeshivah*, Rav Leib Gurwicz, *zt"l*, once told us a story about a *rav* who told him of an interesting experience that occurred to him in the 1920s in Berlin. He went for a walk in the park and came across a crowd listening to a public speech. He stopped to listen and observed the crowd, who were spellbound. This *rav* said the words that were being delivered were spoken with a force and a power that were almost supernatural. The speaker was Hitler, *yemach shemo*. But what was the message of those words? Destruction and genocide!

My *rosh kollel* told me once of a *maggid* whose arrival in town was anticipated with an electric excitement, he was such an astonishing speaker. When his *drashah* was nearly finished, he would look at the packed shul. He had just finished telling them a very sad tale, and the men sat with lumps in their throats and quivering lips. Suddenly he shielded his face with his hand so that only one half of the shul was able to see his expression. Then he stuck out his tongue and made a funny face. The half that could see it promptly burst into laughter. The other half, still moved by his sad tale, were still on the verge of tears. Each side stared at the other, one side unable to understand why the other was not crying and the other baffled why the rest were not laughing.

The *maggid* explained to them what he had done and, more importantly, why he had done it.

"A moment ago I had you all on the verge of tears, and I can make you laugh just as easily. I can make you feel whatever I want! Never listen to someone just because he is a brilliant speaker. His message has to be true!"

In *Vayishlach*, Yaakov confronts his brother Esav. This parashah was always studied by Chazal in preparation for any confrontation history forced us to have with Esav and his children. Whether it was the *Tannaim* in Rome, the Ramban in Barcelona, or the Maharal in Prague, they knew that Esav was the master of deception par excellence. Chazal say that the symbol of Esav is the pig. On the outside, everyone can see his split hooves, and he appears to be kosher. In reality, the inside is as *treif* as can be.

The ultimate occupant of the empty black taxi, Esav, went on to create a world where Avraham's descendants are portrayed as the scoundrels and they as the innocents. We have to remind our-

Beware Empty Black Taxis

selves in every generation to look deeply, beyond the messengers and the kosher wrapping of their products, and carefully examine the product itself. We have to be wary of those like Pharaoh or Avimelech, even if they call themselves "rabbis" and look so sincere but whose words contradict those of the *gedolei hador*.

In the days before Mashiach's arrival, the chutzpah of the material world increases, and nothing is the way it appears. We have to be careful when an empty black taxi draws up and be very, very suspicious of anyone who gets out.

New York, Lockerbie, and Sedom

(Unpublished)

They say the first casualty of war is the truth. The horrors of September 11 and the West's subsequent war against terrorism inevitably mean that the world can expect to witness truth twisted to suit the protagonists' needs. A British foreign secretary traveled to Tehran to seek the support of the Iranians in combating fundamentalist Islamic terrorism. That's like the FBI asking Al Capone to help them stamp out gangsterism in 1920s Chicago.

As time passes and world events become part of history, records and archives become available to historians and the truth emerges. Governments usually take great care, though, to ensure that crucial facts are released well after the people who were pivotal to them are long dead. Sometimes governments set a hundred-year embargo on such information. At the time of this writing, the West has launched its war on Afghanistan. What the future will conjure from that only Hashem knows.

New York, Lockerbie, and Sedom

In the third chapter of *Koheles*, Shlomo HaMelech says that there is a time for everything under Heaven — "a time to be born and a time to die; a time to plant and a time to pluck that which was planted." At the end of the long list, Shlomo HaMelech changes the formula and says "a time of war and a time of peace." He does not write "a time to make war and a time to make peace." Such decisions lie in the hands of Hashem, not those rulers and leaders who think they are going to war.

We cannot see the future, but the Torah commands us in *Ha'azinu* to see the past: "Remember the days of the world; consider the years of each generation...." *Da'as Zekeinim* says the Torah is saying, "Now recall and examine the acts of kindness that Hashem has done to the Jewish people."

Thirteen years ago it was a different act of Arab terrorism that was visited upon an American airliner that shocked the world. Pan Am Flight 103 was flying over the little Scottish town of Lockerbie when a bomb detonated in the hold and sent 259 people hurtling to their deaths (eleven more died in the town itself). I was born in Scotland, and as I listened to the news I felt connected to what had happened, even though I had never actually visited Lockerbie. Little did I know that I was about to become connected to those events in reality.

On the second night after the disaster I was visiting an elderly relative when his phone rang, and he told me that it was for me. One of Manchester's leading members of the *chevrah kaddisha* (burial society) and one of my closest friends was phoning from Lockerbie on his cell phone. In those days cell phones were huge and cumbersome things with very limited battery life. His battery had only a little power left, and he needed to use it to make a crucial call. The *chevrah kaddisha* had spent the day fruitlessly trying to gain access to the Jews who had been killed on the flight. He asked if I could give him the private phone number of Scotland's secretary of state.

It was only recently that Scotland achieved its own parliament and prime minister. Until then it had been ruled directly from London, and the member of the Cabinet who controlled the country was the secretary of state. At that time the man who held the post was Sir Malcolm Rifkind, a cousin of my wife. I couldn't give out his private number, but I promised to phone him myself.

Sir Malcolm's wife was reluctant to let her husband speak to me. He had just returned from Lockerbie, and he had seen sights that had left him profoundly shaken; however, after some persuasion he took the call.

I explained the situation and asked for his help to allow the *chevrah kaddisha* to do their holy work. He responded by saying, "Rabbi Rubinstein, do you really think that after a body has fallen thirty-five thousand feet there is anything left to identify?" I told him that I understood what he was saying, but I was still asking for his help.

The *chevrah kaddisha* were eventually allowed into the makeshift morgue to begin their grim task. What they found over the next few days was little short of astonishing.

In *parashas Vayeira* Avraham petitions Hashem to save Sedom: "And Avraham approached and said, 'Will Your anger consume the righteous along with the wicked? Perhaps there are fifty tzaddikim in the city. Will you also consume them and not forgive the place for fifty tzaddikim that are in it? Far be it for You to do a thing like this, to kill the righteous along with the wicked so that a tzaddik is the same as a *rasha*; far be it for You, the Judge of the entire world, not to do justice.'"

The holy Alshich explains that Avraham was exploring how Hashem might deal with Sedom. Perhaps He might indeed kill tzaddikim together with *reshaim*, or perhaps He might save the tzaddikim due to their deeds, but they would not be able to shield the other people who lived there with them. It might also be that the tzaddikim would merit protection for themselves and the others, too.

New York, Lockerbie, and Sedom

When Avraham said, "Far be it for you to kill the righteous along with the wicked," he was addressing the first possibility. The Alshich writes, "Regarding the first possibility, Hashem might retort that the tzaddikim deserve to die with the others as a result of their failure to protest their behavior. This was exactly the argument of the attribute of justice at the time of the destruction of the first Temple. To forestall such a position, Avraham argued that it would be unjust to act on that basis and both the righteous and the wicked should suffer the same fate. Their crimes were different, and so should be their punishment. If the wicked deserved death for their crimes, then the tzaddikim who were guilty of not protesting those crimes should get suffering, not death. That is why Avraham said, 'To kill the righteous along with the wicked so that a tzaddik is the same as a *rasha*. Far be it for You, the Judge of the entire world, not to do justice.'"

Avraham succeeded in receiving Hashem's assurance that He would not do such a thing, and not only would the deeds of tzaddikim protect them but also those around them. It was only the inability to find even the minimum number of such tzaddikim in the five cities that made up Sedom that condemned the cities to be destroyed. Yet if, as the Alshich says, Avraham established that a tzaddik would not suffer the same fate as a *rasha* even if they could be accused of not protesting their evil behavior, how could that happen, as the Alshich himself reports it did during the destruction of the first Temple?

The story is told in the Gemara: "Rav Acha bar Chaninah says: It never happened that a merciful decision came from HaKadosh Baruch Hu and was transformed into a punishment except once. Hashem told the angel Gavriel to go through the streets of Yerushalayim and write the letter *tav* in ink on the foreheads of the tzaddikim who had groaned and cried over the abominations that were carried out there, so that the destroying angels could have no effect on them. On the foreheads of *reshaim* the angel should write a *tav* in blood so that the destroying angels would kill them. Justice said to HaKadosh Baruch Hu, 'Almighty, what is the difference between the two groups?' Hashem replied, 'These are complete tzaddikim, and these are completely evil.' Justice said, 'Almighty, but the tzaddikim could have protested the others' behavior and didn't!' Hashem answered, 'It was clear to Me that had they protested, the others would not have listened.' Justice said, 'Almighty, that fact was known to You, but it could not have been known to them!' That is why the verse in *Yechezkel* says, 'Old and young, girl, child, and woman, were utterly slain.' "

The Ben Ish Chai points out two problems in the *gemara* in his *Ben Yehoyada*. Why did Hashem instruct that both the tzaddikim and the *reshaim* be marked? If only the tzaddikim were marked, that would have been sufficient to alert the destroying angels whom they could and couldn't touch. The second question is the obvious one. Hashem knew the argument of Justice before He heard it, so why order something that would not work in the first place?

The Ben Ish Chai answers that there was another group of Jews in Yerushalayim, those not obviously tzaddikim or *reshaim*, the *beinonim*. These people would need to be judged according to whether the majority of their actions were good or evil. The different fates of the two marked groups, one in ink and one in blood, were already decided. Justice had misunderstood Hashem's intention. He had already decided that the tzaddikim were guilty for not protesting; they, too, would die when Yerushalayim fell. But He had endorsed Avraham's protest — "to kill the righteous along with the wicked so that a tzaddik is the same as a *rasha*; far be it for You, the Judge of the entire world, not to do justice." Those marked as tzaddikim would die, but without pain or wounds. The Ben Ish Chai explains that the destroying angels would appear in front of them, and their souls would simply leave their bodies. The wicked, on the other hand, would die violently, by the sword. The fate of

New York, Lockerbie, and Sedom

the third group was to be decided separately.

The question Justice was posing to HaKadosh Baruch Hu was, what is the difference between these two groups — the ones that are marked and the one that isn't? When Hashem referred to those with a *tav* of ink as complete tzaddikim, Justice thought that Hashem intended to let them off completely and therefore protested.

The *chevrah kaddisha* in Lockerbie began the grim task of identifying the Jews among the victims. There were seventeen in total. The sights that confronted them in that morgue were too horrific to describe in these pages; my friend told me it took him an entire year to be able to sleep at night. The secretary of state's words to me were appallingly true — "Do you think that after a body has fallen thirty-five thousand feet there is anything left to identify?" Yet as the seventeen Jewish bodies were located, an astonishing thing became apparent. None of them had so much as a fingernail missing! Most had suffered only bruising. A few weren't even bruised.

I told this tale once in a *shiur* I gave in London. Afterward a young lady approached me and explained that her brother had been on that flight. Although he was not very religious, he had taken his tefillin with him in his baggage. His body was found lying in the fetal position, and beside him, impossibly, inexplicably, were his tefillin!

Ha'azinu begins with the words "Give ear, Heavens, and I will speak. Listen, Earth, to the words of my mouth." The Alshich points to the word *va'adabeirah*, "and I will speak," which in Hebrew suggests harsh speech, and to the words *imrei fi*, "the words of my mouth," which suggest gentle words. He explains that Moshe could address the heavens and demand that he be listened to. Angels are not creatures that have freedom of choice. When he was addressing the Earth, though, where human beings, who do have freedom of choice, live, he used gentle words that persuade.

We cannot know the future and what the events of September

11 will bring the Jewish people. We should, however, recall the past and remember the words of the *Da'as Zekeinim*: "Now recall and examine the acts of kindness that Hashem has done to the Jewish people." We should also recall that Hashem never judges tzaddikim like *reshaim*. Now, more than ever, we need to try our best to be counted among the tzaddikim.

Finally, we must remove any possible complaint Justice could have against us by reaching out to those whose actions could condemn them and protesting and trying to draw them back with gentle words that persuade.

Lost in Glasgow

(Hamodia)

When I put down the phone, the memories came flooding back. I hadn't seen or spoken to him in twenty-seven years. We both used to belong to the same Jewish organization in Glasgow, and when we first met I was a "sage" of fifteen years and he was twelve. I was introduced to him by his big brother, who was my close friend. This little brother looked up to me and often sought the guidance of my advanced years. Now he had phoned me completely out of the blue and asked if he could come to me once again for help.

It turned out that he had been living for the past ten years not too far from Manchester, in the beautiful town of Buxton. He had married out, and now, after an acrimonious divorce from his non-Jewish wife, there were complications over custody of their child. He needed to find a good family lawyer and thought that I might know one. I certainly did — I knew several, in fact — and it was easy enough to make a phone call and an appointment on his behalf. Then we started to catch up on the missing quarter of a century.

He was now a completely secular Jew with no connection to the Jewish community. This was the pattern of all his siblings. He was one of the 50 percent of Anglo Jews who vanish and disappear from the Jewish world.

As we talked, he said something that particularly intrigued me. He recalled the old Scottish song "I Belong to Glasgow, Dear Old Glasgow Town" and said, "I love being a Glaswegian. I love people's reaction, especially in England, when they hear a Glaswegian accent. People assume you will have a great sense of humor, be intelligent, and be able to take care of yourself in a fight."

His analysis was correct. I had put the latter part of it to good use once when I was in yeshivah in England and five skinheads were menacing two *bachurim*. I intervened and unleashed my Glaswegian accent. The biggest of the Neanderthals couldn't fathom it. His mind struggled with two opposing concepts: *Jew — He should be afraid of me. Glaswegian — I should be afraid of him.* It was too much for him, and he and his fellow troglodytes departed with no damage done.

I told my old friend that I, too, was proud to come from Glasgow, but I was far prouder of being a Jew. Glasgow is Scotland's industrial center and its biggest city. It has a proud history, particularly in the fields of heavy industry and shipbuilding. It has also made significant contributions to the fields of medicine and science. In the scheme of the world's history, though, Glasgow's story could be painted as a miniature. The story of the Jewish people by comparison would require an entire wall for a mural, and it would have to be an enormous wall at that.

Science fiction abounds with the idea of a time machine. From the genre's earliest writers until today people have imagined being able to travel into the past or the future, perhaps to meet the greats of history. With the publication of Einstein's theory of relativity in 1905, the concept moved from the world of fiction to reality, or, at least, theoretical reality. The science is complex and the inevitable outcome for anyone trying it would be instant death, but it is theoretically possible.

You would, I'm sure, be interested to know that a time machine has already been built, and I have one in my hand as I write this article. It is called a "pen."

The *Chovos HaLevavos* (*Sha'ar HaBechinah*, ch. 5) points out that with one of these machines a person can travel through time. He can go back to the world of thousands of years ago and read what people's concerns were then and what they thought. Through this machine, too, a person can travel to the future and communicate his thoughts and ideas to those who have not yet been born.

Jews have always been time travelers. Certainly one of America's greatest men of letters thought so. Last century he wrote an essay entitled, "Concerning the Jews," in which he wrote:

"If the statistics are right, the Jews constitute but one percent of the human race. It suggests a nebulous dim puff of stardust lost in the blaze of the Milky Way. Properly, the Jew ought hardly to be heard of, but he is heard of, has always been heard of. He is as prominent on the planet as any other people, and his commercial importance is extravagantly out of proportion to the smallness of his bulk. His contribution to the world's list of great names in literature, science, art, music, finance, medicine, and abstruse learning are also way out of proportion to the weakness of his numbers.

"He has made a marvelous fight in the world in all the ages and has done so with his hands tied behind him. He could be vain of himself and be excused for it. The Egyptian, the Babylonian, and the Persian filled the planet with sound and splendor, then faded to dream-stuff and passed away. The Greek and the Roman followed and made a vast noise, and they are gone. Other peoples have sprung up and held their torch high for a time, but it burned out and they sit in twilight now or have vanished.

"The Jew saw them all, beat them all, and is now what he always was, exhibiting no decadence, no infirmities of age, no weakening of his parts, no slowing of his energies, no dulling of his alert and aggressive mind. All things are mortal save the Jew; all other forces pass, but he remains. What is the secret of his immortality?"

Several years ago I was a joint guest speaker for a charity. My fellow speaker was the ex-speaker of Great Britain's House of Commons, Viscount Tonnypandy. The viscount told the tale of the first Jew he'd ever met. It was in his hometown of Tonnypandy in Wales at the beginning of last century, in around 1910. A Jew called Isaacs approached little Geordie Thomas and asked him if he would be willing to come in and light the coal fire on Friday night and Shabbos morning. if he would do this every week, he would receive a threepenny coin. Geordie eagerly agreed and returned home proudly holding his fortune in his hand.

He entered his mother's kitchen, where he found her washing dishes. She observed him out of the corner of her eye as she carried on with her task. When she finished, she turned to him and asked, "Where did you get that, boy?"

"The Jew Mr. Isaacs gave it to me. If I go into his house on his Sabbath and light his fire Friday night and Saturday morning, I get threepence!"

His mother looked at him sternly and said, "Take it back, boy!"

Little Geordie was stunned and replied, "But, Mam, he said I could have it!"

His mother insisted he should take it back. The future peer of the realm looked up at his mother, and his lip started to quiver and tears filled his eyes. He said, "But why, Mam?"

His mother looked at him and explained, "You don't take money from a man to help him serve his God!"

Geordie Thomas trudged back to his benefactor still clutching his threepenny piece and told him why he could not accept the money. The Jew would hear nothing of it and marched him straight back to his mother. Mr. Isaacs and Mrs. Thomas began to argue. In the end, they came to a compromise. Geordie could keep his threepence on that one occasion, but from then on he would light the Shabbos fires for free.

Lost in Glasgow

Viscount Tonnypandy looked at his Jewish audience and declared, "You Jews, you've forgotten who you are! When we in this country were still running around in animal skins, you had already built your golden Temple in Jerusalem. While we were still living in caves, you had already written the book that would inspire the whole world. Never be ashamed of being Jewish! You've forgotten who you are!"

So we can answer Mark Twain's question, "What is the secret of his immortality?" It is because we are not ashamed of being Jewish; we are proud to carry a special responsibility.

The Chafetz Chaim wrote whole *sefarim* spelling out exactly what that special responsibility is. In *Chizuk HaDa'as* (ch. 2), he writes about those he calls "lost sheep":

"It is well known that when we received the Torah from Hashem, we did not accept it for ourselves alone. Each and every one of us accepted upon ourselves the responsibility of strengthening observance of the Torah among every other Jew. Therefore every Jew became responsible for every other Jew.... From this comes the law that every Jew can fulfill a mitzvah on behalf of another Jew even though he has already carried out his own obligation toward that mitzvah, as in the case of Kiddush and shofar blowing."

As the Rosh explains (in *Berachos* 20), "If a fellow Jew has not done a mitzvah, then it as if you have not done that mitzvah either. Similarly, if you have the opportunity to stop a Jew from doing a sin and you do not take it, then his crime becomes your crime."

The Torah has carried us through the millennia, but in every age Jews have lost the way and forgotten who they are and eventually become ashamed of what they are. Instead, they see greatness in the trivial, and as their vision contracts, they are no longer able to view that which is enormous.

Pride in coming from Scotland's greatest city can blind a Scottish Jew to another story, a far, far greater story — his own story. Enchantment with all things Greek led tens of thousands to disappear forever. It happens in every age — Hellenisim, socialism, nationalism, feminism.

It only stops when we reach out and show our lost sheep the way home.

If You'll Take My Advice

(The Jewish Tribune, August 12, 1999)

Being out of town for Shabbos has lots of benefits, chief among these anonymity. Usually a rabbi's Shabbos is spent saying lots of *shiurim*. A weekend away offers the perfect break, a chance to daven, learn, and recharge the batteries with a well-earned nap.

Of course, when you go to shul on Shabbos morning there is always the danger that the resident rabbi will compliment you with an invitation to give the *drashah*. Recently I found myself in such a position.

The rabbi honored me with a seat at the front, but on this occasion I wasn't asked to speak. The reason was that there was no *drashah* scheduled for that Shabbos. Instead the shul had arranged a panel for a question-and-answer session after a *kiddush*. The subject was to be family, and the panel was to consist of the rabbi and someone who works for a Jewish organization that offers advice to couples with marriage difficulties. This struck me as perfect, a straightforward service and a chance to slip away quietly to where the gefilte fish was waiting anxiously to make my acquaintance.

"Englishe" shuls put their rabbis in a box by the eastern wall of the shul. I have sat in many of these. Some are designed to accommodate a giant, with the rabbi revealing nothing more than a forehead to the congregation. Others follow the opposite school, so that the sides press against the visitor's shoulders, and turning the page of the siddur leaves one resembling a sardine attempting to break out of its tin. I was sitting in a rabbi's box that clearly demonstrated that it was constructed during a national shortage of timber.

After davening the shul president approached me and asked for a special favor. The rabbi was not feeling well. Could I step in and take his place in the question-and-answer session? As long as he could find a reasonably muscular congregant to lever me out of the box, I would be delighted, I told him.

The first question was from someone who wanted to know when the "rabbis" were going to do something about *agunos*. As I answered, I noticed that the shul's rabbi, although he was not feeling well enough to participate, felt well enough to be sitting among his congregants wearing an enigmatic smile.

The next question was from a lady who wanted to know why yeshivos and seminaries don't run courses about marriage. I was surprised at the question, particularly since few, if any, in the congregation would have sons or daughters in a yeshivah or seminary. Having spent seven years in Gateshead Yeshivah and having taught in three seminaries, I thought I was qualified to respond.

"Both yeshivos and seminaries attempt to bring out the very best qualities in their *talmidim*. This training develops sensitivity in all aspects of *bein adam l'chaveiro*, relations between people. At the same time, when young men or women become engaged, they get a specific course of instruction, not just in the halachic obligations of marriage but also in how to interact with their spouse. If I compare the basis that secular marriage is built on, I think the answer to the question is that making a marriage work and building a family is absolutely what yeshivah and seminary are all about."

The audience liked the answer; my fellow panelist did not. Before answering the next question, he permitted himself to disagree publicly with what I had said.

"I feel that yeshivos and sems do not equip young Jews for marriage. Young people are taught that they must sit and learn as much as possible and that the wife's role is to stay at home and support her husband, and then everything will be okay. It simply does not work!"

Then he went on to explain his organization's approach and his own qualifications. He had been trained by the non-Jewish Marriage Guidance Council (now called "Relate"), and he had brought the skills he learned there to the Jewish organization he now works for. He had never been near a yeshivah.

"In our organization we try to help couples see what is wrong with their marriage and see if they want to solve it. We do not give advice. We are nonjudgmental."

Lastly, he complained that so few *rabbanim* have been trained like him in counseling. His most disturbing comment of all was when he claimed, "Our organization is seeing increasing numbers of religious couples who are coming to us with difficulties."

One of Manchester's institutions employed an educational psychologist to assess children who were not doing well at school. The children were given a standard IQ test and uniformly produced terrible results. The psychologist could not understand why the results were so poor. The answer lay in the test itself. It had been designed for non-Jewish children. The correct answer to the fill-in question "Fish and ——?" should have been "chips." The Jewish children wrote "mayonnaise"! It was obvious that the test would have to be redesigned to take into account the different background and culture of the children.

Common sense would dictate that religious Jews, with their extremely complex and spiritual outlook, could only be well advised by someone sharing the same experiences and outlook.

There is no doubt that in secular society counseling is a growth industry. The philosophies and trends that have led to so much societal suffering and the breakdown of marriage are being applied to solve the same problems. It is self-evident that advice springing from such sources is totally inappropriate for religious Jews.

A few years ago I attended an intensive counseling course together with several other *rabbanim*. The trainers were a well-known husband-and-wife team who have written books on the subject, teach about it at university and run courses for local authorities. The sine qua non of counseling, we learned, is to be "nonjudgmental." No matter what the client is telling you he has done or plans to do, you must not indicate whether you approve or not. Among other rules, counselors are told it is essential not to become "emotionally involved" with their clients.

The participants of the course had to practice various possible scenarios, with the experts pretending to be clients. All of the scenarios were real ones taken from the trainers' extensive experience. On one occasion my trainer took the part of a heroin addict. Although he had nearly died from his addiction and had eventually given up drugs, he was thinking of starting again. My role was to help him explore why he wanted to do this (nonjudgmentally). If I found that he honestly wanted to go back to drug addiction and was fully aware of the dangers, I was supposed to help him consider "safe" ways to go about it.

One of the rabbis who was with me on the counseling course was finishing a university degree in counseling. He has now completed a master's degree in the subject. We both concluded that what we had just been trained in was the absolute opposite of Judaism.

Being nonjudgmental means you cannot offer advice. To quote my fellow panelist, "You try to get the couple to find the solution themselves." But that is what they have not been able to do, perhaps after many years, and it is precisely why they have turned to someone else. Sadly, the person whose help has been sought

If You'll Take My Advice

may have been trained not to offer the solution, even if it is patently obvious where it lies. Judaism believes in offering advice. The *Zohar* refers to the 613 mitzvos as 613 *eitzos*, 613 pieces of advice!

The first essential in Jewish counseling is that the adjective *Jewish* does not merely describe the ethnicity of the counselors but the philosophy from where the counseling comes.

HaRav Shlomo Wolbe, *shlita*, writes in *Alei Shor* (vol. 2, p. 295): "And not just regarding commentaries on the Torah and halachic decisions do we rely on our sages, but also for life issues for which there is no specific section in the *Shulchan Aruch* do we believe in the Torah sages in every generation."

Any counseling has to have the full endorsement and participation of our *gedolim* and tradition. The sages' approach to people in distress is certainly not, as taught by contemporary counseling courses, to avoid becoming "emotionally involved." After the passing of the previous Gerrer Rebbe, the saintly Pnei Menachem, the following story, among scores of others, appeared in a Jewish newspaper.

A man beset by numerous sorrows and misfortunes commented upon leaving the Rebbe's room that he felt as though stones had been removed from his heart. When this comment was repeated to the Rebbe, the tzaddik replied, "And do you know what happened to those stones? I took them and placed them on my own heart."

There is no doubt that the problems besetting our community now include areas that we have not had to deal with before. *Gedolim* have increasingly addressed this new reality in recent years. We may find ourselves having to turn to professionals and experts as we attempt to deal with these issues. But their expertise has to be applied through the filter of halachah and the judgment of *gedolim* to ensure that it is compatible with who and what we are. If you'll take my advice, organizations that fail this test should be avoided at all costs.

Counted In and Counted Out

(Hamodia)

I drove through the city of Liverpool the other week, and since I was early for the *shiur* I was to deliver, I popped in to see an old friend. He greeted me warmly and took me out into his garden. It was a beautiful early-summer evening. As we chatted, he was struck by a sudden thought and told me that he had to show me something.

He went into his house and returned with a large piece of paper. When he unrolled it on the garden table, I could see it was a family tree. My friend explained that he and his wife had started to research their family, and this was the result of their efforts. The paper was very large, and my friend pointed to the earliest name they had tracked down so far, a Mr. Yeshua Fleishman, who was born around 1860. He had married someone named Sarah, and they had a large family in Russia before immigrating to England. Their children's names were there, too. There was an Avraham and his eight siblings, Dina, Shmuel, Feige, Daniel, Rivka, Rachel, Binyamin, and Miriam. All but one had sailed to England. Feige stayed behind to look after a sick grandmother. Eventually she moved to America. My friend pointed to his own family and his children, one of

Counted In and Counted Out

whom is a *talmid* of mine, and then he made a comment that opened my eyes.

"Look," he said and pointed again at the tree, this time at the third generation of Yeshua Fleishman's family. "The names! Look at the names!"

By the third generation, the Yehoshuas had been replaced by Jasons, the Sarahs with Samanthas. Then he pointed to the next generation, and the anglicized names remained the same, but the size of the families had shrunk. By the next generation many of the families, like autumnal leaves, had dropped off the tree altogether.

Here was the truth so much discussed and fretted about in the secular Jewish world in undeniable picture form. As these people had shrugged off Jewish names and Jewish practice, they inevitable shrugged off their Jewish identities, too.

In *Bemidbar* Moshe is commanded to count the Jewish people. Rashi explains that when they came to be counted each one brought with them their *sefer hayuchsin*, their family tree. Each Jew was proud to point to his document as proof that he and his family had flowered and grown from a branch with roots that traveled all the way back to Avraham, Yitzchak, and Yaakov.

The counting, though, was much more than an opportunity for each Jewish family to prove they belonged. Each and every Jew would pass before Moshe Rabbeinu himself with Aharon HaKohen standing by his side. Each individual would be identified and known to Moshe by his Jewish name. He was then recorded as being part of the Jewish people, and in so doing the Jewish people became part of him. The merits of all the people became available for Moshe to draw on and would act as a protection should he need it.

The failure to realize the importance of being counted among the Jewish people led them to make one of their greatest mistakes and set in motion a set of events that nearly led to disaster. When Moshe was told that he may send in spies to the Land of Israel, Hashem included one caveat: "Send for yourself *anashim*." The

Alshich points out that the word *anashim* means "great men." Moshe was being told to choose the very best he could find. This would minimize the danger that they would bring back a bad report and that he might suffer the consequences. Moshe did precisely that: "All of them were great men, the leaders of the Jewish people."

One of the puzzles of Jewish history is how these *anashim* could bring back such a disastrous report that rejected the Land of Israel. They had seen with their own eyes what Hashem had done to the most powerful society on earth when He brought the Jewish people out of Egypt. What had they to fear from any nation, no matter how powerful?

The Kesav Sofer explains that they did not doubt for a second that Hashem could bring them into the Land of Israel. They doubted if Hashem *would* bring them into the Land of Israel.

After the Exodus, they had made the golden calf. Surely that meant they no longer deserved that Hashem keep His promise. The spies' fear resulted from failing to understand the significance of being counted after the sin of the golden calf. One of the greatest ways Hashem can show the Jewish people that He loves them is to count them. After the golden calf they had counted themselves out of Hashem's affection. In *Bemidbar* Hashem counted them back in, and they failed to realize this.

In *Ki Sissa*, the Torah says that the people must be counted by half-coins and not counted directly "so that there is no plague among them when you count them." Rashi thus reveals another principle about counting Jews: "Counting allows an *ayin hara*, evil eye, to rule over them, and plague may come upon them, as happened in the days of King David."

I was once walking to shul with my son, who was then ten years old. This walk was always a time for him to quiz me on the parashah. Why, he asked, should the Jews suffer a plague because King David counted them? What did they do wrong? Surely King

David should suffer a plague, not his people. The counter should be punished, not the counted.

Fortunately I had looked in the *sefer Ohel Yaakov*, by the Dubno Maggid, the night before, which is where I had first seen my son's question asked. He explains that if someone steals wood and bricks from his neighbor and uses them to build a house, the neighbor cannot demand that the entire building be knocked down so that he can retrieve his bricks. If, however, the thief later knocks down a wall to build an extension, and the man finds his bricks and wood lying on the ground, he may take them back.

There can be a time when the Jewish people are individually on an extremely high spiritual level. At other times, though, they may fail as individuals to live up to the Torah's standards. Being part of the Jewish people protects them. Despite their misdeeds, Hashem will not take that "brick" from the "wall." If, however, someone counts a Jew directly, then that very action has the effect of removing him from the protection of the rest. Counting is by its very nature an act of separating out parts from a whole. Once that protection has been removed, their misdeeds may be punished, and a plague may befall them.

I recall once hearing a close friend telling his wife that he was very tired when he awoke that morning. He had considered going back to sleep and attending a later minyan. Instead he'd forced himself to attend his usual seven-thirty minyan. "It's a good job I did," he exclaimed. "When I got there I found someone who needed help urgently. If I'd gone to the later minyan, it would have been too late!"

One of the reasons Chazal emphasize the importance of davening with a minyan is in case you have insufficient merit to receive the thing you are praying for. You may still have your prayer answered in the merit of the others you are praying with.

Last Shabbos morning I decided to take a slightly longer route home from shul. It is a longer route precisely because the road is full of Jews. I would be guaranteed to be stopped by friends and acquaintances keen to have a shmooze. Yet in walking those streets I had the pleasure of seeing other Jews, and I met a friend who had been desperate to ask me a question about a very important matter.

Unlike those names on that Liverpool family tree that tragically counted themselves out of the Jewish people, we are proud to be rooted firmly in Torah soil and to count ourselves in. Still, we have to remind ourselves that there are a thousand other ways to count ourselves both in and out of the Jewish people. There are always people who will be counting on us. We have to make sure we are available at the times and places we can make ourselves count the most.

Teaching...or Teaching Talmidim

(Unpublished)

A number of years ago I was lecturing at a conference. After I finished my own lecture, I went to hear another participant talking about teachers and teaching. After introducing his subject, he invited his audience to consider a very intriguing question. How many teachers had they had in their lifetime?

The speaker explained that what he meant by the term *teacher* was anyone who had taught them anything, from how to multiply three and three to how to write an essay or how to sail a boat or sew or knit. The audience paused to think and count. When individuals were invited to reveal their results, most had recalled around one hundred teachers from primary school through university, including those who had taught life's other skills, such as how to drive a car.

The lecturer paused for dramatic effect and then asked another question. "Of those hundred or so teachers, how many of them inspired you so much that they actually influenced or changed your life?"

The audience thought again, and when they were invited to answer that question, almost everyone came up with the same answer — one or two. The lecturer concluded his point by saying, "That is how common the really talented teacher is. He is as rare as one in a hundred! That sort of person is so passionate and committed to his subject that his passion and commitment transfer themselves to his students."

Chazal put it like this: "*Devarim hayotzim min halev nichnasim lalev* — Words that come from the heart enter the heart." There is, though, an even greater type of teacher — one whose passion and commitment to his subject is matched by his passion and commitment to his students.

Many years ago in Gateshead Yeshivah the *mashgiach*, Rav Matisyahu Salomon, *shlita*, asked the young married men in his *shiur* to ask themselves what sort of *bachur* they invited home for Shabbos. After we had thought for a moment, he inquired if the answer wasn't that we looked for the nicest boy who would make an enjoyable guest and add to the Shabbos table with his personality and sophisticated *divrei Torah*. "If so," said the *mashgiach*, "you aren't really inviting such *bachurim* to fulfill the mitzvah of *hachnasas orchim*. You are inviting the *bachurim* to enhance your table and do *chesed* for you!" It was the shy *bachur* and the awkward *bachur* who needed the encouragement and warmth of a Shabbos invitation, even though they would not necessarily "enhance" the Shabbos table.

There is no great achievement in teaching a pupil so gifted that he sails through the academic material, mastering it easily and producing superb exam results. Such a child would have succeeded almost regardless of who taught him. The measure of a great teacher is if he can take his passion and commitment to his subject and transfer it to a student who is struggling to absorb it.

An even greater achievement is taking a student who does not want to learn or even refuses to learn and turning him into a vessel that is eager to be filled. A teacher who is truly committed to his *talmid*, and not just his subject, will persevere and exhaust every

Teaching...or Teaching Talmidim

trick and technique there is to overcome the resistance of a student who does not seem to want to succeed.

Everyone knows the story of Rabbi Akiva — or, rather, a man called Akiva — and how he began the journey that would transform him into Rabbi Akiva. One day he noticed a rock that had a hole in it. Wondering how the hole got there, he saw water dripping into the hole. He said, "If water, which is soft, could do this to stone, which is hard, then the Torah, which is hard, can certainly have an impact on my soft heart."

The story reveals an often overlooked fact. Rabbi Akiva was aware of the Torah and its nature before this incident. Up till then he had rejected the Torah, but there existed a trigger, a way to reveal the potential that anyone would have thought was lacking in him until then. Once that key had been found, nothing on earth could stop Akiva from becoming Rabbi Akiva.

Taking someone who does not want to learn and turning him into a person who thirsts for knowledge is one of the most difficult tasks imaginable. The greatest educators know how to do it, though, and, more importantly, they love their *talmidim* enough to want to make the effort.

A *bachur* once told me a story his father had told him of what occurred when he had gone to yeshivah. One of the *talmidim* of the yeshivah was a young man who was extremely popular with the boys. He was very talented and possessed a natural charisma that gave him universal popularity. But for some reason this father could not fathom until this day, he did not get along with his rebbe.

This rebbe was used to instant success. The boy often slept in and sometimes missed learning sessions. Although he did nothing that was actually bad, the rebbe became more and more frustrated at his unusual lack of success. Eventually the rebbe gave up on the young man and asked his father to take him to another yeshivah. Fortunately, the other yeshivah contained someone who decided not only to give this boy a second chance, but to get to the root of the boy's problem and solve it once and for all. The new rebbe succeeded, and the young man followed in Rabbi Akiva's footsteps and achieved great heights in his learning.

Years later the first rebbe met the young man, who was now married with children. "I have to ask your forgiveness," he told him. "If I had persevered the way you did, I would have had the merit of being able to say that it was I who created a *talmid chacham*."

When I first went to yeshivah, I was in the *shiur* of Rav Moshe Schwab, *zt"l*, the old *mashgiach* of Gateshead. One of Rav Moshe's many talents was his gift for raising funds, and he would devote a significant amount of his time and energy to collecting badly needed cash for Europe's largest yeshivah.

While he was away on one of his fund-raising trips, someone came to Gateshead and suggested a *shidduch* for me. I went to discuss the matter with the *rosh yeshivah*, Rav Leib Lopian, *zt"l*. By the time Rav Moshe returned to Gateshead I was a *chasan*.

Rav Moshe took me aside to ask me about the *shidduch*. *Shidduchim* were another one of his talents. I could see that he was hurt, and I knew why. Being in his *shiur*, I should have at least informed him what I was contemplating, but instead I had discussed the matter with someone else. Rav Moshe actually asked me, "And why did you go to Rav Leib?"

The months slipped by, and it was the week before my wedding. I was walking with Rav Moshe while I asked him about some point in the Gemara that I had not understood. After he finished explaining it to me, he said, "You know, it's very important when a young man gets married for him to be able to put his hand in his pocket, take out some money, and say to his wife, 'Here, go and buy yourself something nice!' " He took my hand and pressed 750 pounds in notes into it. I protested that I couldn't accept the money, but Rav Moshe insisted and walked away. This was the *rav*

Teaching...or Teaching Talmidim

whom I had hurt — he was determined not to allow that incident to jeopardize a relationship with a *talmid*.

The next day we were again taking a walk after the *shiur*, and again I was asking for elucidation on the Gemara. After Rav Moshe had finished explaining it, he said to me, "You know that money I gave you yesterday? It was not enough!" and he thrust another 250 pounds into my hand.

Rav Moshe was a rebbe par excellence. Even when a *talmid* had wounded him or made it clear that he didn't actually like him, Rav Moshe never let go.

A friend told me another tale about Rav Moshe, which he had personally experienced. A certain *bachur* had behaved so badly that it was obvious he would have to be expelled. My friend was sent to summon the boy, and Rav Moshe asked him to wait outside. The boy was told that his crime had been discovered and he was no longer a member of the yeshivah. The stunned young man was told to send in the *bachur* who was waiting outside, since he was going to be helping him pack and escort him to the train station.

As soon as my friend entered, Rav Moshe told him what had happened. He told him to help him pack and persuade him that he should come back and beg to be given a second chance. The two soon returned, and the *bachur* begged for a second chance. Rav Moshe refused! And then he called my friend in again.

Once more, he told him to persuade the boy to beg him to reconsider. Once again Rav Moshe refused his pleas and told my friend to persuade him to try a third time. This time Rav Moshe agreed to give him one more chance.

Rav Moshe's strategy paid off, and a boy who could have been a "write-off" learned his lesson and went on to greatness in Torah.

Rav Moshe's love for his *talmidim* meant that many whom others might have given up on remained attached to Torah (and, by the way, Rav Moshe) throughout their entire lives.

Some of *Klal Yisrael*'s biggest *talmidei chachomim* came from backgrounds or went through stages of their lives where the likelihood of them achieving greatness in Torah looked very remote, and, in some cases, impossible. Reish Lakish, the great Talmudic Sage, started life as the leader of a band of thieves! All these people, though, shared one thing in common: they had a rebbe who was determined not to let go until the person they were holding on to changed from a confused young man into a credit to his people.

Avraham's Gift

(The Jewish Tribune, November 1999)

Last summer during our family holiday in Scotland, one of my sons and I headed off to climb Mount Schihallion, which has an altitude of over 3,500 feet. We parked at the foot of the mountain. From the car next to ours emerged a grandfather of about seventy and his teenage grandson. They started to dress for the ascent. Our clothing was of the latest high-tech fabrics; the grandfather wore a yellow nylon jacket. My walking stick consisted of three sections and with a twist could be any size I chose. His walking stick was made of wood. We finished getting ready, and off we strode, covering the ground well — until about halfway up.

Over the years thoughtful souls have piled stones into little cairns, strategically placed to guide you to the top. Very soon I started to wish that instead they had strategically placed intensive care units.

As we collapsed, panting, on top of one of the cairns, I looked down and saw that the yellow-clad grandfather was strolling inexorably toward us. He was calling encouragement to his lagging teenage companion and gave the impression that he was taking a stroll in the park. My son looked at me, and no words were needed. We got up, ready to escape this embarrassing pursuer. At the next stop, we spotted the grandfather not far behind. The end was in sight — both the top of the mountain and my will to carry on. The grandfather strolled past with a cheery "Afternoon!"

Later in the day I thought about this incident, and a worrying thought struck me. My reaction to being overtaken by this old fellow was one of profound unhappiness, even outrage. I realized that I had been affected by society's view of the elderly. I was much younger, and therefore I must be better.

Today managers and workers are made redundant at the age of forty-five; they are told they're too old to ever work again. A few years ago a major British bank was taken over by a Far Eastern one. The British bank had attempted to make its operation appear "lean and mean" and had rid itself of its older staff. When the new Asian owners arrived, they noticed that the workforce was all young. Upon hearing why, they exclaimed, "That's why you were ripe for a takeover. You've lost everyone with experience."

In the contemporary world, old equals useless. Old people are seen as having little value and precious little to contribute. But the Torah says, "Before someone with white hair you should stand up, and give honor to an old person, and you shall thus fear your God; I am Hashem" (*Vayikra* 19:32). Rashi says that the word *zakein*, old person, refers to an old person who has acquired wisdom.

In *Horeb*, Rav Shamshon Refael Hirsch writes: "Alas for the youth who in pert arrogance derides old age, the companion of the past, which is the mother of everything of which he boasts, and wisdom, which should be the father of his actions. Happy are you, young man, if you rejoice in vitality and the strength God grants you while at the same time realizing that they are still unripe blossoms which you must allow to ripen, that you are still only a shoot more rich in hope than in fruit, a shoot which if it is to be blessed one day with fruit must have the past for its soil and wisdom for its sunshine.... Show respect, honor, and civility to the old men and wise men of every nation."

The *Yalkut* in *Chayei Sarah* reports: "Avraham asked Hashem

Avraham's Gift

for old age. He said, '*Ribbono shel Olam*, a father and son may enter a place, and no one will know whom to honor. If you crown him with age, people will know whom to honor.' Hashem replied, 'You have asked for a good thing, and it will start with you.' "

From the beginning of time until Avraham came along there was no such thing as aging. This is what the verse means when it says, "And Avraham was old." He was the first person in history to show his age.

Aging is a badge of honor and respect. It is a point of reference for younger people so they will know whom to approach for advice.

A recent Friday night took me to a different shul from my usual one. I had the flu, and I couldn't face the longer walk to my regular shul. I was invited to sit in the front and sat beside two other *rabbanim*. One I knew well, and he introduced me to the other. He asked me where I had learned, and I replied Gateshead. He asked, "Were you there at the time of the Reb Leibs?" (Rav Leib Gurwicz and Rav Leib Lopian were brothers-in-law and joint *roshei yeshivah*), and I replied proudly that I was.

"I was in the Mir with Reb Leib," he said. I was electrified and started to ask him questions about my *rosh yeshivah* as a young man. Then a thought occurred to me. "Did you hear *shiurim* from Reb Yerucham?" The rabbi smiled, looked at me indulgently, and replied, "Of course."

It was a good job that we had arrived before davening because I couldn't stop myself as the questions came tumbling out. What was he like? How did he present a *shmuess*? Was it true that he sometimes used to take *bachurim* to another location for the *shmuess* simply to get them excited so as to break down the resistance that routine creates?

He answered all of my questions and told me other things that I had not thought to ask about. I felt like someone who had discovered a gold mine — no, three gold mines!

Dancing through Time

We started to daven then, before I could ask him to take me back even a generation earlier to stories he may have heard from Rav Yerucham about his great rebbe, Reb Simchah Zissel, *zt"l*. Avraham's gift had alerted me to the possibility that sitting just a few inches from me was a door through which I could walk into Poland at the beginning of the century and have a look at the great Mir Yeshivah.

The Torah tells us at the beginning of *Ha'azinu*, "Remember the days long gone by. Ponder the years of each generation. Ask your father and let him tell you, your grandfather who will explain it."

Klal Yisrael is built upon the previous generations. Alas for any of us if we allow the world's view to blind us to Avraham Avinu's gift and the key to the past — old age.

Smile

(Unpublished)

In Eretz Yisrael, the Klausenberger Rebbe, who had lost his wife and eleven children in the war, set about the task of rebuilding. One of the most wonderful institutions to rise from the ashes as part of his contribution to rebuilding the Jewish people was Laniado Hospital in Netanya. Today it serves a quarter of a million Jews.

At one of the fund-raising dinners held in the UK by Laniado's supporters, I was asked to introduce their guest of honor, Sir Jimmy Saville, OBE (Officer of the Order of the British Empire, an award bestowed by the Queen on those who have made an outstanding contribution to England; Sir Jimmy received the award for his charity work). I must admit that part of my willingness to take on this role was the opportunity to meet Sir Jimmy.

In the UK he is one of the most famous personalities in the world of entertainment. But he is even more famous for his work outside the media. He has personally raised over 50 million pounds for charity during his lifetime. His favorite charities are hospitals, and he personally raised enough to build a special spinal injuries unit in his hometown of Leeds. At the height of his fame, he lived next door to the Talmud Torah in Manchester. An alumnus of the school told me he recalled Sir Jimmy chatting to the boys and quizzing them about what they had learned and what they believed.

At the dinner, after I had performed my role and introduced the guest of honor, who in reality needed no introduction at all, Sir Jimmy explained how he came to be such an admirer of the Jewish people.

He recalled his mother taking him to an area of Leeds where many Jews owned shops. They entered a store to purchase some material, which his mother planned to make into a dress. The shopkeeper greeted his mother warmly with a smile that lit up his face and asked her where her son went to school and how he was getting on there. More questions followed, and eventually the purchase was made and mother and son left the shop. Outside, little Jimmy, who had listened to the warm conversation between his mother and the Jewish shopkeeper, asked his mother how long she had known the man. His mother replied that this had been the first time she had set foot in the place; she had never met the man before in her life.

Sir Jimmy told his audience, "I thought about that, and even as a little boy, I felt that there was something I could learn from these people. In fact, every good thing I have ever done has been inspired by the Jewish people!"

Many years later, at the height of his fame, he was invited by a Jewish friend to go on a tour of the Land of Israel. By this time he was a flamboyant television personality. The tour included a reception at the home of the president of Israel. Together with many other guests, Jimmy (he had not yet been knighted by the Queen, so the title "sir" was still some way off) stood in line, waiting to meet the head of state.

In a striking suit of bright pink, with his ponytail and gold jewelry, it would be fair to say that he was not exactly inconspicuous. When his turn came, the president shook his hand and asked him, "How are you enjoying your stay in Israel?"

When the president spoke, though, he was not looking at his striking guest but at the people around him. Jimmy Saville decided

Smile

to tell the president exactly how he was feeling.

"Actually, I'm very disappointed!"

This response succeeded in getting the president's attention. He finally looked at his guest and asked, "Why?"

The outlandish figure in the too loud suit replied, "Because you've forgotten how to be Jewish! Jewish people smile at you when they're talking to you, and they look at your face, too."

The president was stunned. "And are there any other things that have disappointed you since you've been here?"

Jimmy assured him that there were. Despite the fact that there was a large line of people still waiting to be introduced to him, the head of state took Jimmy Saville into a room to hear exactly why he was disappointed.

After Jimmy voiced his opinions, the president of Israel asked if he would be willing to do him a favor. Would he agree to come with him to the Knesset the next day and tell the Israeli Cabinet everything he had just told him?

Later, Sir Jimmy was invited to meet Menachem Begin and Anwar Sadat. He would not reveal to his audience what he said to them, but it was enough to earn him a special award from the State of Israel for his contribution to the peace treaty between Israel and Egypt. When he finished his tale, Sir Jimmy Saville produced the gift he was given on behalf of the Israeli people. It was a beautiful little box. He opened it and pulled out a check, his contribution to Laniado Hospital. It was for one thousand pounds.

"Before I hand this over, I just want to tell you all, never forget how to be Jewish. Never forget how to smile!"

Rav Matisyahu Salomon, *shlita*, once pointed out that a person's face is a *reshus harabbim*, a public thoroughfare. You don't see your face, but other people do. A smile is something you give to other people.

On one occasion I went to see Rav Salomon to ask his advice. I had been invited to go across the River Tyne from Gateshead to speak to students in Newcastle upon Tyne. I was not very keen to do it. I told Rav Matisyahu that I was feeling a bit depressed, and I didn't think I would give a very good *shiur*. "Listen here, young man," he replied. "Do you think if I allowed my face to betray how I was feeling every time I walked through the *beis midrash* people would be interested in coming and telling me their worries?"

The Ramban writes in his *Iggeres HaKodesh*: "The Jewish people have been selected to give honor to Hashem. It is obvious that servants behave in a way their master demands and finds acceptable. Our relationship to Hashem is exactly that of servant to master. We are commanded to be a holy people to reflect His holiness...

"But if a Jew behaves badly in business or elsewhere, what will people say? 'Do you see this Jew who has learned and knows Torah? See how corrupt he is.' That is a *chillul Hashem*. Since we are supposed to emulate Hashem's attributes so that His ways can be glimpsed through us, *kiddush Hashem* or *chillul Hashem* rests solely with us."

The Ramban emphasizes that such a reaction to our misbehavior occurs when the world can correctly point at those who have "learned and know Torah" and behaved badly. A Jew who keeps, and claims to keep, nothing of the Torah can hardly be seen as an ambassador of Hashem in the world.

I often quote this *Ramban* to my students and point out that the logic applies to smiling. If the world observes religious Jews walking along the road as though they have just been told that their home has been destroyed, people will say that if they are so miserable (or, even worse, unfriendly) then that must be how Hashem wants them to be. This is hardly an encouragement for others to be impressed with our lifestyle; after all, it appears to produce such misery.

Perhaps we should remind ourselves of some of the things Chazal say about smiling. In the first chapter of *Avos*, the fifteenth *mishnah* says, "Greet everyone by projecting a smiling face." In the third chapter of *Avos*, the twelfth *mishnah* says, "Greet everyone cheerfully." The Rambam comments, "Everyone means everyone! Young and old, master and servant, any and every human being."

The Talmud says: "When the Torah states, 'And you shall love Hashem your God,' it means that the Name of Heaven should be loved through you. You should learn and attach yourself to Torah scholars. Your business dealings should be above reproach. You should speak gently to people. If you do that, people will say about you, 'Happy is the father who taught Torah to his son and produced such a person. Happy is the teacher who taught him Torah and produced such a person. How sad it is for others who did not learn Torah. This fellow who did learn, look how nicely he behaves and how exceptional are his deeds.' It is exactly such a person that the verse refers to when it says, 'You are My servant Israel, and through you I will be praised' " (*Yoma* 86).

There is no doubt that people will say such things about Jews who smile and treat people well — like Sir Jimmy Saville, who rebuked an Israeli president for forgetting to be a Jew and who reminded a Jewish audience, "Never forget how to be Jewish. Never forget how to smile!"

Chinese Whispers

(Hamodia, May 2001)

There is a game which for generations has brought endless amusement to children all over the world. In America it is called "broken telephone." In England it's called "Chinese whispers."

One child thinks of a sentence and whispers it to another, who in turn whispers it to a third. After the message has been passed from lip to ear six or seven times, the last recipient of the message announces what he heard. Invariably it is a very different sentence from the one that started. I remember once watching children engulfed in laughter as they played this game. Of course, for the desired effect to occur, the participants have to be a little less than careful in passing the message across to their neighbors. If the children try very hard to get it right, they usually do and the game loses its point.

There are, of course, circumstances where the relating of a message will inevitably be disrupted by even the most faithful *talmid*. Yehoshua, who the Torah says never left Moshe's side, was so distressed at Moshe's death that he forgot thousands of halachos. Had it not been for the intervention of Osniel ben Kenaz, who deduced the halachos through Talmudic reasoning, they would have been lost forever.

When the Jewish people were under the severest pressure by

the Romans and the *rabbanim* who carried our oral tradition were being slaughtered, there was a danger that the message would get distorted or lost. So the sea of the Talmud flowed into a harbor of parchment and ink so that it could be handed down unaltered to the generations.

Like the children's game, however, the message only travels forward unaltered if the conveyors of the message *want* it to be so. When Hashem tells Moshe at the beginning of *Shelach* that he may send men to spy out the Land of Israel, He uses the words *"Shelach lecha anashim* — Send for yourself men." Rashi comments on the seemingly redundant word *lecha*, "for yourself," that Hashem was not telling Moshe whether it was a good idea or not. It would be his choice. *Lecha* means "it is up to you."

The holy Alshich comments that the word *lecha* here means the same as Rashi's interpretation of *"lech lecha"* — the words Hashem spoke to Avraham when commanding him to leave his homeland. There Rashi says that for Avraham going to the Land of Israel would be *lecha*, "for your benefit." That, insists the Alshich, is what the word means here, too.

Moshe was being warned that there was a danger in this project. If the spies were to bring back a report falsely condemning the Land of Israel, it would have negative consequences that would directly impact upon him. Ultimately it would mean that because of that, not the striking of the rock, he would be unable to bring the Jewish people into the Land of Israel!

The Alshich supplies a parable to explain. Someone walks along a street at night and drops a penny. He shouts up to the people in their houses, "I've dropped a penny. Could someone bring me a light to see where it is?" No one is going to go down to the street to help someone look for a penny. So the man puts his hand in his pocket and pulls out a fifty-dollar bill.

This time the people hear him shouting that he has lost fifty dollars. That awakens the people's sense of pity, and they come down and bring lights. The lights reveal the fifty-dollar bill and the penny, too. The man is able to recover all his money.

The result of the spies' report is that an entire generation of men (not the women, who never believed the spies' report) were fated never to enter the Land of Israel and died in the desert. Their behavior meant that Hashem could not justify collecting their *neshamos* from a spiritually unclean place like the desert. If Moshe was also buried outside Eretz Yisrael, however, when Hashem collected his soul to take it to Heaven, He could at the same time pick up all the other souls of that generation, too.

So Moshe is told to choose *anashim*, "great men," to minimize this danger. Selecting the cream of the people, those totally loyal to Hashem and His servant Moshe, would minimize the risk. As long as they would be "*shelichim*," people who would carry out their mission to the letter and would see themselves as fulfilling Moshe's instructions and agenda, everything would be fine.

The Shem MiShmuel explains how these great men, leaders and princes of the Jewish people, came to replace Moshe's message and ambitions with their own.

The greatness of the spies was in part evidenced by the fact that they were all prophets. When they looked into the future, they could see a *Klal Yisrael* who were no longer led by them. They could see others leading the people in the Land of Israel. It was this that led them to abandon the mission as Moshe's messengers. Now they had their own agenda: to make sure this future did not come about.

What they did not realize was that the glimpse of the future that revealed that they would no longer be the leaders of the Jewish people was a result of their abandoning Moshe's plan and directions. Had they stuck to his agenda, they would have brought back a favorable report, and they would have been the leaders of the Jewish people in the Land of Israel.

Rav Zalman Sorotzkin, *zt"l*, adds an intriguing observation based on the fact that the names of these princes are different from the names the Torah lists in *Naso*, when the princes brought their sacrifices. The Oznayim L'Torah explains that Hashem had told Moshe to choose the very best, but the verse goes on to report that the spies who were sent were *"kol nasi bahem"* — each one a prince in *their* estimation, not in Moshe's estimation. The Jewish people did not have absolute confidence in people who were solely *talmidei chachomim*. They wanted great people, but also people who would be able to tackle the survey of the Land of Israel in a more pragmatic and worldly way. They required people who understood business and commerce and who would be able to look at the land with a shrewd business eye, so they sent different people from those Moshe chose.

I once recall having a long conversation with the son-in-law of a well-known tzaddik. He complained to me passionately about the way his father-in-law's closest chassidim would take the Rebbe's statements and change them to suit their own purposes. I asked him why he didn't tell his father-in-law what was happening. "What?" he replied. "And break a tzaddik's heart?"

In pre-world-war Germany there was a religious Jew who was extremely active on behalf of the religious community. He was wealthy and influential, and his money bought him enough latitude to pursue the running of the community in the way that he thought best. He was certainly a very dedicated *askan*, but he suffered from arrogance and was impervious to those who disagreed with his actions and pronouncements, including *rabbanim*. He was not even above criticizing the town's *rabbanim* in public.

On one occasion he took it upon himself to publicly criticize one of the leading *talmidei chachomim* of the time. One man wrote to the local Jewish newspaper protesting the man's attack. His letter recalled an incident that involved Moreinu Rav Yaakov Rosenheim, who was chairing an executive meeting of Agudath Israel. Dr. Yitzchak Breuer arrived late to the meeting. He took his seat and asked his neighbor whether Moreinu Rav Yaakov Rosenheim *"hut sich schoin geChaim ausert."*

Ausert is the German word for giving an opinion. Dr. Breuer was hinting at the fact that whenever Moreinu Rav Yaakov Rosenheim spoke he reflected the opinion of his mentor, Rav Chaim Ozer Grodzensky, *zt"l*.

"A Torah *askan*," wrote the author of the article, "must understand and be able to reflect the *da'as Torah* of his teachers. His own opinion is not relevant."

Askanim are essential to the Jewish people; they could not function without them. Such people often dedicate huge amounts of their time, money, and energy to their communities. Great *askanim*, though, know the lesson of the spies. The very greatest want nothing more than to reflect the opinion of our *gedolim*. They understand the rules of Chinese whispers and make very sure that the original message that they heard is the one they convey to *Klal Yisrael*.

The Hand, Not the Foot

(Unpublished)

There are several shuls on the street where I live. The largest by far is called, rather grandly, "The Great and New Synagogue," but more usually it is referred to by the name of the house that used to occupy the land, Stenecourt.

It has existed for about a century. Had it followed the trend of its type of synagogue, it should have been closed long ago, or it should be hanging on to an existence supported not by daily minyanim but by wealthy congregants who want to daven on the High Holidays in the shul their grandparents prayed in.

This shul did not go the way of so many chiefly for two reasons. It is located in the heart of Manchester's Orthodox enclave of Broughton Park, and the vibrancy of the surrounding community has been a good ally for the growth of the shul. The second reason is the person who has been the spiritual leader of the congregation since 1944.

He arrived as a refugee from Czechoslovakia. With a subtle hand he has steered the shul delicately to the point where it is one of the most dynamic in the entire United Kingdom. It is busy with *shiurim*, learning programs, and guest speakers from home and abroad and supports several minyanim daily. It must have been blessed, too, with presidents who were wise enough to allow him to craft the direction of the shul. He is also the father and grandfather of children who are proud *bnei Torah*. One of his sons is the registrar of the Manchester *beis din*, a role he juggles with volunteer work in a score of charities and communal activities.

I am often invited to speak there, and on one Shabbos I sat waiting to be introduced by Rav Gavriel Brodie, *shlita*. The rabbi sat in a box beside the *aron kodesh*, and I sat in the front row next to him. Reb Gavriel left his box and turned immediately to mount the steps to the lectern. When he was halfway up, he paused for a split second as he realized that he had left the door of his box ajar. One more step would bring his foot inches from the open door, and I anticipated that he would give the door a little nudge with his shoe, which would neatly solve the problem. I was wrong. Rav Brodie bent down and deftly closed it with his hand. I watched and thought to myself, *Yes, that is the Jewish way to do it — not with a foot, with a hand!*

After three years of learning in Gateshead Yeshivah, I came to realize two things. I finally grasped how to understand *Mesilas Yesharim*, which I had been learning during *mussar seder* every night since I arrived in yeshivah. My second discovery was that you could learn as much from the *ba'alei batim* (laymen) of Gateshead as you could from the rebbes of the yeshivah. These were people whose every action was imbued with Torah and *chesed*.

When my third son was born, it was the second day of Rosh HaShanah. The next day was Shabbos. Since his arrival was a bit early, we hadn't prepared for a *shalom zachor*. This was no problem for the people of our street. Freezers were opened, and cakes and food started to fill our house. There were some items that no one had, so Mr. Stenhouse, the owner of the local kosher store, opened his shop on *yom tov* and invited me to take whatever I needed.

These people had come from families who could tell stories of

The Hand, Not the Foot

hosting Rav Dessler, *zt"l*, in their homes or quote grandparents telling them things heard directly from Rav Yerucham Levovitz, Rav Shamshon Refael Hirsch, or the Sefas Emes.

When I was the UK representative of a *ba'al teshuvah* yeshivah in Yerushalayim, I always told the young men I was sending there that they should stay the three years or so that it would take them to gain the necessary learning skills and then move on to a mainstream yeshivah. There is an infinite amount that one can learn just by rubbing shoulders with those who have always been observant or who have learned closely from those people who are the latest chapter in a book going all the way back to Sinai.

I remember a conversation with a young man who had been a professional violinist before choosing a life of Torah. He told me about "master classes" he used to attend. These special sessions allowed the most gifted and aspiring young violinists to come together with some of the world's most famous exponents of the instrument and learn about technique and approach. He'd watch every single facet of the maestro's approach, from the way he held the bow to how he sat and even his expression as he played. It was by learning and replicating the entirety of the master's approach that he hoped to be able to reach the same pinnacle of musical genius.

Someone once told me that art students sit in front of masterpieces in galleries for days and copy the paintings. They are trying to discover how the master used paints and applied them to the canvas. Even the directions of the brushstrokes are noted and copied.

The Gemara is full of stories of *talmidim* who would follow their rebbes to observe their every move. "That, too, is Torah!"

In Rav Eliyahu Dessler's *Michtav MeEliyahu* (vol. 4, p. 220), there is a short essay called "Refinement of Speech." This, he says, does not mean how to avoid bad language, but rather how one should use words that are permissible. He quotes the well-known *gemara* (*Pesachim* 3a) that talks extensively about use of language.

Two *talmidim* were sitting in front of Hillel. One used the word *tumah*, impure, and the other employed the term *eino tehorah*, not pure. Hillel said, "I am convinced that the one who used the phrase 'not pure' will go on to teach Torah in Israel." That *talmid* was Rabbi Yochanan ben Zakkai!

Rav Dessler explains that this story and several like it come to teach us that the most subtle levels of refinement of speech reflect the essence of that person's soul. Someone who aspires to reach the very highest levels in Torah should devote all his efforts to that level of sensitivity to language.

The Alshich points out an intriguing contradiction in the Torah. When Eliezer went in search of a bride for Yitzchak, he said a prayer that contained an appeal. "Behold, I will stand beside the well of water, and the daughters of the men of the city will come out to draw water. And it will be that I will say to the girl, 'Bring down your pitcher, and I will drink.' And she will say to me, 'Drink and also your camels I will give to drink.' That is the girl You have selected for Your servant Yitzchak."

The verse reports that just as Eliezer finished speaking Rivkah came out. The Torah is exhaustive in repeating her lineage, though we already know it from previous *parshiyos*.

"Rivkah, who was born to Besuel the son of Milkah the wife of Nachor, the brother of Avraham, came out."

But the contradiction is contained in what happened next.

"And the servant ran to meet her, and he said, 'Give me a little water from your pitcher.' And she replied, 'Drink, my master,' and she hurried to put her pitcher in her hands and gave him to drink. She finished giving him to drink, and she said, 'Also for your camels I shall draw water until they have finished drinking.' "

Eliezer had been shown that he had found the perfect match for Yitzchak — or had he? The conditions that he suggested to Hashem in his prayer were not fulfilled! The true bride for Yitzchak

The Hand, Not the Foot

was to say, "Drink and also your camels I will give to drink." Rivkah did not say that. She gave him to drink, and only after he had finished did she say, "Also for your camels I shall draw water until they have finished drinking."

The reason was that Rivkah knew something Eliezer did not. You do not speak of a human being, who is the image of Hashem, in the same breath that you mention an animal. That is why she waited until he had finished drinking and only then mentioned the camels.

But Eliezer was not Avraham's servant in a domestic sense; he was his *talmid muvhak*, his most devoted disciple. Eventually Avraham would give Eliezer permission to establish his own yeshivah, confident that what would be taught would be faithful to the teachings of his master. Yet this young girl's refinement of language was exactly as the Torah would expect it to be, something that Eliezer had not yet absorbed despite all his decades of devotion and learning with Avraham. The reason lies in the Torah's emphasis on Rivkah's lineage.

When Avraham was taken from the cave in which he had been hidden by his mother, she sent him to the yeshivah of Shem and Ever to study Torah. No parent sends his child to a school unless he is confident about what will be taught there. Avraham's mother was clearly well aware of what was taught at the yeshivah which Avraham attended.

The *Kuzari* points out that there was an unbroken chain of prophets from Adam HaRishon through Noach until Avraham. Avraham's family was part of an unbroken chain of believers in a world of idolatry. That is why Haran said to himself as his brother Avraham was being taken to the furnace, "If he survives, I will be on his side, and if not, on Nimrod's." How could he even consider that Avraham might survive the flames? Haran, too, knew of Hashem, although his belief was weak.

The female side of Avraham's family carried no such weakness. Avraham's mother passed it to her daughter Milkah, who passed it to her granddaughter Rivkah.

It was this belief in Hashem and the Torah taught by Shem and Ever, passed from mother to daughter, that gave Rivkah an innate sensitivity to Torah values and modes of speech that Eliezer had not yet acquired. He would learn it, though, through his contact with her.

The longer the chain, the more weight lies behind each link. By attaching ourselves to teachers whose every action reflects countless generations of Torah-observant Jews, we give ourselves the opportunity to discover sophisticated levels of Torah values that we might never have found on our own.

The greatest exemplars of Torah are those who are a direct link or who have absorbed and understood from those who are a direct link in an unbroken chain to Har Sinai. From teachers like those, we will understand that Torah permeates every human action, from being careful in our speech to closing a door with our hand, not our foot.

Virtual Chesed

(Hamodia, November 10, 2000)

Not every Orthodox Jew has the luxury of walking a few yards from their front door and finding a minyan waiting for them. Of course, in Yerushalayim or Boro Park or Golders Green, we are a bit spoiled in this regard and take such things for granted. Elsewhere, though, seven or eight Jews can often be found standing patiently, waiting and hoping that two or three others will arrive and transform a group of individuals into a minyan.

Someone in New Jersey recently e-mailed me an original question. These days many computers come equipped with cameras that transmit in real time the picture of the person sitting in front of the screen. "What," asked my friend, "would be the halachah if ten Jews around the world were to link up via the Internet to form a virtual minyan? Each would be able to see the others, and, significantly from a halachic point of view (see *Pesachim* 85b), they would be able to hear each other." Unfortunately, the *Shulchan Aruch* has already decreed the necessity of all the members of the minyan being in the same room. A virtual minyan is not valid.

Rav Moshe Cordovero, in his beautiful masterpiece, *Tomer Devorah*, explains why.

"All of Israel are a family, each one connected with the other. That is because each Jew's soul is connected with every other Jew's soul. There is a fraction of each Jew's soul contained within every other Jew's soul. That is why, if a Jew is among the first ten who appear in shul to make up a minyan, even if a hundred subsequently join them, the first ten receive the reward equal to a hundred who have come to pray! The reason is that each individual contains another nine fractions of those others within him. He is in reality already ten people, and so are the others in the minyan. Ten times ten equals a hundred, and the reward they gain for coming together is the reward of hundred people coming together, not ten!"

The closer the contact, the greater the connection that is established. In *Vayeira*, even the pain of his bris is nothing compared to the pain Avraham feels because there is no one available for him to do *chesed* to. So Hashem sends him three guests. The reaction of the master of *chesed* gives us a taste of how *chesed* should be performed. He runs to greet them and begs them to accept his hospitality. Having secured their agreement, he personally prepares part of the meal. The Midrash reports that even at the pinnacle of his power Shlomo HaMelech's table could not compare to the sumptuousness of Avraham's table. The luxury and largesse of Avraham was used to produce one effect only — to bring his guests close to Hashem and draw them away from the cruelty and emptiness of a world of idolatry.

Avraham could easily have instructed any of his servants to carry out the preparations. But that sort of "virtual *chesed*" would not have done. It would have detracted from the quality of the *chesed* itself. "Actual *chesed*" is best achieved when we engage in it directly, when we connect ourselves with the person receiving the *chesed*.

This point is made by the Chafetz Chaim in his *Ahavas Chesed*. He writes that the Torah begins and ends with *chesed*. Hashem Himself prepared Chavah's hair to make her appear beautiful to Adam. Hashem Himself buried Moshe Rabbeinu. It was the fact that He did it Himself that makes the *chesed* so special.

When I first moved to Manchester, I gave a public *shiur* on a

Virtual Chesed

Shabbos afternoon to a large group of people. After Shabbos one of Manchester's greatest *rabbanim* and tzaddikim called to offer an apology. He told me that he had intended to come to listen to me but had been unavoidably prevented from doing so by an emergency. I was astonished that one of the *gedolei hador* would have even thought of honoring me this way. In fact, I think if he had walked in, I might have fainted!

A few years later, in Bournemouth, I was spending Shabbos at a hotel where I was lecturing to a large group of young people. On Friday night my *shiur* was based on *Michtav MeEliyahu*. The door opened, and in walked Rav Mordechai Miller of Gateshead Seminary. Rav Miller is the most outstanding teacher of the works of his rebbe, Rav Dessler. I am one of his *talmidim*. It was Rav Miller who first introduced me to *Michtav MeEliyahu*. He sat down and smiled approvingly throughout the *shiur*. Afterward Rav Miller approached me and said, "They told me you are speaking again tomorrow. What time? I'd like to listen to you again!"

Both incidents conjure incredibly warm memories. Of course, the second one generates the warmest memories. Circumstances allowed Rav Miller to actually make that connection. I still feel profoundly honored that he did.

Rav Dessler says in his famous essay on *chesed* that everyone is born with a strong sense of self-love. The more you give to someone, the more you see yourself in the person. Since you already love yourself, you come to love the other person, too. According to Rav Dessler, the effect of *chesed* is connection. The more sincere the *chesed*, the stronger the connection that will be established.

A close friend of mine and I were once traveling together to speak at a seminar. We were discussing this lesson of Rav Dessler's, and he expressed a concern. "According to Rav Dessler, when you do *chesed*, ultimately you are not really doing it for the other person but because you see yourself in him. So you are really helping yourself, and that is not true *chesed*!"

In the light of Rav Moshe Cordovero's insight, seeing yourself in the person is not an artificial projection that allows you to feel connected to him. There is already a piece of you in the other Jew. The *chesed* you do for him simply allows you to discover it and see it. Helping someone else is helping yourself because, again to quote *Tomer Devorah*, he is you.

Rav Dessler illustrates his point with a startling example. The Torah prohibits cruelty to animals. There is a specific Torah prohibition not to overload a donkey. Yet the Gemara in *Bava Metzia* says if you see your friend unloading an already overloaded donkey and someone you detest starting to load a donkey, you should help your enemy load his beast rather than assist your friend in unloading his! As Rav Dessler explains, this act of kindness will start the process of removing your hatred for the fellow. You will see yourself within him. In reality, part of you was within him all the time. Your act of kindness reveals that fact and allows you to connect with someone who previously you would have had no connection with at all.

The "actual reality" required of true *chesed* is discussed further in *Tomer Devorah*:

"The *Zohar* explains that there are angels whose sole purpose is to record the *chesed* that Jews do. When Heavenly justice demands that we deserve punishment, these angels reveal our acts of *chesed* and mercy tempers justice. It was this process that saved the Jewish people from extinction when the Temple was destroyed and Heavenly justice demanded our end, too. Hashem told the angel Gavriel that despite everything else we may have done Jews still performed *chesed* with each other. That averted the worst."

There are, of course, times when "actual *chesed*" is not appropriate. The Rambam gives examples to illustrate this point.

The best form of charity is when you set someone up in business. The next best is when the person receiving the charity does not know who his benefactor is and the benefactor doesn't know

Virtual Chesed

to whom the money went. This is because there could be a danger that the act of *chesed*, instead of creating a closer connection between two individuals, will have the reverse effect. The recipient could feel embarrassed and ashamed when he sees the person who helped him. The giver could feel superior to the person who needed his help. Nevertheless, such charity would still be considered "actual *chesed*." The goal is still to create connections between Jews, not to impede them.

I witnessed an example of such *chesed* every day for months in an unusual way — through little brown envelopes. A well-known Manchester philanthropist phoned me three months ago to ask a favor. A lady was facing bankruptcy, having struggled for years to nurse her late husband. Several *gedolim* had signed a letter that would be printed in the press asking for help. I was asked if my name and address could be used for donations to be sent. Of course I agreed, and I have watched day after day as scores of little brown envelopes have landed on my mat. Each week the organizer of the appeal comes around to collect the envelopes, and I always need to use two hands to give the bundle to him. Though the original advertisement appeared months ago, *Klal Yisrael* has not forgotten, and the little brown envelopes continue to arrive.

Chesed is almost always best done directly so that the recipient feels that we care. The greater the *chesed* and the greater the quality of the *chesed*, the more merit those recording angels will have to write down and the better our insurance policy will be. In times like these, we need to try our best to keep them very busy indeed.

A Very Stubborn People

(Hamodia, 2000)

Two years ago I spent two weeks lecturing in South Africa. The high spot of the tour was a *Shabbaton* set among the stunning African countryside. One of the participants was a young man who had recently become religious. He attended all of my lectures, but there seemed to be something about Judaism that was troubling him. At the last event, an "ask the rabbi" session, I finally discovered what it was.

He explained that he was deeply disturbed by the treatment meted out to some of the greatest of our *gedolim*, sometimes by other *gedolim*. In particular, he could not understand how the Rambam could have been so criticized and attacked, especially after writing *Moreh Nevuchim*.

Of course, this type of situation was not confined to the Rambam. He could have referred to the hand of suspicion that was pointed at the Ramchal and Rabbi Yonasan Eibeshutz in the aftershock of the earthquake caused by Shabsai Tzvi, who rocked the world with his false messianic claims and ultimately converted to Islam. In fact, he could have referred to the histories of countless *gedolim* in history.

A Very Stubborn People

I gave him an answer that I knew he would not understand at first. I said that what he was referring to was a true and painful chapter in our history. (Rabbeinu Yonah was supposed to have written *Sha'arei Teshuvah* to make amends for his erstwhile opposition to the Rambam.) "But despite his distress and knowledge that his critics were mistaken," I continued, "the Rambam would have ultimately been quite content and even happy that he was suffering such an attack."

HaKadosh Baruch Hu describes the nature and character of the Jewish people in the Torah. After the making of the golden calf, He says, "*Hinei am keshei oref hu* — Behold, it is a stubborn nation." Obviously Hashem knew that this was our special trait long before anyone thought of a golden calf. We are, after all, the descendants of Avraham, Yitzchak, and Yaakov, who stood alone against the entire world.

The *ba'alei mussar* point out that *middos*, character traits, are neither good nor bad; they are neutral. How we use them determines whether they become good or bad. Rav Dessler says that even *azus*, brazenness, a *middah* we pray every day to avoid ("*shetatzileini hayom u'vechol yom mei'azei panim u'mei'azus panim* — that He should save me today and every day from those who are brazen and from brazenness") still has a positive function.

After the famous incident when Avraham smashed the idols, Nimrod condemned him to be chained in a dungeon for ten long, cold, damp, dark years. He still had no proof that his belief in a Creator was correct. At any time he could have saved himself by denying what he held to be certain truth and walked away a free man. At the end of those ten years he was again brought before Nimrod and invited to renounce his claims. Again he refused. Avraham was placed in stocks in the city and made to watch as the people brought wood for the burning of this "heretic."

His mother, Amselai bas Karnevo, came and begged him to give in, and once more he refused. It was only after the miracle, when the flames could not touch him, that Hashem spoke to him for the first time, and He said to him, *"Lech lecha"* — leave your homeland.

Reb Simchah Zissel asks why this incident is only hinted at in the Torah and is not given a whole parashah in its own right, like *akeidas Yitzchak*. He answers that this, Avraham being thrown into a fire rather than deny his belief, was the necessary test before he could receive the Torah. Avraham had to prove that he could carry the Torah to the next generation. Avraham had to be "stubborn." This was only part of the process of the preparation and transformation of Avraham to be able to receive the Torah. It was the person he became and what he managed to achieve through the ten tests that merited to be mentioned explicitly in the Torah.

If Hashem wanted to find a people who would be able to carry the Torah through the millennia unswervingly, despite the Crusades, the Inquisition, pogroms, and even the Holocaust, He would have to find a people who was stubborn. Such a nation would be deeply suspicious of anything or anyone who seemed to deviate from its oral tradition. The criticism and suspicion the Rambam and so many other *gedolim* faced attested to the great care the nation takes in guarding its Torah. It attests to the tenaciousness of the Jewish people.

We have no shortage of *sefarim* that inspire us with the lives of our *rabbanim*, Rebbes, and *roshei yeshivah*. Every Jew, though, is a story, and always when I hear the phrase *pashute Yid*, a simple Jew, I think, *There is no such thing*.

When he was eighty years old, Morris Wide married a member of my wife's family. It was his third marriage and her second. Morris eventually moved to Eretz Yisrael where, at the age of ninety-six, he returned his soul to Heaven.

Morris was born in Breslau, Germany. Once, while he was sitting at our Friday night table, one of my sons asked him if he had ever been a soldier. Morris looked at him and asked, "In which war?

A Very Stubborn People

In the first war I was in the German artillery. In the second war, again I was in the artillery — the British artillery!"

During the 1930s he managed to escape to Britain. He knew the British would only accept people who had a skill the country could use, so he got someone to teach him the rudiments of carpentry and joined other refugees in a special camp called the "Kitchener Camp." He became a naturalized citizen and immediately started the process of having his wife and six-year-old son join him. He was in London filling out the relevant forms when Britain declared war on Germany. He never saw them again. After the war he moved to Rhodesia and married again. When his second wife passed away, he returned to Britain and settled in Manchester.

When he and his new wife made their last move — this time to Eretz Yisrael — he was obliged to travel back to Manchester for prolonged stays in order to settle various business affairs. Every Friday night he spent Shabbos with us.

On one return trip he suffered from deep-vein thrombosis because he had been sitting too long in one position and spent two weeks in the hospital. He was released on Friday and upon crossing a busy road was knocked down by a truck. I was called to the hospital, and we waited for the results of the X-ray. The doctors thought he had fractured his skull and broken his hip and leg. The outlook for a man of his age was gloomy.

The X-ray results came back. He had not fractured his skull, nor broken his hip nor even his badly cut leg.

Morris came home to us and had his usual Friday night meal. He was in extreme pain from his leg, and the next day I passed his room and peeked in to see if he was all right. Morris was sitting on his bed stretching his damaged leg. From his face, it was apparent that the pain was excruciating. It brought tears to his eyes and robbed him of his breath. He tried again. If anything, the pain seemed worse. But, despite the agony, Morris kept stretching the damaged leg, again and again.

Dancing through Time

By Sunday morning our patient was demanding to be taken back to his own apartment. Eventually we had to give in. We borrowed a wheelchair and together with a friend lifted him up the stairs to his front door. I told him I would pop in later that afternoon to make sure he was all right. There was no need. Two hours later, Morris, stick in hand, walked past our house.

A fortnight later he went back to the hospital for a routine X-ray on his leg to check on the thrombosis. It was then that they discovered that the leg was broken after all. They had failed to notice the fracture after the accident. Since Morris was doing fine without a cast, they decided to leave him as he was.

Morris was the perfect gentleman and a faithful Jew who not once during his entire front-line service during World War I allowed himself to eat *treif*. When he was in the hospital for the last time, at the age of ninety-six, he summoned a nurse.

"Does this hospital have a minyan on Shabbos?" The nurse replied that it depended on who were the patients in the hospital at any given time. Morris insisted that there must be a minyan. "It is my bar mitzvah Shabbos, and I have read the Torah portion without fail on this Shabbos for the last eighty-three years!"

Whenever I think of Morris, I remind myself of the Jewish nation's special attribute and how it could be used positively.

The young South African had his answer. The Rambam and the other *gedolim* knew that only a people totally dedicated to protecting their Torah could subject them to such close scrutiny and inspection. The source of that process, their very stubbornness, would become the essential *middah* that would produce hundreds of thousands of Morris Wides. It would be the essential *middah* that would carry the Torah through three and a half millennia and bring the people back to Yerushalayim.

When the Cub Becomes a Lion

(Unpublished)

On my first trip to South Africa I found that the organization that had invited me wanted me to speak on as many occasions as I could manage. South African Jews are truly thirsty for Torah, and the two lectures a day I had originally arranged to give soon evolved into four a day and on one occasion even five.

After a *Shabbaton* in the beautiful Drachensburg Mountains, the family I was staying with drove me back to Johannesburg. There were three cars altogether, two for the family and myself and one full of people who had come for the weekend.

My host decided it wasn't fair that I was not getting a chance to see the beauty of his country, so he decided that we should stop off at the Lion Park, which is about an hour north of Johannesburg, to give me a taste of the real Africa.

We collected a brochure as we drove through the park gates. It described how the lions are looked after and warned us not to drive too fast in the enclosures where the beasts lived. Sometimes the lions had attacked swiftly moving vehicles. We drove slowly, very slowly.

Dancing through Time

Lions lay alongside the road. One or two were draped over the lower limbs of trees. A lioness wandered up to my door and gave a bored look at our moving cage and then walked away. Eventually we finished the tour of the enclosures and entered the tourist area. There was a picnic area and a shop with hundreds of toy lions in every shape and size. This was also the place where the brochure said you could get your picture taken cuddling a lion cub. The brochure showed a picture of a little blonde-haired girl cuddling a fluffy ball. The caption revealed that this fluffy ball was a baby lion.

The lion cubs are separated from the pride after they are born. This is to protect them from the adult lion, which might accidentally kill its own cub. At the age of six months, the young lions are reintroduced back into the pride.

I read all this with interest, and I made up my mind that a picture of Daddy cuddling a fluffy ball of a lion cub would be exactly the thing to take home to my little daughters.

Our party arrived at the cage that housed the cubs. There were three altogether, and they sat, or rather lay, on a little hill. The attendant sat outside eating sandwiches, and we all gathered around the cage to get a look and take pictures.

My host asked if I wanted to get into the cage and have my picture taken with the cubs. The answer would have been an immediate yes, except that these cubs were not the fluffy balls from the brochure. In fact, later that day, these animals were due for release back into the pride.

I don't know if you know what a lion looks like at six months. It is about the size of an Alsatian dog. I decided that I did not want to get into a cage with three large lion cubs, after all. The problem was that the nine-year-old son of my host did want to have his picture taken carrying a lion cub, and I didn't want to look like a chicken in the eyes of a nine-year-old. On the other hand, I didn't want to look like a chicken in the eyes of a lion either.

When the Cub Becomes a Lion

We entered the cage. My young friend and I sat on the little hill next to the lions, I beside the beasts and he beside me.

I came to the conclusion that a lion is really just a great big pussycat. All one had to do was deploy "pussycat psychology" to show this king of the beasts who was the real boss. I leaned over and started to tickle the nearest lion behind the ear while doing a rather good impression of a cat purring. The lion's head snapped around. His teeth snapped, too.

The tourists outside were delighted. "Oh, look," someone said. "It nearly bit him," and they started to click their cameras. By now I was feeling as though my spine had been removed and overcooked spaghetti substituted for it instead.

The bored attendant, who had now finished his lunch, entered the cage. He came over to where I was now standing, preparing to make a dash for the door. "Would you like to have your picture taken holding the lion cub?" he inquired.

I started to answer no, but while I was still at *n* and before I had got to *o*, he picked up one of the beasts and pushed it against my chest.

My right arm struggled to hold the lion around its ribs, and my left arm cradled it under the neck. Most of it, though, was dangling in midair. It was obvious the lion had outgrown this sort of stuff and no longer wanted to be picked up by tourists. It wanted to be put down, and it indicated this to me by biting me on the arm. I put it down.

I still have a nice scar on my upper arm that required three stitches. When I tell people that I was bitten by a lion, they give me an amused smile.

I think one of the biggest mistakes we parents make is not spotting the point at which our cub has become a lion. At bar mitzvah dinners of boys from nonreligious homes, the young man often begins his speech with the words "Today I am a man." These words, delivered in a voice that has not yet broken, often evoke smiles and chuckles. Yet having watched four sons reach this stage, I know that just a few months later they will be marching up to their father and, in a very deep voice, asking if they can borrow his beard trimmer. A boy may not be a man at thirteen, but he is on the verge of becoming a man.

Parents often find themselves baffled when their children reach this stage. Where did the son or daughter with whom they had so much in common and who gave them so much *nachas* disappear to? The son and daughter can't comprehend why their parents don't understand them and why they expect them to do things they are no longer interested in.

The teenage years are very difficult for young people. Perhaps they are more difficult in our days than in times past. There are so many pressures exerting themselves on our children and so many dangers. One threat to the relationship between parents and children, though, is the same today as it was when *Klal Yisrael* began. Shlomo HaMelech warns of it when he says, "*Chanoch l'na'ar al pi darko* — Educate each child according to his path." Shlomo was making it clear that inevitably the child's path will be different from that of his parents — it is his path, not yours.

Rav Eliyahu Dessler, *zt"l*, explains in his *Michtav MeEliyahu* that each of the three *Avos* had a character trait that was unique to him. Avraham was the epitome of *chesed*. Yitzchak was the personification of a different quality, *yiras Hashem*, fear of Heaven.

Doesn't this seem strange? Wouldn't it have made more sense for Yitzchak to follow in his father's footsteps and developed *chesed* even further? Rav Dessler's answer solves an age-old question raised by Rashi.

When Rivkah was unable to have a child, both she and Yitzchak beseeched Hashem. The verse reports that it was Yitzchak's prayers that succeeded rather than Rivkah's. Rashi says this was because "the prayers of a saint who is the son of a saint are greater than the prayers of a saint who is the child of someone wicked."

When the Cub Becomes a Lion

The words of Rashi don't seem to accord with the way we see things. The struggle of someone who has come from a bad, even terrible, background and has then gone on to reach greatness seems more heroic than someone who has it handed to him on a silver platter.

I knew a young girl who had become religious. Every week her parents literally dragged her down the driveway to the family car. She was forced into the back seat to ride to shul on Shabbos. Today she is happily married to a *kollel* man and has a fine young family. Her journey through life and her determination to arrive at the right address makes someone who had Shabbos handed to him on a silver platter appear as though he's had it very easy.

Rav Dessler's explanation about Yitzchak developing a different *middah* solves the puzzle. The greatness of Yitzchak was that even though he was Avraham's son and could have followed in his father's footsteps, he was not content to do that. If he had followed in his father's path, this might have indicated that his dedication to Torah was shallow and superficial. Instead, Yitzchak struggled to forge his own path and went on to erect an edifice that was truly an expression of his individuality and commitment to Hashem.

This is a theme Rav Dessler returns to again and again. When Lot was saved from the destruction of Sedom, the verse says that Hashem remembered Avraham and saved Lot: "And it was when Hashem destroyed the cities of the plain that God remembered Avraham, and He sent Lot from the midst of the conflagration when He overturned the cities that Lot had lived in" (*Bereishis* 19:29). Rashi says the reason Hashem "remembered" Avraham and saved Lot was because Lot knew of Avraham and Sarah's deception in Egypt, when they pretended that they were brother and sister. Hashem remembered that Lot chose not to inform on them.

Avraham was Lot's rebbe, his brother-in-law, and his uncle. Even the worst and lowest sort of human being would not inform Pharaoh of their deception. Why was that the reason that Lot was saved? There were certainly far, far better reasons for saving Lot.

The Midrash says that Lot had not two but three daughters. One made the mistake of offering hospitality to a stranger who had entered the city. This was a capital crime in Sedom, and Lot saw her tried and sentenced to death. The form of execution was as cruel as the Sodomites could invent — she was to be eaten alive by insects. Lot was forced to witness her death. Despite all this, when the angels appeared in Sedom as strangers to the city, Lot was still willing to offer them hospitality, endangering his life and that of his family for this mitzvah. Why was this not the reason that Lot was saved?

Rav Dessler explains that Avraham was the embodiment of *chesed*. Anyone who came into contact with Avraham was immediately influenced, and his own *middah* of *chesed* was transformed and elevated. Lot was such a person. His willingness to sacrifice himself for the mitzvah of *chesed* flowed from Avraham's teaching and example.

Lot's real test lay in the fact that he loved money. That was why he settled in Sedom after he separated from Avraham. There was good grazing to be had around Sedom. His flocks would flourish there and bring him wealth. The knowledge that he had only to drop the tiniest hint about Avraham's deception — a tiny hint that he could have pretended to himself was unintentional but would have resulted in Avraham's death — was a huge test for Lot. The reward of dropping that tiny hint would have been great wealth. He would have ended up being the only living relative of Pharaoh's new wife. Such a position would have allowed him to gather unimagined fortunes.

Thus Rav Dessler writes: "Everything a person does as a result of the education he received from others, even if it motivates him to perform a mitzvah at the highest levels, does not reveal his own true level of achievement in Judaism" (*Michtav MeEliyahu*, vol. 3, p. 167).

By fighting and winning his own battle against his true nature, Lot gained himself credits in Heaven that could be drawn upon and save him and his family from the destruction of Sedom.

The last time I heard the late Manchester *rosh yeshivah* speak in public before his passing was at the bar mitzvah of one of his grandsons. It is obvious that the words he chose were given particular consideration for this special occasion. After he explained a question in halachah to the bar mitzvah, he smiled and said, "You may look around at your family and become disheartened. Your father is a great *talmid chacham*. Your uncles, brothers, and cousins are already *talmidei chachomim*. You might think, *How can I make my mark surrounded by so many people who are so far ahead of me?* You should know that you are unique, and you will make your own way and become a *talmid chacham* in your own right."

"*Chanoch l'na'ar al pi darko* — Educate a child according to his way." Yitzchak's way was not Avraham's way. Yaakov's way was not Yitzchak's way. Yaakov's twelve sons each had a path that was unique and special. Yehudah's path was kingship; Levi's was to serve in the Beis HaMikdash.

In a very real sense, a child is an extension of his parent. This is hinted at in the fact that children look like their mothers and fathers. They also often inherit talents and temperaments from their parents. Inheritance of material possessions, too, allows a child to stand in his parents' shoes and carry on their work. A father or mother may want nothing more than that the child occupy those shoes and follow exactly in their footsteps. The Torah, though, expects more than that. Children are expected to take what they have been given by their parents and fit that legacy to their own uniqueness. And fathers and mothers must allow them the freedom to do so.

If a father loves learning Gemara, he may be disappointed if his son inclines more toward halachah. Personally, I have always loved the commentary of the Alshich, but all of my sons enjoy other commentators. This is their *derech*, the way they feel they can develop their *avodas Hashem*.

Dancing through Time

As long as a child's *derech* is one of the many paths that lead to the very top of the mountain, a wise parent will be happy to allow him to make his own way. The point at which he starts to assert his individuality and seek out his own path is when they become individuals according to halachah.

That's why parents have to watch out for the moment when the cub becomes a lion.

Not Seeing the End

(Hamodia)

Vayeishev begins a story that comes to a climactic conclusion in *Vayigash*. The brothers' hatred of Yosef increased when he told them his dream. They were convinced that far from being a prophecy, this dream was merely his sleeping mind's reflection of the inappropriate ambitions of his waking thoughts. They were unable to see how the story would end and that they would, indeed, gather and bow to the king whose corn stood high while everyone else's withered. They went on to make one mistake after another. First they tried to kill Yosef, then they tried having animals do it for them, and finally they sold him as a slave.

Rav Eliyahu Dessler, *zt"l*, explains why it was part of Hashem's design that misinterpretation and misunderstanding should follow miscalculation so that the brothers were "unable to speak to him in peace."

Yaakov knew that his children would have to face exile in Egypt. He also knew that Egypt held the potential to completely destroy any vestige of the Jewish people. He spent years in preparation to ready his children for their forthcoming exile.

When they brought Yaakov to Egypt, the Torah calls Yaakov's children *"bnei Yisrael,"* the sons of Yisrael, not *"bnei Yaakov."* He had succeeded in enabling his children to reach the highest spiritual heights. They could now be designated by the name Yaakov Avinu was given to signify his own spiritual triumph.

Yosef, too, had to spend these years in preparation. Whereas Yaakov had to prepare *bnei Yisrael* for Egypt, Yosef had to prepare Egypt for *bnei Yisrael!* As king, he would be able to alter Egyptian society in several significant respects, which would blunt the effects it would have on his people.

Yosef first had to reach the spiritual level whereby Hashem would perform miracles through him. Through Yosef's efforts, Egypt's food would survive a famine in which all other food rotted whether it had been stored safely or not. For Yosef to be worthy to be the vehicle for this miracle, he, like the finest steel, would have to be cast into the forge several times and worked anew before returning again and again to the flames. Therefore he had to be betrayed and sold as a slave and specifically by those who should have been his fiercest protectors, his own brothers. His destination had to be Egypt from where no slave could ever escape and who treated slaves with extreme cruelty.

When Yosef's fortune at last seemed to turn and Potifar promoted him, he was faced with an extreme test in the form of Potifar's wife. When he passed this, he might have expected Hashem to reward his victory. Instead he was thrown into jail, and despite his innocence, the name "Jew" was besmirched because of him. Then, when he seemed to find a way out, his trust was betrayed by the wine butler, who paid Yosef's kindness by celebrating his return to office with a bout of amnesia. Throughout all this, Yosef never for a moment wavered in his faith and accepted it all with love and trust in Hashem.

These tests produced a Yosef who was worthy of being the vehicle through which Egypt was changed enough to save the Jewish

Not Seeing the End

people. When Yosef revealed himself to his brothers, he reported, "And now, it wasn't you who sent me here; rather, it was God, and He made me a father to Pharaoh and a lord to all his household and a ruler throughout the land of Egypt."

"And now" — now Yosef and his brothers could see what Hashem had planned all along. Before the end was revealed, though, Yosef's journey was a long and hard one.

Reb Yisrael of Ruzhin once said, "At the end of days, before the coming of the Mashiach, Hashem will take a string of faith and stretch it around the world. Many people will try to hold on to it, but as the days of Mashiach draw near, Hashem will command two angels to grasp both ends and shake it violently. It will become more and more difficult to maintain a hold on the string, and as time goes by many, many, will slip and fall. I am telling you this, my brothers, so that those living at that time will know and take heed."

There is a saying, "Forewarned is forearmed." Knowledge of what's waiting around the corner allows us to prepare and be ready to meet it. Not knowing what awaits us makes any task or journey profoundly more difficult. Rashi explains that this is why a component of Avraham's ultimate test was the instruction to go to "one of the mountains that I will show you." Hashem increases the challenge he sets for his tzaddikim by starting them on their journeys before they know where they will lead. Without the guarantee of a final destination and the knowledge that the hard road will come to an end, the journey might seem too daunting to attempt.

This point is never truer than when, in *parashas Vayechi*, Yaakov wanted to reveal to his sons what would happen at the end of days, when the Mashiach would arrive. He wanted to, but the Shechinah left him, and his ability to do so was removed. But Yaakov could reveal the glimpse of the future he had been shown as he watched the angels ascending and descending the ladder. He knew that their journey and that of their children would be a long and dark one.

Dancing through Time

It was a vision of a journey that would last thousands of years. It was a long road, but along that road was displayed place names he could read. There they could find a little respite before being compelled to take to the road again. Many of the place names were written in bloodred. Toward the very end, he could read road signs with names like Auschwitz and Treblinka. Despite not knowing when and how the journey would finish, his sons were willing to make it and keep moving forward.

A few months ago I received a phone call from someone who wasn't Jewish. She had heard me broadcasting on the BBC and wanted to ask a favor. Her au pair was a young woman from Russia named Tanya, and she was Jewish. Tanya had always wanted to meet a rabbi and see a synagogue. Could I think of anyone who might help her?

I arranged for Tanya to come to my house two days later. She entered nervously and sat down with a notebook in her hand. She had lots of questions. Before she began, I asked her if she really had never met a rabbi before nor seen a synagogue, and she confirmed that it was true. She told me that she came from Siberia, from the city of Irkutsk. Then she asked her first question: "Why is Sabbath on Saturday?"

I spent a great deal of time answering every conceivable question from "How do you prove that God exists?" to "If Hashem knows what I am going to choose, how do I have freedom of choice?" This last question was so unusual coming from someone who knew nothing that I paused for a few seconds thinking how to reply. I asked her if she knew the story of Creation in Genesis. She looked puzzled. I asked her if she had heard of the Garden of Eden. She shook her head. Then a thought struck me. "Have you heard of the Torah?" She had not. She had, though, heard something about God.

It was a rare and a wonderful opportunity to face a fully mature adult whose Jewish knowledge was that of a two-year-old. The one hour I had set aside for Tanya became three and a half hours. I

Not Seeing the End

told her about *Bereishis* and how there were two Torahs, not one. I explained how Jewish law works and introduced her to Rabbi Akiva and the Vilna Gaon.

She met Sarah and Esther and learned of kashrus and rabbis and even why Sabbath is on Saturday. I told her, too, how you can prove God exists and how, even though He knows what you are going to choose, you still have freedom of choice.

Her trip to a synagogue and seeing her eyes as I opened the *aron kodesh* and showed her a *sefer Torah* was a memory to be treasured. Later I drove her around the *frum* area of Manchester. Staring at the Jewish schools, yeshivos, sems, and the bustle and rush of Jewish life, she asked me one last question: "What do you do?"

I wasn't sure what she meant and asked her to elaborate. She explained that her sister now lived in Israel, and she wrote to her occasionally. She had heard things about religious Jews, so she wanted to know for herself "what we do."

I told her that we laugh a lot and worry about things like the mortgage and the phone bill and whether we will be able to afford a well-earned vacation. I explained that we particularly worry about our children, and sometimes we argue with our spouses. We try to make what the Torah says the compass by which we steer our lives. "Apart from being religious," I concluded, "we're very much like everyone else."

Tanya understood what I was saying and laughed. "I thought so," she said. "I just had to check it out for myself."

I invited Tanya to spend a "Saturday Sabbath" with us, but she told me that she had to work on Saturdays. I asked her to keep in touch and perhaps come for a midweek meal. She assured me she would try to get the time off.

A week ago I received an e-mail from Russia. It was from Tanya, who was now back in Irkutsk. She wrote that she could not get the time off to come for that meal. She missed England, since the temperature in Irkutsk was now below freezing. Then she wrote: "Several days ago my mother took me to the local synagogue for a lecture. I enjoyed the lecture very much. We celebrated Sabbath's beginning (it was Friday). I am certainly going again next Friday. The rabbi asked me about England, and I told him about you. He asked me if it was possible to invite you for some talks or lectures...."

I was astonished. These Jews had suffered invasion by Hitler, *yemach shemo*, and the terror of Stalin. They have endured decades of atheism so that they don't know what the Torah is and why Shabbos is on Saturday. Not only are they uncertain where the Jewish road leads, they are unclear about where it began. Yet when they have the first opportunity to get back on that journey, they stride forth, sometimes leaving the rest of us behind.

I'm hoping to make my first trip to Siberia in two months' time. Not, as they might think, to strengthen them, but rather to be inspired. I'm quite sure I'll return with more than one story that will help us all on that journey whose end we know will come soon, even if we don't know exactly how or when.

Seeing through the Satan

(Hamodia)

It was the most remarkable *siyum* I had ever attended. One of my ex-students had kept alive his connection with his tutor in Project SEED. The two, the *ba'al habayis* from Manchester and the young man, now living in London, decided to learn a tractate together even though they were separated by 210 miles. For the cost of two pounds a week they had learned *Rosh HaShanah* via one-hour sessions on the telephone. The young man had traveled back north for Shabbos, and together with a minyan of others I was invited to attend and speak at the *siyum*, which was celebrated at the *seudah shelishis*.

After completing the Gemara, my *talmid* stood up to recite the *Hadran*, the concluding ceremony. Perhaps because of the unique nature of the event, I found myself listening with particular attention to words I had heard hundreds of times. "*Modim anachnu lach...* — We are grateful that You have appointed our role among those who sit in the *beis midrash*."

The Gemara in *Bava Basra* says that Iyov wanted to free the world from divine punishment: "If a person has done wrong it is only because of his evil inclination. Hashem gave us this evil inclination;

therefore it is not our fault." Iyov's friends pointed out the flaw in his argument. It is true that Hashem gave us an evil inclination, but he also gave us the antidote. "*Barasi yetzer hara barasi lo Torah tavlin* — I created the evil inclination; I created its antidote, the Torah."

Rav Eliyahu Dessler, *zt"l*, makes a brilliant but troubling remark on this *gemara*. "But the *yetzer hara* will not let you learn Torah!" How, then, can we ever get the essential medicine? He answers that you cannot go to the *beis midrash* to learn Torah in a positive way with pure intentions, because the *satan* will stop you. You can get to the *beis midrash* if you have ulterior motives — by seeing that what the *satan* is offering as alternatives are a series of false promises and unachievable goals. That motivation brings someone to the *beis midrash*, and once he tastes Torah, the *yetzer* is in trouble, because "*mitoch shelo liShmah ba liShmah*" — doing something with ulterior motives brings a person to do it with pure intentions.

Let's see what Chazal say about this and look at our own experiences to see if this does not ring true.

The *satan* might point out that those who devote their lives to Torah tend to be poor. Instead of going to yeshivah, go into business and you will have lots of money. Chazal point out, "Someone who desires money will never be satisfied with money."

The *satan* might tempt us with an enormous house and a beautiful new car. Chazal remind us, "The more possessions you own, the more worries accompany them."

When you're rich, he tells us, people will respect you and you will be well respected. Chazal observe, "The more you chase after honor, the more it flees from you."

Like most salesmen, the *yetzer hara* sets before us a tantalizing package. As long as we are not dazzled by the glitter, we may have enough sense to examine carefully the fine print that comes with his exciting offers.

Last year I invited an old friend to address my students in Hillel House. He looks like any yeshivah man. A smart suit, black

Seeing through the Satan

hat, and small *peyos* behind his ear. When I first met him ten years ago, though, he looked very different. Then he was a Hollywood film star. He told his young audience the story of his journey.

Born in London, he was educated at an exclusive school. Then he went to drama school and became an actor. He found work touring with a famous show. He and a friend decided they could write something just as good, and they did. It became a hit and still fills theaters here in England and abroad. Tiring of the world of acting, he decided on a career move. He opened a recording studio. It was the first of its kind in Europe. Because it was so technically advanced, it attracted some of the most famous names in pop music.

My students sat there looking at this Orthodox rabbi who had produced some of the biggest selling records of popular culture, and their jaws dropped.

His success got him an invitation to travel to America and produce pop groups there. His all-expense paid flights were first class on the Concorde. Chauffeur-driven stretch limousines waited to take him from place to place. Success followed success. Once again something in him made him move on, and he was soon touring a one-man show around America to great critical acclaim. Eventually he arrived in Hollywood. Agents fought to sign him up. He made films and became a star.

One day, as he was being driven to the film studio (in the inevitable stretch limousine), he thought about his life. He had fame and fortune. In his grand Hollywood house he had a stable of cars, Mercedes and Porsches. The cars were, of course, exchanged for new and shinier ones every year; his personal relationships had the same turnover. As he considered his life, one thought crossed his mind and troubled him profoundly. *Is this it? Is this all there is?* Ten years later he teaches Torah in Yerushalayim.

Few people who listen to the evil inclination's promises ever come anywhere near to getting all that was offered. For those who do, life is empty. What the *satan* promises is a lie.

Rav Dessler secures this fact with an astonishing *Ibn Ezra* on *Esther*. After Haman was hanged, Achashveirosh turned to Mordechai and told him to write whatever he wished as a royal edict, which the king would sign and seal. The previous edict, which stated that the Jews were to be killed on the thirteenth of Adar, could not be annulled.

Mordechai displayed his genius in the wording he chose. He wrote that the king had dictated the first edict at Haman's hand, instructing that on the thirteenth of Adar the Jews should kill their enemies. Then Haman had changed the text and the order, writing instead that the Jews should be killed by their enemies. In this way the first edict was not contradicted, Haman was seen to be the liar and now hung from a gallows as a reward, and everyone thought the king had never intended to have the Jews harmed.

Our tradition teaches that the word *king* in the megillah really refers to HaKadosh Baruch Hu, the King of kings. Haman was the embodiment of the evil inclination. The message is that the way to defeat him is by exposing him as a liar.

Sometimes, Rav Dessler writes, two people will arrange between themselves that whenever they say yes they mean no, and whenever they say no they mean yes. Reb Mendel of Vitebsk wrote, "It is a fact that whatever the *satan* promises us, he really means the opposite."

As I sat at that special *siyum* and listened to the words of the *Hadran*, I heard them with a clarity I had not managed before. "*Anu mashkimim...v'heim mashkimim...* — We arise to words of Torah, and they arise to words that in truth mean nothing." Only the words of Torah are true; the words offering alternatives in reality offer nothing at all.

Rav Dessler's insight adds a new weapon to help us resist the *yetzer*'s best efforts. With just a little thought, it is possible to see through the *satan*.

Please...Help Yourself

(The Jewish Tribune)

When I first met Yair, he was among the hundreds of students who had been unable to study law at an Israeli university. To keep the number of applicants and therefore lawyers down, Israel requires the highest possible academic grades for entrance to a law school.

Someone realized that Israeli law is mostly based on English law, and if you have an English law degree, you can do a one-year "conversion" course and circumvent the problem. Once this loophole had been discovered, hundreds of Israelis appeared in England after completing their army service. English universities were only too keen to accept them. Strangely, despite the fact that he came from an antireligious family, Yair was willing to suspend his suspicions of religious Jews when he found himself in *chutz la'aretz*.

I met him when he arrived in Manchester, and we became very friendly. The relationship was based on acceptance of our individual lifestyles and a willingness to disregard each other's beliefs. He could still go home on holidays and join his parents on anti–*shemirat Shabbat* demonstrations, which they joined because they objected to what they saw as religious coercion. I was still allowed to think and believe all the things a religious Jew believes.

One night he phoned me to say he was in serious trouble. He had gone to have tests at a hospital for certain symptoms that could indicate a very serious disease. He told me he was convinced the results would prove positive. He could not face the prospect of a long and drawn-out illness. He was contemplating taking steps no Jew should ever take — ending his own life.

I told him to wait until I arrived, and I drove to where he was and brought him home. This situation was surprising to both of us. One minute he was a healthy twenty-three-year-old, the next a scared young man. I managed to convince him that I did not believe the test results were anything to worry about. His symptoms indicated a thousand other things besides the worst. I suggested he stay with us the few days he was waiting for the hospital's answer. Then I broke the rules upon which our relationship was based. I told him, "Look, you don't believe in the Torah. Just in case I'm right, why not give Hashem a motive for helping you now? Why not take on a mitzvah?" I asked him if he would wear a set of tzitzis if I gave it to him, and he agreed emphatically.

When the Jewish people stood at the edge of the Red Sea with an Egyptian army racing toward them, Hashem said to Moshe, "Why are you crying out to Me? Speak to the children of Israel that they should travel forward." Rashi comments that Hashem was saying that this was not the time to pray; at this moment praying was a mistake!

The Ohr HaChaim questions the verse more poignantly. "Who else should the Jews cry out to except Hashem? Especially at times of crisis." He explains that the angel who defended Egypt made a complaint in Heaven at this crucial moment. "It is true that my people the Egyptians are unworthy idolaters, but so are the Jews!" referring to their behavior in Egypt. What was required was an act that would change that truth. Prayer was the wrong response.

Please...Help Yourself

The Alshich explains the concept in dramatic and uncompromising terms in *Beha'aloscha*: "It is the way of people who are foolish and have little understanding to cry out to Hashem when troubles befall them. They say, 'Hashem, please save us, because no one can save us except You.' Instead of making things better, they are making things worse."

He explains that when we pray for help Hashem opens up our "account" book to see if we have made any deposits upon which to draw. If the account is empty, all our prayer has succeeded in doing is emphasizing that fact. There are times to ask Hashem for help and times that require us to help ourselves. Prayer without commitment to change will only get us into hotter water. We should start the process of *teshuvah* first, before praying.

Rav Chaim Shmuelevitz, zt"l, remarks on a strange abrogation of normal Jewish behavior that occurred when the Jews stood at the Red Sea. Historically the Jewish people have been willing to give up their lives to die *al kiddush Hashem*. From Ur Kasdim, when that element of our nature was germinated in us by Avraham Avinu, until the present day, loyalty to God's will and His Torah has taken precedence over the desire to live. Yet Chazal say that at the sea the Jewish people experienced an outbreak of what might best be described as "gentlemanliness." Each tribe turned to the other and said, "After you," and received the reply "Oh no, I insist — after you!"

Finally Nachshon ben Aminadav went into the waters, and the miracle of the splitting of the sea occurred. Rav Chaim points out that had the command been to die *al kiddush Hashem*, the Jewish people would have advanced into the waves. The command, however, was to go into the water and change it into dry land!

As far as Nachshon was concerned, if Hashem says the water will become dry land, then of course the water will become dry land. The rest of the people were not yet on Nachshon's spiritual level; they could only follow his lead.

Rav Chaim illustrates Nachshon's perspective with a beautiful story. Imagine a young mother who lives in a village in Russia. The Germans are approaching, and she sweeps her baby up into her arms and flees. She runs into a forest and eventually comes to the foot of a mountain. She climbs up the mountain and down the other side. Now she has to cross a long, arid plain and, after fording a river, finds refuge in another Jewish village. If at any point of the journey you were to ask the child, "Where are you now?" whether it was the forest, mountain, plain, or river, he would reply, "I'm in my mother's arms." If Hashem said that the sea would become dry land then Nachshon already saw it as dry land. He was "in his mother's arms."

It was that action that created the subsequent "investment" in the account of the people, which they could now draw on. Now they could move forward from Egypt to Mount Sinai.

I went with Yair to the hospital for the results of his test. When the doctor called him into his office, he looked at me with sad and worried eyes. Yair seemed to freeze, then shook his head and slowly got up and disappeared behind the door. A few minutes later the door opened. The tears in his eyes contrasted beautifully with the smile on his face. The results were negative.

We have kept in touch over the years. Yair is now a happily married lawyer living in Eretz Yisrael with one lovely little boy. I have the last picture he sent me of him standing beside his wife as she holds her son. If you look at the picture carefully, you'll notice that the boy is wearing his tzitzis out, just like his father.

Flight AA 176 Los Angeles to London

(The Jewish Tribune, August 2001)

The flight from Los Angeles to London would be flying via Israel through the night. I had just spent two very enjoyable weeks giving *shiurim* and enjoying the unparalleled hospitality of the LA community.

The aircraft filled with passengers. A group of Israelis moved along the aisle, talking and joking very loudly. One of this group, a man in his sixties, moved toward my seat, scrutinizing his ticket and working out where his seat might be. Somehow I had a feeling that he would be sitting next to me. The nearer he got, the more his face betrayed that he, too, had come to the same conclusion. Eventually he stood beside me and slowly looked at the vacant seat, then at me, and then back at the seat. He turned to the stewardess and asked, "Is there another seat on the plane?"

The stewardess replied that the flight was full. My neighbor looked again at his seat and walked away. He was determined that he wasn't spending ten and a half hours sitting beside a rabbi. The rest of his fellow countrymen were seated eight rows forward, and he spied a seat there. He asked if it was free, and his new neighbor, although not an Israeli, answered, *"Kein!"*

"Atah medaber Ivrit? Yofi! You speak Hebrew? How nice!" he exclaimed and sat down covered in smiles.

The plane took off at around 7 P.M., and the passengers, who were already tired, took out books or stared at the overhead video screens.

Anyone who has ever traveled on an El Al flight to Israel knows that there is a clear, almost genetic difference between the way Jewish people fly and the way non-Jewish people fly. As soon as the seatbelt sign goes off, Jews leap from their seats. Those in first class swap seats with those in second. People clutter up the aisle, sitting on seat rests or standing as they chat to relations and friends. This does not happen on other airlines. But on American Airlines Flight 176, everyone was going to get a little taste of a more relaxed attitude to flying.

The Israelis milled around and joked and shouted. Those who had their views of the video screens blocked (no bad thing actually) were getting very annoyed. Tired passengers started telling their boisterous fellow travelers to sit down and were perplexed when these exotic people (who, thank God, people thought were Spanish) pressed the tips of their fingers together and stretched out their hands wearing a slightly pained expression. (This is actually the Israeli gesture for "One minute!") The "Spaniards" weren't actually doing anything wrong; they just weren't doing anything wrong loudly.

An outraged South African called over the stewardess and demanded that something be done. Other passengers concurred. Eventually the stewardess told the complainers that the police had been radioed in Heathrow and would be waiting to meet the plane.

A few hours into the flight, the Israeli who should have been my neighbor came and sat down beside me in his official seat. I decided to tell him that he and his friends were behaving in an unacceptable way. He found this claim baffling. "What law have we broken?" he asked rhetorically.

I struggled to explain the English law called "behavior likely to lead to a breach of the peace" in Hebrew. I told him that the police would be waiting to meet the flight and that he should tell his friends that they must speak to the English police respectfully, admit they had been too loud, and apologize. He smiled at me indulgently, but he did as I said and was met with gales of laughter from his friends.

Half an hour later he was back. He leaned across and astonished me by saying, "*Du redst di mama lashon?* — You speak Yiddish?" I answered in the same language that I did speak Yiddish and asked how he came to speak the *mama lashon*.

"Vizhnitz!" he replied, pointing to his chest. "*Ich steim fun Vizhnitz* — I come from a Vizhnitz family."

We spoke for the next hour and a half in Yiddish, and an amazing thing occurred. He spoke Yiddish, and he became a Yid!

A language is more than a collection of words. It expresses attitudes and outlooks, too. When returning to the language of his childhood, this man returned to its attitudes. In Yiddish he understood that they had been wrong in upsetting the young women and had perhaps been too loud.

In *Va'eschanan* Moshe tells the children of Israel that his entry to Eretz Yisrael was barred because of them: "Hashem was angry with me *lema'anchem*." Rashi translates *lema'anchem* as "because of you." It was because of the people that Moshe was forbidden to enter the land. They had caused him to stumble and hit the rock. Moshe's love for the children of Israel led him to accept Hashem's verdict although he could have pleaded. His burial outside the Land of Israel meant that Hashem would appear there, so to speak, to collect his soul and bring it to Heaven. This would allow Him to collect the other souls of the generation who died in the desert because they believed the spies' report. They would not have merited that Hashem came just for their souls. If Moshe had continued pleading with Hashem, He would have had to accede to his request. That would have meant that the souls of those buried in the desert would be left there. Moshe realized that his sacrifice would be necessary, and he accepted God's decree.

Moshe's unconditional love for the people and his willingness to sacrifice himself for us is shown in many other places in the Torah.

When Hashem proposed destroying the Jewish people and starting again from Moshe, his response was "And now if You can bear the sin of this people...but if not, then erase me please from Your book that You have written."

When Moshe returned to Hashem after the apparent failure of his first mission to Pharaoh, he said, "*Lamah harei'osah la'am hazeh lamah zeh shelachtani* — Why have you done evil to this people and why did you send me for this?" The Midrash says that the angels wanted to kill Moshe for saying this, but Hashem replied, "No, he learned it from Me."

When Moshe and the Elders approached Mount Sinai, they saw a vision of Heaven — the floor was made of sapphire bricks. Rashi says that these bricks acted as a constant reminder to Hashem that the Jews were enslaved in Egypt building with bricks. Hashem doesn't need to be reminded of anything, so what was the purpose of this vision?

Reb Simchah Zissel explains that they were being taught a lesson. If you want to understand and feel someone's suffering, you have to picture it in your mind. To truly fulfill the mitzvah of *nosei b'ol im chaveiro*, bearing someone's pain with him, you have to see yourself as though you are the person suffering.

Moshe knew this, and when he spoke harshly to Hashem over his failed mission, he was not speaking for himself. He was expressing what the people were saying as they witnessed their hopes for the end of the exile collapse and die. Moshe saw himself as the Jewish people.

One time in the Torah Moshe's reaction seems totally out of character. In *Beha'aloscha*, the *eirev rav*, the mixed multitude, "desired a desire." The Jewish people joined in and also expressed this mysterious longing, which superficially seemed to be a craving for meat. Chazal tell us, though, that their true agenda was a regret over the Torah's limiting of whom they could marry. They wanted to challenge this, but were not brazen enough to state openly what they really wanted.

Moshe's reaction is astonishing. He said to Hashem, "*Lamah harei'osa l'avdecha v'lamah lo matzasi chein b'einecha lasum es massa kol ha'am hazeh alai* — Why have You done evil to Your servant and why have I not found favor in Your eyes that You have put the burden of this people on me?" (*Bemidbar* 11:11). Moshe seems to be rejecting the Jewish people and his role as their leader.

The Alshich disagrees with the direct translation of this verse. The translation of the word *lasum* is not "that you have put." That would be the translation if the word were *shesam*. The true translation of the verse is "Why have I not found favor in your eyes to put the burden of this people on me?"

Moshe understood perfectly what their real agenda was. He also realized that they were too embarrassed to declare it openly. Perhaps if he could bring them the meat they claimed they wanted, he could arrest this rebellion before it could go further.

A tzaddik is able to interact with the Jewish people in a way that reflects his spiritual level. That is why the food Moshe had brought — the manna — was miraculous. Moshe was requesting the ability to supply them with food that was below both his unsurpassed spiritual level and dignity. Such was his love for the people.

We may understand Moshe's motivation, but we might question his tactic. After all, as they say in English, "Give a person an inch, and he'll take a mile."

Dancing through Time

I heard recently from a *rav* in New York the story of a boy who, although he came from a sincere, *frum* family, had gone off the rails and abandoned Judaism. His father did not know what to do. Keeping him at home posed dangers for his other children. Throwing his son out meant severing any chance that he might do *teshuvah*.

One Friday, close to Shabbos, the father entered his son's room. "I don't want you to go out tonight," he told him. The boy had taken to going to the very worst places on Shabbos. This request from a parent with whom he was in open rebellion was about to receive the usual rejection when the father continued, "I know where you go on Shabbos, and it's a dangerous place."

The boy sneered.

"Listen," the father went on. "What you do inside your bedroom is up to you, but I don't want you to go out on Shabbos."

Then the father produced something he had been hiding behind his back — a small televison set. With tears in his eyes, he handed it to his son and quietly left the room.

The young man later said it was that act that caused him to do *teshuvah* and come back to Torah and mitzvos. "I knew," he said, "how much it killed my father to give me something he despised as much as a television. It made me realize how much I had hurt him — and how much he loved me."

When Moshe would give the Jewish people the meat they demanded, perhaps they would also realize how much he loved them and was willing to sacrifice for them.

In *Va'eschanan* we see that he was willing to give up the thing he wanted more than anything else in the world — to enter the Land of Israel — and he gave it up willingly for the people he loved more than he loved life itself. Moshe demonstrated that you have to love Jews unconditionally, even when they don't deserve it.

The flight from Los Angeles was nearly ready to land, and I went over to the South African who had been so angry with the Israelis.

"Howzit," I said, using the greeting of his *mama lashon*.

"Are you from South Africa?" he asked. I replied negatively and explained that I had spent two weeks lecturing there recently and that I visit at least once a year.

We began to chat about Johannesburg and Cape Town. "Are you flying on to JoBurg from Heathrow?" I asked. He replied that he hoped to spend a week sightseeing in London before returning home. "That's great!" I enthused. "You'll see such wonderful places in London," and I started to list well-known spots.

"It's a pity," I went on, "that you'll lose so much time from your trip."

"What do you mean?" he replied.

"Well, I heard you say that you are going to offer yourself as a witness against those Spaniards. That means you'll lose at least one day in the police station filling out forms, and they'll probably want you back the next day for identification."

The South African looked horrified. "That's ridiculous," he exclaimed. "All right, they were behaving badly, but not too badly. They were loud, but not too loud!"

We landed and started to file off the plane. The English police were standing beside the stewardess, who pointed at the Israelis. Then she pointed at my new South African friend and said, "That's the man who said he'd be a witness."

"Sorry," he blurted, "but I have to make my connection to South Africa," and hurried off the plane.

You have to love Jews unconditionally, even when they don't deserve it.

The Chesed Bank

(Hamodia, August 17, 2001)

Chazal state it quite clearly. The Torah begins with *chesed*, and it ends with *chesed*. At the beginning of the Torah we see that Hashem Himself prepared Chavah's hair to make her appear beautiful to Adam. At the end, Hashem himself buried Moshe Rabbeinu.

The Chafetz Chaim introduces his *sefer Ahavas Chesed* by pointing out that these words of Rabbi Simlai are only the introduction to the story. The truth is that the whole of the Torah is *chesed*, and he cites some of the different categories of *chesed*. There is the *chesed* of lending people things. It might be the loan of a car or a money loan. There is *chesed* when we give of ourselves, opening our homes to strangers or accompanying guests on their way. In fact, any help we provide to others is *chesed*.

I once knew a university student from Liverpool. He was an easy young man to like, and, although not religious, he clearly possessed the prerequisite to becoming so. "*Derech eretz kadmah laTorah* — Respect for others comes before Torah." He was a mensch.

After two years of university, he approached me and asked if I could give him a bit of help. His degree was in business, and the course required a year abroad where students could work in commerce or industry and gain experience. The university had found

The Chesed Bank

him a job in Boston, Massachusetts. He needed help finding a place to stay. I smiled and assured him that I was sure that I could help.

A few phone calls later I was able to tell my young friend that his accommodations were all arranged, and not only that but it would be very cheap, too! I told him that there was an apartment in the shul of the Bostoner Rebbe that he could use.

His reaction to my efforts was, not surprisingly, guarded. He suspected that I had put him there so that the Bostoner chassidim, well known for their outreach work, would, as he put it, "try to make him *frum*." I assured him that no one makes anyone *frum*. People choose to make themselves *frum*. Of course, his new landlords might be keen to help him make exactly that decision, but I didn't feel it necessary to share my suspicions.

The *Yalkut Shimoni* points to the great *ba'al chesed* Avraham Avinu and says that a person can show no greater love for his fellow human beings than to bring them close to Hashem. This is what Avraham Avinu did for countless thousands.

My young friend accepted my arrangements and eventually accepted the invitations of his hosts to attend the daily minyanim and to come for Shabbos and *yom tov*. *Chesed* is contagious. In a very short while, those who receive it want to give it themselves.

A few years later, when he was back from yeshivah, he told me something his *rosh yeshivah* had once told him. "There is a *chesed* bank. Sometimes in his life a person will need to draw on it. Later, if he used what he withdrew wisely, what he took out will have grown and he will then be able to put it back in."

The act of paying into the *chesed* bank, though, does much more than just repay a debt. The second *mishnah* in *Pirkei Avos* says, "The world stands on three things, on the Torah, on the Temple sacrifices, and on acts of kindness."

The Alshich looks at the order and suggests that *chesed* should come first. After all, *chesed* like that of Avraham existed before the Torah was given. He quotes an enigmatic *midrash* on *Shemos*: "Before *mattan Torah* the world existed on only one pillar — *chesed*. When the Torah was given and a second pillar was added, the world started to topple until Hashem added the third pillar, that of the Temple sacrifices, and the world rested on those three."

Why should the world be happy resting on one pillar but totter when a second was added? The Alshich explains that before the Torah was given moral and ethical lapses were judged more leniently and the world was able to rest on only one pillar. Once the second pillar, Torah, was added, the pillar of *chesed* moved from its central position, and the world now balanced, not on one pillar, but on two.

People were now commanded to keep the Torah's laws. If they were to break those laws, the Torah could no longer hold up the world, so a third pillar was added. The sacrifices of the Temple allowed those who had violated the Torah to atone, and so together these three would keep the world standing.

But the sacrifices in the Mishkan and the Temple would atone only for offenses against the Torah that were committed accidentally, not for those done intentionally. If there was a time or a generation when the Jewish people were guilty of consciously transgressing the mitzvos, how would the world stand if not by Hashem's *chesed*? To bring the *chesed* of Hashem "measure for measure," we need to make sure that the *chesed* bank receives a sufficient number of our deposits in all the areas the Chafetz Chaim mentioned.

This is why, says the Alshich, *chesed* comes last in the list. The Mishnah is establishing an essential and fundamental Torah principle — the ultimate insurance policy for *Klal Yisrael* is created when we do *chesed* for each other. Only that will release Hashem's *chesed* to us.

About a year ago I was speaking in New York. I asked my host where I could buy a jacket, and he directed me to a small shop. The shopkeeper was a chassidic Jew of about my age. He asked what I

The Chesed Bank

required and soon disappeared to return with a choice of clothes. Eventually I found what I was looking for. As he packed the jacket, I handed over my credit card and asked him if he could charge me five dollars more than the jacket cost since I had no money with me and give me back the five dollars in cash. It was a very hot day, and I wanted to buy a Coke. The shopkeeper looked at me and begged me to allow him to make me a coffee. I replied that I didn't want to put him to any trouble, and I couldn't take up his time; another customer might come in at any moment.

My new friend looked at me and said, "There was once a Jew who went to see a Rebbe. The Rebbe asked him if he would like a cigarette, and the Jew replied that he didn't smoke. The Rebbe asked him if he would like some snuff, and the Jew replied that he didn't take snuff either. The Rebbe asked him if he would like a cup of tea, and the Jew said he didn't want one. The Rebbe looked at the Jew and exclaimed, 'Reb Yid! How can I do a *chesed* for you then?' "

The shopkeeper raised an eyebrow at me, and I smiled and said I would accept his cup of coffee. As I drank the coffee, my new friend asked me about myself and then told me another story.

He had a little boy who had been born with a very serious illness. By the time the boy was three he would require major surgery. That was something any parent would dread. Someone mentioned to him that there was a famous Chinese practitioner of alternative medicine visiting New York and that he specialized in the complaint the child had. The shopkeeper felt he should try to see this man, and an appointment was made.

The Chinese healer explained that he was in New York for only one week, which was not very much time. He suggested that they start his treatment, and if the parents saw an improvement they should bring their son to Hong Kong for two months.

After a week a distinct improvement was apparent, and the shopkeeper called his travel agent to find out about flights to Hong Kong.

The travel agent told the shopkeeper that he was crazy to even consider spending two months in Hong Kong. "There are no religious Jews in Hong Kong. And how will you get kosher food?" The shopkeeper discussed this problem with his wife, and they felt that, given the problems outlined by the travel agent, they would have to wait for the operation after all.

A week later a rabbi wearing a Homburg and black trousers and holding a briefcase entered the shop. It was a very cold day, and the rabbi was in shirtsleeves. The shopkeeper was soon able to remedy the situation and then asked the rabbi, just as he had me, "Let me make you a coffee."

The rabbi accepted the offer happily, and as he drank they, too, began to chat. The shopkeeper asked the rabbi where he was from and found out that this customer was a *rosh kollel* from Israel, fund-raising in the States. "Forgive me for asking," said the shopkeeper, "but weren't you a little foolish to come to New York in the winter in only your shirt?" The *rosh kollel* explained that he had a coat, but he had taken it off in a taxi and the taxi driver had driven off before he had a chance to collect it from the back seat.

"Ah!" said the shopkeeper. "And are you going straight back to Israel after New York?"

"Oh no," replied the *rosh kollel*. "I'm flying on to Hong Kong."

The shopkeeper was amazed. "Are there religious Jews in Hong Kong?" he asked. He was told that indeed there were. Soon he explained why he was asking, and soon the *rosh kollel* was making phone calls to various friends in the Far East. With no difficulty, accommodations that provided kosher food was arranged.

The shopkeeper told me that the two months were a great success, and when they returned to New York they took their child to see the surgeon who was to perform the operation. The surgeon could not believe the change in the child and said, "I don't know what you did in Hong Kong, but you don't need me anymore."

My new friend poured me a second coffee and said, "I don't

The Chesed Bank

believe that *rosh kollel* left his coat behind by accident. I think Hashem made him lose his coat so that he could come in here and tell me that there are religious Jews in Hong Kong so that my son was saved by the surgeon's knife."

My friend was right, of course, but the act that led to him learning that he could go to Hong Kong after all and the incredible chain of events that cured his little boy was the simple offer of a cup of coffee.

Have a Safe Journey Home

(Unpublished)

The journey was quite simple really. The distance from the Baltimore-Washington Airport, where I was collecting a car, to Philadelphia is about a hundred miles. It should take only around two hours for the whole trip — if you know where you are going, that is.

If, like me, you have never driven between American cities in your life, and you aren't actually sure where Philadelphia is, the journey might not be so simple after all. (I'll ignore the fact that absolutely every single vehicle was driving on the wrong side of the road.)

Everyone I spoke to in Baltimore assured me that the trip was easy and it was impossible to get lost. I was not convinced, and I thought about how big the U.S. is and that I'd probably end up in Alaska.

I confided my lack of confidence to a friend, and he told me I had nothing to worry about. He had a special program in his computer that printed driving instructions between any two places in the United States.

He brought me over to his terminal and started to type. The program appeared. There were two sets of boxes to fill in. One said

Have a Safe Journey Home

"From" and the other, "To." My friend typed in "Baltimore-Wash. Intl. Airport, Baltimore, MD" in the "From" box and "262 S. 16th Street Philadelphia, PA" in the "To" box. A tap on the Enter key with his index finger and a perfect set of instructions plus three maps appeared on the screen.

The distance from the airport to the Etz Chaim Center, where I was due to speak was not "about a hundred miles"; it was precisely 107.45 miles. The estimated journey time was two hours and two minutes.

The instructions went into extraordinary detail to make sure I'd arrive at my destination. There were twelve instructions in all. The first said, "Start out going northwest on DAILY PARKING toward AIRPORT EXIT by turning left. 0.06 miles." I stared at those directions. Not 0.05 of a mile or 0.07 of a mile, but precisely 0.06 of a mile.

I sat in my hired car and studied the directions and map. It was all there, and I couldn't really go wrong. Then doubt crept into my mind. *Suppose the instructions aren't accurate? What if they are out of date?* I read them three or four more times, and since I had absolutely no way of arriving where I needed to be other than by doing what was written in front of me, I turned on the engine and headed for the airport exit, trying to imagine what 0.06 of a mile felt like. Sure enough, there was the airport exit. This was actually working! I promptly turned left (0.25 of a mile).

The next direction said, "Take Interstate 195 west." I missed it and was seized by total panic. I had no idea where I was or where I was going. The map that came with directions was specifically matched to those directions. It did not show you anywhere else outside the places it wanted you to be. The Alaska threat loomed over me, and I wondered what was the Eskimo word for "help."

There was only one thing to do. Somehow I had to turn around and head back to the place I'd started from and begin all over again, this time being more careful not to miss the turn. Back at my starting point, I slowly retraced my route, and this time I saw the sign for the interstate highway, exactly where the amazing computer program had said it would be.

By now I was starting to trust this piece of paper and the program that created it. I decided that the only thing that could get me in trouble was if I doubted its accuracy and worried if it could be relied on.

Instruction number eight told me to "leave the highway at Exit 14 toward PATTISON AVE. 0.48 miles." But the numbers on the exit signs did not match the directions. I was looking for Exit 14, but these exit numbers were much higher. Then I noticed the next exit sign had a smaller sign underneath that announced, "Formerly Exit 13." My heart leaped. The directions weren't as up to date as they should have been and certainly needed correcting, but I was still going to make it.

Sure enough, five minutes later there it was — "formerly Exit 14," good old Pattison Avenue. Three more instructions and 3.34 miles later, I found the rabbi who'd invited me standing outside and waving enthusiastically.

A number of years ago a friend phoned to ask for my help. A heartbreaking case was being heard in the High Court in London. It was a custody case over a young Jewish child. The details of the case were both complex and tragic, but two families were claiming the child — one Jewish, the other non-Jewish.

Both families' claims were finely balanced in the eyes of the law. The lawyer representing the Jewish family decided that the court had to be made aware that the child was not only claimed by its Jewish family but the entire Jewish people!

At that time, no legal definition existed in English law as to what a Jew actually was. Before the community could claim the child as one of its own, the court would have to accept a definition of what made a person a member of the Jewish people.

Several *rabbanim* were asked to write a submission to the judge

Have a Safe Journey Home

that would emphasize the importance of each and every Jew to the Jewish people. This was where my help was needed. My submission went something like this:

"Religion for a Jew is analogous to a father who sends his son on an errand. The child will have to travel to a particular destination and afterward return home. The boy has never been to this place before; he has never even heard of it. The father's instructions will have to be exact, and the child must listen carefully. Otherwise the errand will fail.

"Jewish law is actually called 'halachah,' literally, 'a way to go.' The journey is not made alone. There are those who have been told to accompany the child and others whom he must accompany. Each and every traveler has a unique contribution to make to the group and to the mission he is engaged in. If one of the travelers is missing, the lack of his contribution may cause the entire enterprise to fail.

"There is a crucial Jewish teaching: 'All of Israel are a part of each other.' Had one Jew been missing at the giving of the law at Mount Sinai, no Jew would have received it. Each Jew is essential to all Jews.

"There can even be people who join the group as it passes from place to place. These newcomers may bring specialized local knowledge and open the eyes of the caravan as it continues on its travels. (Moshe's appeal to his father-in-law, Yisro, that he should not leave the Jewish people was that "you will be to us as eyes." Coming from a different background than the rest of the Jewish people, Yisro would see things they might miss. His role could prove essential and its omission disastrous.) Some of the travelers will prove to be natural leaders, and the others will turn to them for guidance and interpretation of the original instructions."

The father in my analogy was, of course, Hashem. The journey was that of Jewish souls in this world. Only through their faithfulness to the instructions and their attachment to the group could they hope to return successfully to their final destination. There is no other way for a Jewish soul to find its way back.

Rav Yitzchak Eizik Sher of Slabodka uses this idea to explain why Jewish women were determined to bring children into the world in Egypt, even though the boys would be killed at birth. It is because only through making the journey here could the souls hope to return home.

The instructions of the Torah are precise. David HaMelech says, "*Toras Hashem temimah* — The ways of the Torah are perfect." The Jewish people have gotten themselves into trouble only when they have decided that the "program" may contain flaws or inaccuracies. We get into trouble only when we worry if it can be relied on.

I would have been undeniably mad to continue driving on when I failed to find the correct turning after I left the airport. Where would I have been going?

Historically Jews have veered off the road countless times and continued straight on until they reached a dead end. They did so without even considering where they were headed.

Mesilas Yesharim addresses this phenomenon in the second chapter: "The idea of *zehirus*, watchfulness, is that a person is careful in his actions, that is, he is alert and considers whether his actions and his road are correct or not...."

The prophet Yirmeyahu pointed to this as the failure of his generation. He said, "No one regrets his mistake and asks, what am I doing? All of them repeatedly race along like a horse rushing headlong into battle" (*Yirmeyahu* 8:6). The computer's directions were not perfect and needed updating. The Torah, though, *is* perfect, and halachah is constantly applied to new conditions by those "natural leaders" whom "the others will turn to for guidance and interpretation of the original instructions."

The journey of the Jewish people would be impossible but for those very rare *neshamos* like Rashi and the Rambam or, in our own times, Rav Moshe Feinstein and Rav Yaakov Kamenetsky. They were sent along to match the directions to the changing road and guide the rest of us.

Rashi tells of what happened when Esav and his army of four hundred came to finally settle the score with Yaakov Avinu. They were met by angels, who started to attack them, then asked, "Who are you?"

"We are Esav's men," they replied, only to be hit harder.

"Leave us alone. Esav is the son of Yitzchak!" The angels hit them even harder.

"Esav is Avraham's grandson!" But the angels continued their attack.

"He is Yaakov's brother!" they called, and the angels left them alone.

To have a connection to Torah it is not enough to have once been attached to tzaddikim. The attachment to tzaddikim, the Torah's guides, and through them the Torah itself, has to lie in the present.

The Chafetz Chaim calls Jewish souls who have lost their road "lost sheep." "There are some," he writes, "to whom Hashem has given special abilities to make sure that the lost sheep find their way back to the road. Such people should be given a special title — *ro'ei Yisrael*, guides of Israel."

It is essential for the Jewish people to consider where our road is taking us and to make sure we turn to the *gedolim* of our own time so that the program is applied to the changing signs and circumstances of our times. If we find ourselves taking a wrong turn, the sensible thing to do is to go back to the point where we were on course and get back on the right road. With perfect instructions from the Master map maker and *Klal Yisrael*'s guides warning us where the detours and roadblocks are, we can't fail to arrive at our destination and eventually come safely home again.

There Are No Prophets — Not Even You

(Unpublished)

One Shabbos night, early in our marriage, one of the Shabbos candles went out after just a few minutes. We started to worry. Could this be a sign that something untoward was waiting for us just around the corner? As soon as Shabbos was over, I phoned my *rav*, the Gateshead *rav*, *shlita*, and told him what had happened. There was a warm smile in his voice as he assured me that this was discussed in *sefarim* and there was absolutely nothing to worry about.

Very often things occur to us that seem to indicate that a divine message is being delivered. It is important to remember that since the time of the second Beis HaMikdash prophecy has been removed from the Jewish people. There are no prophets anymore — not even you!

The Rambam reveals (*Hilchos Yesodei HaTorah*, ch. 7) exactly how the process of prophecy worked. A prophet needed to be someone who was exemplary in character. He or she had to be ut-

There Are No Prophets – Not Even You

terly focused on spiritual matters, and prophecy occurred either in the form of a dream or a vision. The message he received was neither precise nor literal. The prophet had to consider and interpret what the symbolism of the vision meant. Prophets could not prophesy whenever they chose; they had to prepare themselves for prophecy, and this could be achieved only if they were in a state of happiness. It was for this reason that music was often used prior to prophecy, as in the case of King David and King Shaul. The prophecy itself might be a message solely for the individual prophet or one that he had to publicize to others.

In the case of Moshe Rabbeinu, the normal standards of prophecy did not apply. His prophecy was superior in every way to any other. There is, though, another form of prophecy that occurs frequently throughout the Torah, but, interestingly, the Rambam omits mention of it entirely. The Ramban refers to this form of prophecy in his commentary on the Torah. The verse says:

"Yaakov traveled and came to the land of the people of the east. He saw that there was a well in the field, and there were three flocks of sheep lying beside it, because from that well the flocks were watered, and the big stone was on the mouth of the well. All the flocks would gather there, and they would roll away the rock from on top of the well and water the flocks, and then they returned the rock onto the well in its place.

"Yaakov said to them, 'My brothers! Where are you coming from?' And they replied, 'We are from Charan.' And he said to them, 'Do you know Lavan ben Nachor?' and they said, 'We know.' And he said to them, 'Is he well?' And they said, 'He is well. Behold, Rachel his daughter is coming with the flock.' And he said, 'The day is yet long. It's not the time to gather in the flocks. Water the sheep and go and shepherd them' " (*Bereishis* 29:1–7).

The Ramban writes: "This episode was a glimpse into the future. It was preordained that Yaakov should arrive exactly at that time, when there were only three flocks by the well and when the stone was on top of the well. It was a hint that Yaakov would be successful on his journey and eventually would have children whose future was contained in this episode. The well alludes to the Beis HaMikdash. The three flocks hint at the Jewish people going up to the Temple three times a year. From this well the flocks would draw divine inspiration, or it was a hint that '*ki miTzion seitzei Torah* — the Torah came from Zion,' for [the Torah] is likened to water."

So although every detail of the story actually happened, Yaakov could see that there was a parallel story unfolding, one not of the present but of the future.

The Alshich says that far more of the future was being revealed to Yaakov than that. The Jews would indeed one day go to Yerushalayim, which was like a well, but their sins would cause the "big stone" (the *yetzer hara* is often likened to a stone) to block the flow of the well. This would be at the time of the destruction of the first Temple, when the sin of idolatry corrupted the Jewish people.

The words "And all the flocks would gather there" refers to the return of the Jewish exiles, who begged Hashem that the "big stone" of idolatry be removed from the Jewish people.

The words "And they would roll away the rock from on top of the well and water the flocks" revealed that the Temple would be rebuilt, and again Torah would flow to the Jewish people.

"And then they returned the rock onto the well in its place" — this showed Yaakov that the Temple would be destroyed a second time. On that occasion, the stone is not called a "big" stone. The sin of *sinas chinam* (baseless hatred) was not as irresistible as idolatry.

"And Yaakov said to them, 'My brothers! Where are you coming from?' " Yaakov was not only inquiring from the men in front of him where they lived; his question sought clarification of the message he had been shown until now. Yaakov was saying, where was *Klal Yisrael* "coming from" that could have caused a second Temple to be destroyed?

There Are No Prophets — Not Even You

Their reply continued Yaakov's tour of his people's future. "And they replied, 'We are from Charan.' " The Hebrew word *charan* means "anger." It would be the anger people would feel for one another that would cause *sinas chinam* and lead to the second destruction.

"And he said to them, 'Do you know Lavan ben Nachor?' " The word *lavan* means "white." The prophet Yeshayahu says that Hashem will make the sins of the Jewish people white as snow, even if they are "scarlet." Yaakov was asking if the Jewish people would be aware of the process that would be required at the time of the Mashiach to whiten the sin of *sinas chinam*. That would be a Lavan ben Nachor. *Nachor* means "rebuke" and hints that the cleansing process would be achieved through the suffering caused by the pain of the epoch of Mashiach.

"And they said, 'We know.' " The Jewish people would indeed be aware of the birth pangs of the Mashiach.

"And he said to them, 'Is he well [*shalom*]?' " Yaakov was asking if the *shalom*, peace, that would exist during the time of Mashiach could not be created among them by themselves.

"And they said, 'He is well [*shalom*], and behold, Rachel his daughter is coming with the flock.' " They showed Yaakov that instead of working on themselves and doing *teshuvah*, the Jewish people would put their hope in Rachel crying for the return of her children from exile to redeem them.

"And he said, 'The day is yet long. It's not the time to gather in the flocks. Water the sheep and go and shepherd them.' " Yaakov protested this response, and he told his children that this approach would mean that the exile would be very long and pointed to an alternative. They should (and could) remove the stone that was their *yetzer hara* themselves and water the flocks.

I don't know why the Rambam omits this type of prophecy, but I can certainly imagine a good reason for doing so. Since the Jewish people know that prophecy has been removed, no one is likely to think that a daydream contains a message from Heaven. But people might worry that events and coincidences that occur to them during their lives might be a message, telling them what they should or shouldn't do.

About twenty years ago one of my very closest friends in Gateshead was considering a major life decision. He occupied a position very successfully but felt that his talents were not being fully realized. (Since he went on to establish a major and successful institution, his suspicions were obviously well founded.)

At that time he felt that he should move to Eretz Yisrael. He had started to discuss his plans with Rav Matisyahu Salomon, *shlita*, but before a decision had been reached, a strange thing happened. He was walking down one of Gateshead's side streets, and he saw an elderly non-Jew walking toward him. This old man stopped and proclaimed, "Why don't you go and live in Israel? You don't belong here. Go and live in Israel!"

My friend was astonished and rushed back to Rav Matisyahu to tell him of this incredible event. After all, this was the very question he had been struggling with, and here was a clear sign, almost prophetic in nature, pointing the way.

Rav Matisyahu listened carefully as my friend told his tale and then asked a question. "You might be right that this is a sign, but what makes you think it comes from there?" He pointed toward Heaven. "Maybe the sign was sent from there!" He pointed down, toward the ground.

Five years after that first Shabbos candle went out, it happened again. By now we had three sons, and although I remembered clearly what the Gateshead *rav* had told me, we still found ourselves worrying. Eventually I decided to phone the *rav* and hoped that he had forgotten that I had already asked the same question five years before. When I asked the question, the *rav* immediately said, "You've already asked me this," but he went on to assure me once more that there was nothing to worry about.

There Are No Prophets – Not Even You

We felt much better, until the next Friday night, when the same thing happened again. When it happened on the Friday after that, which was also Yom Kippur, my wife and I were becoming rather frantic. It was obvious to me that this was no ordinary occurrence, and I didn't allow the *rav*'s words of assurance to provide the comfort they had previously. It was clear to me that this was a message, and it seemed to hint at something terrible around the corner. The following week was spent worrying what might happen on the next Shabbos, and, sure enough, a candle went out.

On this last occasion my wife actually saw it happen. Our two-year-old had managed to climb onto the end of the sofa. He stretched himself as far as he could toward the sideboard. From there he was just able to blow out the shining bright flame, exactly as he had done on the previous weeks.

There are no prophets anymore — not even you or me.

The Flight to Teshuvah

(The Jewish Tribune, September 1998)

A few years ago, on the tenth of September, Flight BA 6219 took off from Johannesburg bound for Durban. It was the month of Elul. The flight had been delayed by a half-hour and then another half-hour and then another, until it was two hours late. The pilot explained that there had been a failure in an emergency backup unit, and given the poor weather conditions, they could not fly without it.

Finally, the plane picked up speed as it moved along the runway, and we experienced a great deal of shaking as it left the ground. I was sitting by a window watching the color and patterns of the African fields below and thinking about which *shiur* would be appropriate for this leg of my two-week visit. Then a thought struck me. We were told our cruising altitude would be thirty-five thousand feet. Why was I still able to see the fields? We were flying no higher than four thousand feet!

"Ladies and gentlemen," came the captain's voice over the loudspeaker, "this is your captain. There is nothing to worry about."

There are certain professions that use key phrases that you should watch out for. If a doctor says, "You may experience some

The Flight to Teshuvah

discomfort," he means you're about to suffer excruciating agony. If a dentist tells you, "I'll only be a few more moments," he means you'll be writhing in pain for another ten minutes. When a pilot tells you, "Ladies and gentlemen, you have nothing to worry about," he means you are in very, very serious trouble. On this occasion the trouble was the fact that they suspected that both front wheels had burst on takeoff. We would be flying for another fifty minutes to use up the fuel (you really don't want to be in a plane crash if the aircraft is full of fuel). *Yom hadin* seemed to have arrived a little early for me and Flight BA 6219.

We were prepared for a crash landing. This was not the "Tie your life jacket in a double bow at the side" routine. In this briefing we were told, "Take off your shoes, ties, and glasses, put your hands on your head, and press as hard as you can into the seat in front of you." Even the stewardesses lost some of their composure.

Fifty minutes is a very long time when you're really doing *teshuvah*. The *machzor* notes that our sins are too many to remember. I found, however, that I could recall exactly what I had done wrong. A dying man is supposed to see his whole life pass before him. I pictured myself back in the *beis midrash* of Gateshead Yeshivah. Once again I was walking up and down the aisles. In my mind's eye I looked to the side and saw a *bachur* whom I had not thought about for eighteen years. I saw my *rosh yeshivah*, Rav Leib Gurwicz, *zt"l*, sitting in his place at the front.

I considered my family, and my composure broke as I thought of my children. Strangely, I was able to say the Shema and *vidui* with peace of mind. I was reconciled to whatever Hashem decided should happen, although the words "*Mi bamayim u'mi ba'eish* — Who [shall die] from drowning and who from fire?" from the Rosh HaShanah prayers came to mind. I asked Hashem that it should not be by fire.

I had also entered into some serious "negotiations" with Him. There were those areas that I would be putting right if I survived the crash. The story would also be a very powerful one for *shiurim* — if I got the chance to write more *shiurim*.

The fifty minutes had passed, and BA 6219 went totally dark as we began our descent. All the lights were switched off in case fuel vapor connected with a live circuit. The captain changed his mind about us not having to worry and shouted through the microphone, "Brace! Brace! Brace!" We hit the ground illuminated by the flashing red lights of the emergency vehicles, which pursued our progress along the runway. Though bumped and bruised, we were down and safe. The Heavenly court had found sufficient merit for me and the other passengers.

The Midrash says that the world was created on Rosh HaShanah. In the ninth hour after Creation, Adam was commanded not to eat from the fruit of the Tree of Knowledge. In the tenth hour he sinned. In the eleventh hour he was judged. In the twelfth hour he left the garden having been pardoned.

Rav Avraham Grodzensky, *zt"l*, wonders where we see that he was forgiven. Adam and his children suffered forty curses, including death. He answers that the *din Torah*, the judgment itself, was the pardon!

The Mishnah in *Makkos* states that a *beis din* that administers the death penalty more than once in seventy years is a *"beis din chavlanis,"* a bloodthirsty *beis din*. The *Sanhedrin* would search for any and every way to make sure the accused was found not guilty. Any merit, any excuse, would be examined to see if it could be used. A *din Torah*, even if the outcome could be the death penalty, is also an opportunity to be acquitted.

Rav Avraham points out that the process of Adam's *teshuvah* is not recorded by Chazal, but he does not find this omission strange. The closer you are to someone and the more you know him or her, the more you will regret that you hurt the person. Regret will automatically prompt abandonment of the hurtful behavior.

No human being knew the nature of Hashem like Adam

The Flight to Teshuvah

HaRishon. He named every creature in the world. The names he chose defined their nature and being. He named Hashem, and Hashem endorsed his description. *"Ani Hashem,"* He said, "the Merciful." Adam's knowledge of Hashem and his closeness to Him made *teshuvah* inevitable.

A few days ago I held a baby in my arms. The mother and father had come to discuss some worries they had prior to returning to Eretz Yisrael. I had named the baby at the bris and had spoken at the *seudah* and at the *pidyon haben*. I felt like a grandfather. When they got up to leave, the father put mittens on the baby's hands. "This will stop you from scratching your face," he said. And I remembered that babies scratch their faces.

It had been only a few years since our youngest child was born. She has a sister and brothers, but I had already forgotten that babies scratch their faces. What unbelievable *chesed* Hashem has done to me, and yet I had let the knowledge of it slip away. The blessing of wife and children. The blessing of yeshivah and being close to *gedolim*. A home, an income, surviving a plane crash, and more and more and so much more.

If we try to remember all of the *chesed* Hashem does for us, Rav Avraham Grodzenky's formula is activated — *charatah* and *azivas hacheit*, regret and abandonment of the hurtful behavior, to the Source of *chesed*, our Father in Heaven.

Hidden Fruit

(The Jewish Tribune, October 21, 1999)

Recently I picked up a book that someone had lent my wife. It was called *Saba Marches On*, and it was written by Manchester's indefatigable Mr. J. H. Sinasohn. It is the story of his father, Max Mordechai Sinasohn, and his journey from being a soldier serving in the German army in the First World War to a fugitive fleeing from the soldiers of the same army in the Second World War. The book introduces — or I should say reintroduces — us to many of the exceptional personalities of that time who transformed Anglo Jewry. There are glimpses of greats like Rav Moshe Schwab, Rav Eliezer Kahan, and Rav Moshe Schneider, among many others. Many were great Jews who were *rabbanim*. Many were great Jews who held no rabbinic title, like Reb Sender Herman and Dr. Judith Grunfeld. Many are inspiring and guiding the community still.

One of the stories in particular stood out because it was so bizarre, almost surreal (though I have heard several people recall almost identical experiences). After the outbreak of the war, before the Nazis declared Berlin *Judenrein*, Jews were allowed to shop for food only during one strictly controlled hour per day. Needless to say, by the time the Jews arrived, the best produce was already gone, and what was left was at best unwholesome.

As the war progressed and food was scarce, the situation be-

Hidden Fruit

came markedly worse. Still, the Sinasohns did not suffer the worst consequences of such a diet because of an amazing discovery. The grocer from whom Mrs. Sinasohn shopped hid fresh fruit and vegetables at the bottom their box of food twice a week. This grocer was a member of the SS.

During the first war he had served in Russia and been taken prisoner. Some unknown Jews had helped and cared for him. This investment of *chesed* was now paying back dividends more than twenty years later.

A friend of mine in Yerushalayim told me of an astonishing story a Jew once shared with him. This person had been in a concentration camp. He and some fellow prisoners were cutting timber when an SS sergeant marched him away into the nearby woods. One can imagine the terrible thoughts that must have run through his mind at that moment. His worst fears, however, never materialized. The SS man instead asked the terrified Jew if he remembered him.

Two little boys in Germany had lived on the same street. One was a Jew who came from a comfortable home and always had sweets to eat. The other, a German, came from a poor home and never had treats. The Jewish boy always sought out this poor boy and shared his good fortune. Much had changed since those far-off days. Now his friend stood before him in an SS uniform with the wish that his boyhood friend succeed in the escape he had engineered for him.

He did succeed. A life — indeed, lives — were saved. This Jew went on to have a family because of a few candies and a kind heart.

I remember a *mussar shmuess* that Rav Matisyahu Salomon gave in Gateshead Yeshivah many years ago. He recalled a story that may have been no more than a rumor. It was that Hitler, *yemach shemo*, had the seed of Jew hatred, which would grow into the most terrible horror in human history, planted in him when he worked as a house painter. He was said to have been employed by a

Jewish family who had treated him badly. "The story may be true, and it may not," said Rav Matisyahu, "but the likelihood of creating a Jew hater by treating him badly is certainly true."

A few weeks ago I heard Rav Matisyahu speak again. He quoted an amazing *Smag* (*Hilchos Hashavas Aveidah* 74). It says that it is essential for a Jew's business dealings to always be above approach and beyond the letter of the law regardless of whether he's dealing with Jews or non-Jews. If a Jew's records reflect that ideal, then when Hashem wishes to bring Mashiach the world will say that indeed the Jews deserve their redemption. "See how honestly and fairly they deal with people!"

If *Klal Yisrael* fails to achieve that renown, the nations could legitimately protest at our behavior and stop the Mashiach's arrival! "Look at this people and how they behave toward others with sly practices and deceit. And God is bringing the salvation for them?" As Rav Matisyahu put it, "The Creator cannot bring Mashiach if bringing Mashiach would be a *chillul Hashem*!"

The world's impression of the way we behave could be a legitimate measure through which our exile is prolonged.

The Chafetz Chaim, in his *sefer Chomos HaDas*, points out that Avraham Avinu was certainly not the first or the only one in his generation to know and believe in Hashem. Avraham went, after all, to learn in the yeshivah of Shem and Ever, who were prophets. The critical difference between Avraham and the other prophets of that time was his determination to bring knowledge of Hashem to the whole world. The others kept such knowledge to themselves. The Chafetz Chaim puts it like this:

"But Avraham Avinu...who loved Hashem more than any of the other prophets, understood what would be the results of their approach. No man lives forever. Therefore, with the passing of those few giants who held the knowledge of HaKadosh Baruch Hu exclusively, it would be lost. So Avraham struggled with all his strength to demonstrate Godliness to the whole world."

Hidden Fruit

Avraham Avinu's behavior toward others was the magnet that drew the world toward Hashem.

Once a young man in Gateshead asked the *rosh yeshivah*, Rav Leib Gurwicz, *zt"l*, if Jews had an obligation to carry the message of the Torah to the nations. "Should we be knocking on the doors of our neighbors to inform them of the seven mitzvos of Noach?"

Rav Leib replied that ultimately we do have such an obligation. The current state of our people is such, though, that we have to concentrate our efforts on bringing Jews back to mitzvah observance first.

A Jew can perform one of the greatest of all mitzvos, *kiddush Hashem*, sanctification of God's Name, simply by doing acts of *chesed* and showing consideration in whichever society he finds himself. Treating people like a mensch (a smile is a good start) may be an investment that another Jew might find himself needing to draw on someday. It might even be an investment that produces other hidden fruits and hurries Mashiach on his way.

Happy Families

(The Jewish Tribune, June 17, 1999)

There was a couple whom my wife and I knew reasonably well. We lived in Manchester; they lived in another town. Whenever we met at *simchah*s, we enjoyed a pleasant time chatting about this and that. Then one day we heard that they'd gotten a divorce. My wife was truly shocked and said, "I can't understand it. They seemed to get on so well."

I remembered something I'd heard somewhere and replied, "If people lived in glass houses, then you could say that."

How many times are a husband and wife in the middle of a very serious exchange of words (to put it very politely) when the doorbell rings? The husband walks toward the door still firing hurtful comments over his shoulder. "You're only like that because you take after your mother!" He has just received his wife's reply about his own family, and then he turns and opens the door. The noise level in the home, which a few moments before was at the same level as a thermonuclear explosion, subsides into total quiet, and a smiling and cordial host greets the visitor on the doorstep.

"Oh, hello, Chaim! Look, dear, Chaim's here!"

A second smile from his wife as the unsuspecting Chaim walks into this most perfect and happy of homes.

My wife once heard Rav Matisyahu Salomon explain the mechanics of *kibbud av va'em*, honoring one's parents. He said that the mitzvah applies to the parents! Children will learn how to perform this mitzvah if they see their mother and father treating each other with respect.

What children see in their homes produces not just the raw material that will evolve into an adult, but in reality it produces the adult himself. A psychologist friend told me about a recent study done in America. Doctors had listed several disastrous childhood experiences, which included violent father, divorce, and substance abuse. Each childhood experience was given a score, two points for a violent father, for example, and then a final total was tallied. Adults who had a score of zero went on to adult life with incredibly better health than those who had significantly higher scores. They enjoyed dramatically lower rates of cancer, heart disease, obesity, and diabetes.

I read the paper with profound concern. How we bring up our children or, rather, how we fail to bring them up can actually bestow on them a legacy of poor health and even life-threatening diseases.

I once asked the Gateshead *rav*, *shlita*, for advice on bringing up children. He told me that it is essential to set aside time for each and every child. Each one has to feel that he or she is special to his mother and father. Someone who was in yeshivah with me told me what he had discovered when he and his brothers were sitting *shivah* for their father. While they were discussing their childhood, each brother confided that from their tenderest years until their father's death he was convinced that their father loved him best. It was this discovery that made them realize how lucky they were to have been brought up in such a home.

Rav Matisyahu Salomon once told me of a young man who had come to see him for help. The young man explained his problem: he hated his tefillin! The meaning of this strange declaration was that he had thoroughly gone through all the halachos of tefillin. He knew what were considered kosher tefillin, and he knew what made them invalid. He had become terrified that his *batim* weren't perfectly square or the straps were insufficiently black or the parchment inside had become invalid.

Rav Matisyahu pointed out that after we finish reading from the *sefer Torah* it is replaced in the ark with the words from *Mishlei*, "*Deracheha darchei no'am* — The Torah's ways are pleasant." If we have read the Torah and the results are that our lives are miserable, we misread the words. *Yiddishkeit* is meant to be pleasant; when we bring up our children, they should be shown that.

Recently it has become apparent in many communities that, in addition to people like me who specialize in *kiruv rechokim*, outreach, we are increasingly in need of people gifted in the infinitely more difficult art of *kiruv kerovim*. Significant numbers of young people from observant homes are drifting away and getting lost.

The reasons for this tragedy are multifaceted, but it is certainly hard to imagine another time when the corrosive values of Esav have found so many different ways to insinuate themselves into Jewish homes. Never before have homes needed so badly to be places that are warm and pleasant.

On April 17, 1835, Rav Shamshon Refael Hirsch sent off the manuscript for the work that would become famous as *Horeb*. He wrote that it was meant mainly for "Israel's thinking young men and women." In the chapter entitled "Guarding against Immorality," he writes:

"And as for you, Jewish parents, do not forget that it was at the time when you were young that the decline began. Sin has made giant steps since you were young; keep guard over your children! Some already move in the direction of this sin in the tenth, ninth, eighth year. Test the schools, the playmates, the servants, the friends of the house! Know that vice enters the circle of youth by every way. Become the friends of your children! Give them early warning! Stand by their side in their battle! Do not leave them just in those years when the battle is hottest!"

Happy Families

If moral decline started when *Horeb's* readers were young, Rav Hirsch is referring to the beginning of the 1800s! How would he react if he saw what a walk on a deserted street, empty of people but festooned with billboards and posters, would reveal to our children today? The central role of a Jewish home as a place that is happy and warm has rarely been so needed. Such a home is a sanctuary where children feel guilty about flouting the values taught there and that will always be a place they are happy to be part of.

Sadly, I have been consulted several times by parents whose children have wandered from the *derech*. It is not within the scope of one article to address all the possible causes and all the possible cures. One thing is obvious, though: the happier and more secure the home, the less likely it is to occur.

This does not mean, however, that people are fated to be congenital *nebbechs*. One of the most exciting things I ever read in any *sefer* was Rav Dessler's point that the opposite of the Hebrew word *ra*, evil, is not *tov*, good, but *er*, "catalyst" or "awakening."

It is true that statistically bullies were themselves often bullied, and often abusive parents were themselves abused. But it doesn't have to be that way. Avraham Avinu the monotheist had a father who sold idols. A man who thought himself a god, Pharaoh, brought up Moshe Rabbeinu. The Jewish nation were prepared for receiving the Torah by a 210-year-stay in immoral Egypt. The paradigm of *tznius*, Ruth, came from a nation that was a byword for immorality.

Bad experiences can be used positively to push us in the opposite direction. They can awaken a rejection of that which we ourselves suffered.

When a young couple are told that they are going to have a baby, many things in their lives will change. The news will not, however, bestow perfection on the new mother and father. They will carry their shortcomings with them into parenthood. But they need not transfer those same shortcomings to their own children.

Dancing through Time

The most important advice any Jew can take to create a happy home for himself and his children is found in *Pirkei Avos*: "*Asei lecha rav.*" Get yourself a rabbi! This is especially important when a couple is committed to making their marriage a success but have reached an impasse from which they feel they can't escape. They might arrive at the conclusion that the husband thinks his wife behaves badly because she takes after her mother, and the wife doesn't have a high opinion of her husband's relations either. This is where a *rav* comes in. No one has to behave badly just because his parents were not the perfect role models. One can find a role model in his *rav*, and if he wants to change, he can.

The Mishnah says "*rav*" in the singular. The more the advice, the more the confusion! If the *rav* gives advice we don't like, we still have to heed it, as it says, "If your *rav* tells you your right hand is your left hand, believe him!"

How do you find such a *rav*? How do you find out who is the best specialist in any field? Ask other people, especially those who had the same problems. Suppose you live in West Hollywood, Los Angeles, and the *rav* lives in Bnei Brak? Well, there is always the phone and the fax, and perhaps he can recommend someone nearby whom you didn't think of.

The greatest gift we can give our children is a happy home. The Torah provides the advice to make that ambition a reality. It is essential that the smiles our friend Chaim sees after he passes through the door are the same ones that were there before he rang the bell.

Avoiding Mistakes

(The Jewish Tribune)

I once heard a quote from a member of Britain's House of Lords. I suppose it must be a well-known saying, but it was new to me. He said, "Someone who hasn't made a mistake hasn't made anything!"

Rabbi Avraham Twerski makes an interesting point about discovering an exciting truth from a non-Torah source. "Do not think that it is not in the Torah — you just haven't merited finding it there first." This particular truth appears in countless places throughout our *sefarim*, although I have to admit that this particular noble expressed the point rather well.

Vayakhel deals exclusively with the construction of the Mishkan and starts by saying, "Moshe gathered all the congregation of the children of Israel and said, 'These are the things that Hashem has commanded you to do.'" The Torah then interrupts the instructions for the building of the Mishkan and continues with a warning about making a mistake:

"Moshe gathered all the congregation of the children of Israel, and he said to them, 'These are the words that God commanded you to do. Six days you will do work, and the seventh will be holy for you. A Sabbath of Sabbaths to God. Anyone who does work shall be killed. Do not ignite any fire on the Sabbath no matter where you may live.'"

Rashi says we might make a mistake and think that the construction of the Mishkan was a license to break the laws of Shabbos.

Rav Zalman Sorotzkin, *zt"l*, wonders why Rashi is concerned that the people would think they could profane Shabbos to build the Mishkan. He supplies a brilliant insight.

The Mishkan (and its successor, the Temple in Jerusalem) and Shabbos share a common purpose. Both are vehicles for allowing a Jew to have a profound spiritual experience, to come closer to Hashem and feel he's done so. The difference between them is that Shabbos presents this experience at a certain time. It represents *kedushas hazeman*, the sanctification of time. Every seven days, throughout the year, spiritual batteries can be recharged.

The Mishkan occupies a geographic location. It represents *kedushas hamakom*, the sanctification of place. It is not bound by time. A Jew can experience the effects of the Mishkan every one of the 354 days of the Jewish year. The Mishkan and Temple also manifested clear, miraculous phenomena. Shabbos does not operate that way. A person could easily compare the two and imagine that Shabbos had been superseded by the Mishkan.

The Torah knew, though, that there would be times when we would no longer have a place occupied by the Beis HaMikdash, whereas Shabbos is eternal. Wherever Jews have gone, Shabbos has gone with them. Shabbos can be found in Siberia or San Francisco. Shabbos was with us in the century when men first set foot on the soil of America and in the last century when they set foot on the soil of the Moon. *Vayakhel* therefore starts the instructions of the Mishkan by restating the supremacy of Shabbos, ensuring we don't make a mistake.

The Alshich points out a simple reason that the construction of the Mishkan could not displace Shabbos. The Torah's instructions were given on the day after Yom Kippur, when Moshe descended from Mount Sinai. The Mishkan was Hashem's statement

Avoiding Mistakes

of forgiveness for another mistake, the making of the golden calf. At that time there was a gathering that led to a disaster: "And the people gathered against Aharon." Now there would be another gathering to put it right — at the Mishkan and, later, the Beis HaMikdash.

For the making of the golden calf they volunteered only one gift, gold. For the Mishkan they would volunteer thirteen different gifts, gold, silver, copper, and so on. Thirteen is the numerical value of the Hebrew word *echad*, one. The Jewish people and Hashem would now come together and be unified, repairing the breach the golden calf had made. The gifts and the construction would be exclusive to the children of Israel. Those who caused the previous mistake, the mixed multitude, would be excluded.

In correcting one mistake, though, they mustn't make another. Until it was completed, the Mishkan didn't have *kedushah*, sanctity. The construction of the Mishkan was a preparation for the time it would be holy. Something without *kedushah* can never supersede something that possesses it. Shabbos already had *kedushah*; the construction could not override it.

Rav Yerucham Levovitz, *zt"l*, points to a more subtle process involved in the making of the Mishkan that could have led them to violate Shabbos. He notes that Rashi's words in *Vayakhel* echo his earlier comment in *Shemos* (31:13): "Even though you will be busy and preoccupied with your zeal for the work, Shabbos is not suspended because of it."

Three new ingredients, busy-ness, preoccupation, and zeal, all made such a mistake a possibility. But weren't they busy, preoccupied, and zealous for a great mitzvah? Yes, and that was exactly the problem.

David HaMelech expressed this concern in *Tehillim*: "Even though I am traveling in the path of the Torah itself, in that path there lies a snare waiting to entrap me" (*Tehillim* 142:4). Rav Yisrael Salanter once illustrated this problem with a story that I've witnessed with my own eyes in slightly different forms many times.

A great *maggid* comes to town. A Jew in the town is excited about the opportunity to hear wonderful words of Torah and poignant stories. Perhaps he'll come away with the sort of inspiration that will propel him toward being a better Jew. As he approaches the hall, there are lots of other people keen to gain the same inspiration. People start pushing and shoving to get in. Someone pulls at his sleeve and pushes him. He promptly pushes back just as hard. More pushing and shoving follow.

Before this Jew set out, were he to be asked if it is permissible to damage or wound another Jew, he would be amazed at the very question. The very thought of hurting a fellow Jew would upset him. Now, though, he is trying desperately to hear the *maggid*, and all that is forgotten. After all, he is trying to do a mitzvah!

I was once at the *levayah* of a great *rosh yeshivah*. The *aron* (casket) was carried with dignity and solemnity from the yeshivah, and the procession of thousands wound its way down a hill and around a corner. Those carrying the *aron* had been selected from among the *rosh yeshivah*'s family and closest *talmidim*. At various stops along the route, new shoulders had been appointed to come forward for the great mitzvah of carrying their rebbe to his burial. At the last stop someone from the *chevrah kaddisha* called out, "*Kol hakodem zocheh*. The first to reach the *aron* can have the mitzvah of carrying it."

A section of the crowd surged forward. The *aron* swayed and nearly fell. It was one of the most disturbing sights I ever saw. The eldest son of the *rosh yeshivah* cried out in Yiddish, "This is a disgrace to my father!" and slowly order was restored.

The son was right. It was a disgrace, a disgrace *l'shem mitzvah*, for the sake of a mitzvah! Not one person in that huge crowd wanted anything other than to honor the memory of his great teacher. Had the *aron* fallen, they would never have forgiven themselves. And yet, on the road to do a mitzvah lay a snare. Their pre-

Avoiding Mistakes

occupation and zeal for one great mitzvah caused every single *middah* and *hashkafah*, as well as all the other 612 mitzvos, to be swept aside.

Even the greats of the Jewish people's greatest generation had to be warned of the mistake they could come to make when building the Mishkan and the trap that lay before them.

Someone who hasn't made a mistake indeed hasn't made anything. But mistakes can be the greatest teachers and can allow us to avoid making the same mistakes again, despite being busy, preoccupied, or zealous. From there we can go on to build something special for ourselves and *Klal Yisrael*. It requires a determination to carefully bypass the snares along the way and remember our obligations to all the mitzvos.

Judaism and Magic

(Unpublished)

The worst part about getting to your destination via a connecting flight is that more often than not either you arrive too late and miss it or you arrive on time and the next flight is delayed. The latter is exactly what happened recently while I was sitting at Newark Airport waiting to board a flight to Cincinnati. The boredom was lifted when my cell phone rang. At the other end of the line was a reporter from the *Philadelphia Inquirer*.

He inquired (a good thing for a journalist from a paper with that title to do) if he could have an interview with me about a talk that I was due to give in his city in a week's time.

I was scheduled to speak at Philadelphia's Etz Chaim Center, an organization that reaches out to Jews who have not had the opportunity to discover what Judaism is all about. The subject they had chosen was entitled, "Harry Potter: Judaism's Perspective on Magic, Sorcery, and the Occult."

It is difficult to be oblivious to the Harry Potter phenomenon, no matter who you are or where you live. Articles have appeared about it in even the most religious Jewish newspapers, and since the first book has been made into a film, posters advertising the existence of the young Mr. Potter have appeared all over the world.

In case by some miracle you are still unaware of who H. Potter,

Judaism and Magic

Esq., is, allow me to give you a brief introduction.

A young author, J. K. Rowling, wrote her first book in a café in Edinburgh, the capital of Scotland. It went on to become a multi-million best-seller and is probably now, four books later, the best-known children's story of all time. Critics have hailed it, Hollywood has bought it, and chances are that the Harry Potter books, of which seven in all are envisioned, will remain on children's bookshelves for decades to come.

Harry Potter is an orphaned child who is brought up by his cruel and wicked uncle and aunt. He is bullied by his cousin and made to live in a cupboard underneath the stairs. Harry's real story has been kept from him throughout his childhood. His mother and father were actually a witch and wizard. They were murdered by an evil wizard who tried to kill Harry, too. Like all good children's stories, though, the truth will come out, and Harry soon finds that he too has magical powers and is invited to join the Hogwarts School of Witchcraft and Wizardry. The school is situated in a castle in Scotland, which is magically protected from the eyes of ordinary people by a spell or two.

The castle contains ghosts that on the whole get along quite well with the pupils. Hogwarts students spend all their time (leaving aside the occasional adventure with bad wizards) learning how to utter curses, make charms, and brew potions. (They also learn how to fly broomsticks, of course, but I don't feel the need to state the obvious.)

Being asked to lecture on the subject, I had to familiarize myself with Harry and his friends, and there is no doubt that as a children's book it is brilliant. But the reaction of religious Jews to the Harry Potter books is obvious. No matter how brilliant, it does not reflect a Torah outlook.

Interestingly, Harry Potter stirred up quite a bit of opposition in other quarters, too, particularly in America, where religious non-Jewish schools banned it. They were worried that it would trigger an interest in the occult among their pupils. The principal of one such school explained to the press why he had banned the book: "We don't believe in magic."

A simple enough explanation from a Christian principal, but what about Jews? Our religion does believe in magic!

The Torah says, "When you come into the land that Hashem your God is giving you, do not learn to do the disgusting things of the nations. Do not let be found among you anyone who passes his son or daughter through fire or practices stick divination or predicts the future or reads omens or practices magic" (*Devarim* 18:9).

There is a debate among the commentators as to whether magic is mere trickery or something real and powerful. Whatever its true nature, it clearly exists, or the Torah would not have to ban it.

The Rambam says, "The Jewish people did not believe in Moshe as a prophet of Hashem because of the miracles he did, for anyone who would believe because of the miracles had foolishness in his heart. This is because it was possible that the miracles in Egypt were done through magic" (*Hilchos Yesodei HaTorah*, ch. 8).

This clearly suggests that magic in those times was real and potent.

When Moshe first confronted Pharaoh and turned his staff into a snake, Pharaoh ordered his magicians to do the same and they did. *Yalkut Shimoni* reports that Pharaoh went further. He told his wife to turn her staff into a snake, and she did so. Pharaoh turned to the teenage boys who were in the crowd and invited them to do the same, and they turned their staffs into snakes. He then ordered children brought in from the kindergarten to do so, and they, too, were able to turn sticks into snakes.

Egypt was a society totally based on occult forces and the ability to control those forces. Though the Egyptian magicians were no longer able to match Moshe's miracles by the plague of lice, this does not undermine the Rambam's statement. It would still be pos-

Judaism and Magic

sible to assume that Moshe's miracles were the product of magic. Moshe, after all, was brought up in Pharaoh's palace and lived there the first forty years of his life. Perhaps he learned his powers from his Egyptian teachers but was so talented that he was greater in their own arts than they were themselves.

Ghosts are certainly not alien to Judaism. In *Shmuel*, King Shaul is desperate for guidance as to how he should confront the approaching Philistine army. He has lost the gift of prophecy, and after his order to massacre the *kohanim* of the city of Nov, the *Urim and Tumim* will not answer him. So King Shaul turns to a witch! He asks her to summon the ghost of the prophet Shmuel. Not only is she able to open the door between the two worlds, she produces two spirits — Shmuel and Moshe Rabbeinu. Although she can see them, she cannot hear them, whereas Shaul can hear them but he cannot see them.

How did such phenomena occur? The Rambam answers in *Hilchos Avodah Zarah* that Hashem created the planets, the *mazalos*, to control events in this world. These are often portrayed at the back of a Sukkos *machzor*, and the names and shapes of the constellations match almost identically the ones that appear in the astrological columns of newspapers like the *Philadelphia Inquirer*. For example, the *mazal* of the month of Av is *aryeh*, lion. The non-Jewish month is August, and its constellation is Leo the lion.

The Talmud states (*Shabbos* 146) that the planets exert an incredible influence over events and occurrences in the world. The Rambam says both idolatry and magic trace their origins back to this source. Familiarity with the mechanics of how planetary energy controls events in this world would allow people to manipulate that energy for their own purposes.

The Egyptians' chief god was the sheep. This incredibly sophisticated society knew, of course, that a sheep is only a fluffy animal. They revered the animal because one of the twelve *mazalos* is the *tleh*, the sheep. Egypt knew how to access the energy of the *mazal* called *"tleh"* and utilize it to perform wonders. Sheep reminded them of their god.

The power of Egypt was so intense that the Jewish people was nearly destroyed by it. That is why the Exodus occurred exactly when it did. The time when the Earth is closest to the constellation of the *tleh* in its elliptical orbit around the sun is the month of Nissan. The fifteenth of Nissan is the middle of the month, when our planet is at its closest possible point to that constellation. That is the time when its influence reaches its zenith. It was then that this power and influence was crushed.

So the Jewish people, and through them the entire world, were shown the truth about the power of the planets. The *tleh* was only one of the *mazalos*; there are another eleven. Above the world of the *mazalos* and their power is the sphere of the angels, and ultimately above everything is Hashem Who made all these and gave them their power and purpose in the first place.

Mr. Potter's curses also resonate in the Torah. When Bilam comes to curse the Jewish people, Hashem changes the words coming from his mouth, transforming the curses to blessings. I once heard Rav Mordechai Miller of Gateshead ask why Hashem had to do this. "Let Bilam the wicked curse until he is blue in the face. It's not as if Hashem has to respond to his curses and allow his words to come true, is it?"

Rav Miller supplied a surprising answer to his own question. Had Bilam succeeded in uttering the words he intended, Hashem would have had to allow them to come true!

The world was created with freedom of choice. This demands that the truth is not obvious and clear. It is for this reason that this world is called *"olam"* in Hebrew. The root of the word *olam* means "hidden." If there is to be a world with freedom of choice, Hashem has to hide the reality of His existence so that people can choose to search for it.

That's what the verse means when it says, *"Zeh le'umas zeh asah haElokim* — For every positive force that Hashem created in the world, there is an opposing and parallel negative one" (*Koheles* 7:14).

This led Chazal to comment that when the Torah says, "*V'lo kam navi od b'Yisrael k'Moshe* — There would never again be among Israel a prophet like Moshe" (*Devarim* 34:10), it does not mean there could not be someone who was like Moshe among the nations of the world — Bilam!

Freedom of choice could not be maintained if we all had access to astonishing phenomena and insights like those commonly given by prophets. In addition, there are those who can perform similar wonders — their abilities would flow from the *mazalos*.

When the Jews returned from the Babylonian exile, the *Sanhedrin* addressed a prayer to Hashem that the ability to manipulate the power of the planets be removed from men. Their request was granted. As a direct consequence of that, the power of prophecy was taken away, too. "*Zeh le'umas zeh asah haElokim*" — if one went, the other would have to be taken in order to maintain freedom of choice.

So today there is no magic — at least, not the sort of magic that could suspend the laws of nature and turn water into blood. Harry Potter remains a fantasy with echoes of a time when the world was indeed populated with real witches and wizards.

There is, though, in all the fuss generated by the tremendous sales of this book, something of a challenge to religious Jews. Many of us have made sure that our children have no contact with young Mr. Potter and his adventures. Still, by now the vast majority of the Jewish children of the world will be more familiar with the details of the story of Harry Potter than the details of the story of the Exodus!

At the same time, there has been renewed interest in the subject of magic and the occult, and books on those subjects have been given an unintended boost by the efforts of J. K. Rowling. It is essential that Jewish parents be aware that Judaism can deal with the issues brought back to the world's attention — or, at least, the attention of the children's world — by Harry Potter.

Nonreligious parents will be able to get that information only from religious parents, which is why, after all, Harry Potter and Hogwarts School of Witchcraft and Wizardry affects religious Jews, whether they have read the book or not. And that is why rabbis are giving talks entitled "Harry Potter: Judaism's Perspective on Magic, Sorcery, and the Occult."

A year ago I received a phone call from a television producer. He introduced himself and asked for my help with his latest project. He was producing a series of programs entitled "The Weekend," which would explore what people did when they reached the end of the week. He wanted one of the programs to be about the Jewish Sabbath. I told him I was willing to help, and he mentioned that he knew a little about religion since his father had been a priest. I soon found out that his father had actually been the Archbishop of Canterbury, the leader of the Anglican Church throughout the world.

The producer friend arrived with a film crew to interview me about the "Sabbath." I painted a picture of a Shabbos table and the singing and questioning of the children about the week's parashah. I told him of Shabbos walks, when mothers and fathers have a chance to hear about their children's week. I explained that it was a time when phones, e-mails, and faxes can't disturb you.

Questions followed, and after the half-hour I had been told the interview would take, the producer asked if I minded if he asked me more questions. I told him that I didn't mind, and for another hour I answered questions that obviously flowed from his own interest rather than the program's requirements.

Finally, this son of a "prince of the church" asked his last question. "Rabbi Rubinstein, I'm not Jewish, and none of the film crew here is Jewish. Is there any hope for us?"

Judaism and Magic

For an hour and a half he had been hearing what Judaism has to offer and gaining a glimpse into our world. Now he was comparing it to what his world was offering to even these successful professionals in one of the most glamorous jobs in the world, and this was his conclusion: "Is there any hope for us?"

The Rambam explains the point at which the Jewish people did become convinced that Moshe was a prophet: "when we stood at Mount Sinai, and we saw with our own eyes and heard with our own ears Hashem speak, saying, 'Moshe, tell them this mitzvah.' "

When the Jewish people were exposed to the real thing, every phenomenon they had experienced until then was now seen in its proper context. They could distinguish between the limited and the limitless.

The Torah has an answer to every question and offers so much more than any other society could ever hope to. Jews who have enjoyed the privilege of being taught what the Torah is have a duty to pass on its teachings to the Jewish parents whose children might be seduced by the sorcery of Egypt or the beauty of Greece or the power of Rome — or even the magic of Harry Potter.

The Stamp of Approval

(Hamodia, November 3, 2000)

What you think about when you think of a place very much depends on who and what you are. The city of Antwerp might be familiar to some as the second biggest port in the world (Rotterdam is the biggest). This gave birth to a well-known saying in Belgium: "The Scheldt River owes its existence to God, and Antwerp owes its existence to the Scheldt River." An art lover knows Antwerp for its not inconsiderable contribution to the history of art. So there are in reality many Antwerps.

Through its Jewish population, Antwerp has another, quite different claim to fame. Antwerp is one of Europe's capitals of Torah and Chassidus. A few weeks ago I found myself speaking in one of Antwerp's Jewish schools. Afterward several of the teachers took me into the director's office, where I heard about the activities and goals of the dedicated staff on behalf of the six hundred Jewish souls in their care.

As we talked, I noticed a bookshelf beside the director's desk. Lying flat beside the shiny white volumes was a very old and very large leather-bound tome. It was about the size of a *yeshivah*

The Stamp of Approval

bachur's Bava Kama, and on the brown leather cover I could clearly see a gold embossed Star of David. Fleetingly, it crossed my mind that this must be a very old shul *machzor*.

A few moments later the director picked up the book, put it on the table in front of me, and related its history. The school had been founded after the First World War, when Antwerp's Jewish population was roughly double the size it is today. This book had been "the schoolbook," in which the record and history of the school was recorded. It was chilling to notice that during the Second World War, when the school had been occupied by the Nazis, all the pages on the Jewish history of the school had been carefully cut out. The director closed the book and showed me the nearly invisible swastika that had been stamped on top of the golden Star of David. During the war the Germans had removed the gold from the Star of David so that it was nearly invisible. Their evil emblem had been covered in gold and shone out. The school had been transformed into an SS headquarters.

After Antwerp had been liberated, the school became a center for returning refugees. The back of the book contained the names of American and British soldiers who had visited the school. Some had come to offer help; others came just to show their sympathy and support. The director turned to a new page and said that the school would be honored if I wrote something on it.

I felt a very large lump in my throat. I had just finished teaching Torah to Jewish children in a building in which the Nazis had tried to stamp out everything that being Jewish stood for. Now, in a book where a swastika had tried to stamp out the Star of David, I was going to write words of blessing.

The Gemara says, "*Ma'aseh avos siman l'banim* — The lives of the patriarchs were a template for the lives of future Jewish generations." The first attempt to stamp out the Jewish people started with Avraham, although at the time he was still called Avram and he was forty-eight years old.

Dancing through Time

The Torah states, "And it was, when the whole world was one language and one speech [*devarim achadim*]" (*Bereishis* 11:1). "*Devarim achadim*" is translated enigmatically by the Midrash as "words about the ones." The leaders of that generation were very wise and knowledgeable. They were well versed in the power of the occult. The Midrash says that their ability to see into the future revealed to them two "ones." The first "one" was Avraham, whom they saw as unique and separate from the entire world. The other "one" was contained in a prayer destined to be heard soon: "*Shema Yisrael Hashem Elokeinu Hashem echad!*"

The holy Alshich says that the greats of that generation knew other crucial truths, too. They knew that a future Jewish people would share a unique unity, that *"kol Yisrael areivim zeh lazeh* — all of Israel would be responsible for each other." They knew that a continuous flow of energy from Heaven to this world sustains and maintains it and without that energy this world would end in an instant. They were also able to see that in the future that energy would flow to the world through the people who would say the prayer of Shema, declaring Hashem's Oneness.

In opposition to this, Nimrod devised a strategy, a way to guarantee that Heavenly energy would still come to earth and allow for the existence of the world even without a *Klal Yisrael*. He shared his plan with Avimelech and the other leaders of the peoples of that time. It was a plan whose ambition was nothing less than to stamp out Hashem's design for there to be a Jewish people.

Thus the Torah reports that the people moved to the east. Humanity's change of location reveals other fundamentals that they understood. "*Zeh le'umas zeh asah haElokim* — For every positive creation in the world, there is an equal and opposite negative creation." They moved to a place that was the negative parallel of the Land of Israel. They built a city and a tower meant to be a parallel of Jerusalem and the tower of David. They placed one idol on their tower, and all the peoples of the world abandoned their own idols and forms of worship for a new, universal idolatry. They produced all these ingredients to make themselves into a copy of a united *Klal Yisrael*. The idol they planned to place on top of the tower was the *satan*. There would be a copy of *Klal Yisrael*'s worship, but it would be a copy.

Avraham Avinu had clashed with Nimrod before, but he realized the tremendous danger now and prayed for Hashem Himself to intervene. And Hashem declared, "Behold, they are one people and one language for all of them, and this is what they have begun to do. And now nothing will be able to be withheld from that which they attempt to do."

If not for the intervention of Hashem, their plan would have succeeded! So they were scattered, and their one language was replaced with many tongues. Their unity was demolished, as was their tower and their plan.

Rashi points out the difference between Hashem's reaction to Noach's generation and His reaction to the generation of the Tower of Bavel:

"The generation of the flood did not defy Hashem, while the generation of the tower defied Hashem and tried to fight against Him. Yet the first was destroyed, and the second was not. This is because the people of the generation of the flood were thieves who fought among themselves, and ultimately that is why they were lost. The generation of the tower manifested friendship and unity. This demonstrates how Hashem hates *machlokes*, strife, and loves peace."

As I write this article, I witness the same phenomenon. The riots that began over who owns the Temple Mount have been declared by the Palestinians to be in reality a war over Jerusalem. It is not the Temple Mount, but the whole city that is theirs and not ours. As a Palestinian spokesman said recently on the BBC, "There will be peace only when the Jews leave all of Jerusalem, which is Muslim and solely Muslim territory."

Dancing through Time

When I visited Eretz Yisrael a few years ago, after an absence of some time, I was immediately struck by an obvious difference in the Palestinians. A transformation had occurred. It was noticeable in the dress of the women, who now wore headscarves and long dresses, as dictated by their religion. It was noticeable in the eclipse of the secular PLO by the Islamic Hamas. The Palestinians had found an identity they had not possessed before.

At the same time, the State of Israel was suffering from exactly the opposite process. The Jewish nature of the state was becoming more and more eroded. Israelis were losing their identity in a devastating manner that finally culminated in former Prime Minister Barak's "secular revolution."

At a break during the davening on Yom Kippur, a friend, referring to the situation in Israel, asked me, "Why can't they (the non-religious) see it? The Torah's words from *Bechukosai* are happening in front of our very eyes."

He was talking about the verse "If you will walk in My statutes...five of you will chase a hundred, and a hundred of you will chase ten thousand...and if you do not keep My mitzvos...you will be beaten before your enemies...." Yet maybe this is exactly the point. Who is the message really meant for?

I once heard Rav Matisyahu Salomon, *shlita*, quote the Brisker Rav, saying that Hashem allows such things to happen not for Jews who can't see and don't understand to sit up and take notice. The alarm call is meant for those Jews who are familiar with the portion of rebuke and do understand. The alarm call today is being sent to us!

The generation of the Tower of Bavel nearly succeeded in displacing *Klal Yisrael*. That near success was achieved through their unity — a unity that was a copy of what a soon-to-be *Klal Yisrael* would be built upon.

We say it in the Shabbos *minchah* prayer: "*Atah echad v'shimcha echad u'mi k'amcha Yisrael goy echad ba'aretz* — You are One and

The Stamp of Approval

Your Name is One, and who is like Your nation, Israel, one nation in the land?"

When another people comes along and tries to stamp out *Klal Yisrael* and superimpose their symbols on top of ours, there is one focus and one effort we have to concentrate on in order to defeat it. We must realize that we are being sent a wake-up call, that we must make a supreme effort to heed Rashi's lesson and avoid *machlokes*, strife. It is up to us to treat each other with true friendship and ascertain if any of our actions are causing pain to our fellow Jews in any way. We can regain Hashem's stamp of approval by returning to the nature passed on to us by Avraham Avinu and becoming again Hashem's "one nation on earth."

The Further Away You Are, the Louder the Call

(Unpublished)

When our children were younger, my wife and I devoted a lot of time and effort to a special Jewish youth organization. This organization catered to teenage Jews of ages ranging from fourteen to eighteen. Most came from nonreligious backgrounds. Over the years many of these young people grew in Judaism as they grew in years. Today many of my old students from those days are now *rabbanim*, *rebbetzins*, and *mechanchim*.

Many came from troubled homes. The combination of being financially comfortable (the favored euphemism for the very rich) and not religious meant that many of the parents were divorced, and their children had suffered greatly.

The organization organized a two-week camp in the summer and winter. My job in the camp was to teach three *shiurim* every morning, and I was keen to pass on as much of the knowledge that I had gained in Gateshead Yeshivah as possible. But there was more

The Further Away You Are, the Louder the Call

to it than that, as the head of the camp was kind enough to advise me. Every night the kids invaded the staff room, where they'd sit around and shmooze with the rabbis and their wives. It was these late-night gatherings (which sometimes went on until three or four in the morning) that built up trust in these teenagers. That in turn motivated them to hear the lessons in the *shiurim*.

I became very close with one young man named Daniel. I listened to him speak of his problems with his parents and his confusion as to how to react to his brother, who had married a non-Jewish girl in Hong Kong. Two weeks at the summer camp and one week at the winter camp allowed me to forge a strong friendship with Daniel.

Many years after our first meeting, Daniel phoned me one night. He was now eighteen, and the coming summer was to be his last at the camp. I asked him if he wanted to spend a Shabbos with us the following week, and the line went silent. Finally he told me that he had started working, and he had to come in on Saturdays, so he would not be able to spend a Shabbos with me.

I felt devastated. I thought back to all the evenings and early mornings spent helping this young man and how sure I had been that he had chosen a religious life for himself. After a while, I determined I wasn't going to give up. He had said that he would be at the forthcoming summer camp, and that meant he would be sitting in my *shiur* for two weeks. I still had a chance to reach him.

Although I had already written the *shiurim*, I filed them away and started all over again with one person in mind.

My young friend knew he had disappointed me, and at first he was reluctant to approach me as he had done in the past. I made it my business to seek him out and demonstrate that as far as I was concerned nothing had changed between us. He soon felt confident that his news had not destroyed our friendship, and things were back to normal. My strategy was to attempt to reach him through the words of the *shiur*.

Even after many years of attending these camps, the teenagers in the group still had enormous pieces missing from their Jewish education. I started to paint a picture that showed that events and occurrences that happen to a person are a test sent by God.

I got them to tell me the number of tests that Avraham Avinu had faced, and they answered, "Ten!" I told them they were wrong. There were not ten, but millions! Every incident in Avraham's life was a test.

On the last day of camp, I decided to take the bull by the horns. I told them a story that had happened to me.

I was working for a Jewish businessman who had one burning ambition. He wanted to live in Israel. He did not, though, want to go through the usual experience that accompanies those who make aliyah and face a huge drop in income. He wanted me to become the manager of his businesses. He would live in Israel on an income not vulnerable to the Israeli economy.

I was promised a luxury apartment and a Mercedes Benz, and that, he assured me, was only the beginning! There was only one thing standing in the way of this fairy tale coming true. I would have to give up my own burning desire, and that was to go to yeshivah.

My gaze turned to the young man for whom the entire series of *shiurim* had been written. I said, "But we have learned that everything in life is a *nisayon*, a test. Imagine Hashem sends you a job that is a dream come true. The only thing is, the job involves violating Shabbos. It is a test! And if you pass the test and turn down the job, don't you think Hashem can send you an even better job, which doesn't involve you violating Shabbos?"

After the *shiur* was over, a different young man, whom I had very little to do with, approached me and with a very serious expression asked me, "Tell me, Rabbi, are you annoyed with me?" I asked him what he meant, and he asked again even more seriously if I was annoyed with him. I answered in all honesty that I hadn't a

The Further Away You Are, the Louder the Call

clue as to what he was talking about. He looked unconvinced, but he asked if he could speak to me in the staff room later that night.

When we met, he explained that unlike most of the kids in the organization he came from a home that kept Shabbos. He was eighteen and had just graduated from high school. Although the results of the exams would not be known for a month, he was convinced that he had failed and the university he'd hoped to attend would now be closed to him. He told me he had applied for a management trainee course with Marks and Spencer. Very few applicants were ever accepted, and competition for places was fierce. Once Marks and Spencer trained you, almost any management position in British industry became open to you. This young man had been accepted for the position. It would mean that he would have to work on every second Shabbos.

When he finished his story, he asked very solemnly once more if I was annoyed with him. He had been listening carefully to the *shiurim* and thought that it was him I had in mind.

We sat and spoke for another hour. During that time, somehow, with a lot of help from Above, I dissuaded him from taking the job and managed to get him to agree to learn in yeshivah instead. Together with another rabbi at the camp I arranged to pay for his flight (his parents were not prepared to countenance such a choice), and we helped him with his application to a yeshivah with a good reputation for boys with his sort of background, and off he went.

I was in regular contact with the yeshivah we had chosen, and soon I heard disturbing reports. It had not proven a good choice after all. The nature of the young man I sent there was that he thrived on praise. One of the *rabbanim* there had decided that instead what he needed was to be taken down a peg or two. The effect was devastating. Before I could fly out to Israel and repair the damage, I heard he had left.

The cycle of the year had now come full circle, and it was just before the next summer camp when he phoned me. It was the first time he had phoned since his return from yeshivah. We began to talk, and it was obvious that he saw himself as a failure. I told him that in my honest appraisal of the situation, it had not been his fault at all. The yeshivah was to blame (something the rabbi involved admitted freely).

When we finished talking, I had gone some way to repairing the damage to his self-esteem that his Israel experience had caused. He told me that he intended to come and spend a few days at the forthcoming camp, and we agreed to carry on our conversation there.

When we met a few weeks later, it was in the same staff room in which he had spent so much of his youth. This time I was able to have far more success in assuring him that he had not been to blame.

Eventually my young friend declared that he believed I was right. He still had three or four outstanding philosophical difficulties with Judaism that he felt were a barrier to him moving forward. He asked if he could discuss them with me. It was very late, but I knew this was not the time to go to bed, so I invited him to tell me what they were.

He began by asking a classic question in *hashkafah*, and since that question was the very first subject I was discussing in the next day's lecture, I invited him to come and hear it explored there. He assured me he had intended to come anyway.

That left us free to move on to the next issue. I had already typed out my *shiur* notes for the next day's lecture, and his next question appeared as point two on the sheet! I chuckled and explained that by coincidence that was also being discussed the next day and invited him to move on to the remaining topics. His last two worries appeared as points three and four in my *shiur* notes!

When I told Rav Matisyahu Salomon, *shlita*, this story, he told me that it must be publicized. Although the hand of the *Ribbono*

The Further Away You Are, the Louder the Call

shel Olam was unusually conspicuous on this occasion, we shouldn't be too surprised at such occurrences.

The first blessing of *Shemoneh Esreh* concludes with the words "*Melech ozer u'moshia u'magen baruch atah Hashem magen Avraham* — King, Helper, Savior, and Protector, blessed are You, Hashem, Protector of Avraham." The blessing describes Hashem as a king who is a helper, a savior, and a protector. Each definition speaks of a different and distinct aspect of Hashem's interaction with *Klal Yisrael*.

Rav Yitzchak Blazer, *zt"l*, explains that if someone "helps" you, there is a relationship. Both you and the other person are working together to achieve a goal. If someone "saves" you, you are not contributing anything. Perhaps a sign that warns that a river has dangerous currents has fallen over. Because you don't see the warning, you decide that this is a good place to swim. You soon find yourself in serious difficulties and start to drown. Someone who is a strong swimmer sees you, and just before you go down for the last time, the swimmer comes to get you and pulls you to shore.

If someone "protects" you from danger, you are unaware that you were in danger in the first place. Someone saw you coming along holding your towel and swimming costume and noticed that the warning sign had fallen down. He picks it up and puts it back up. This keeps you from getting into trouble in the first place.

If we were to consider which of the three ways that Hashem intervenes in people's lives we would hope He would apply to us, we would probably prefer Him to be our Protector. Most of us would hope to avoid the pain of a *nisayon*. Indeed, that is something we daven to avoid every morning in *shacharis*.

There is, though, a danger in Hashem shielding us from our problems. If He interacts with us as a Protector, then we wouldn't know that He had helped us. We would be in danger of thinking that our trouble-free lives are due to our own efforts and talents and conclude that we can manage quite well on our own without Hashem's help.

That's why the blessing concludes with the words *"magen Avraham."* With Avraham, who was on the very highest spiritual level, Hashem could behave as a *magen* without the danger that Avraham would come to forget Hashem. Avraham knew that absolutely everything comes from Hashem. This is why he was willing to die *al kiddush Hashem* at Ur Kasdim before Hashem called out to him for the first time with the words *"lech lecha."*

It occurred to me that we can derive from this that the further away someone is from Hashem, the more obvious Hashem would have to make His intervention in his life. The further away someone is, the louder the call will have to be to reach him.

Rav Chaim Friedlander, *zt"l*, says exactly this in the first essay on Chanukah in his *sefer Sifsei Chaim*:

"One of the earliest miracles mentioned in the Torah was when Moshe replied to Hashem's command that he go and save the Jews, 'They will not believe in me nor listen to my voice.' Hashem said to him, 'What is that in your hand?' So the miracle of the stick turning into a snake came at a time when Moshe was in danger of slipping from his spiritual level, as witnessed by him offering the argument 'They will not believe in me.' Until that statement, Moshe did not require the demonstration of a miracle. The *Avos* stood at the most lofty spiritual level and therefore did not require miracles and wonders. This was because even without them they recognized and knew the Master of the world. Of course, miracles occurred for them, too. Avraham was saved from being burned in the furnace at Kasdim, and Yaakov split the river Jordan to cross it and face his brother Esav. The purpose of these types of miracles were not to strengthen faith, however. They were merely to aid them in the tasks they had to perform."

Not too long ago I received a very excited phone call from a friend of mine who is the *mashgiach* of one of Gateshead's

The Further Away You Are, the Louder the Call

yeshivos. He told me that he *had* to send me a fax. After I got it he would phone back and tell me the story behind it. I awaited the fax, and what arrived was an enlarged copy of a telephone calling card. The phone rang again, and my friend told me its history.

A young man from America had been spending his summer in Israel and, much to his own surprise, ended up, instead of scuba diving in Eilat, learning in a *ba'al teshuvah* yeshivah. As the time to return to the final year of university came, he spoke to his *rosh yeshivah*. He no longer wanted to resume his secular studies. His time in yeshivah had proven a great success in every sense, and he wanted to continue and go further.

The *rosh yeshivah* disagreed. He was concerned about the effect that abandoning his studies would have on the boy's family. His advice was that he should return home and finish his degree and then come back to yeshivah.

The young man went home and finished his degree, but when the time arrived for him to return, the passage of time had dulled the glow of his enthusiasm. He phoned his *rosh yeshivah* to discuss his misgivings.

"I know I should be booking my ticket and coming back, but frankly I'm no longer sure it's the right decision."

The *rosh yeshivah* listened and told him, "But you know it's the right decision."

The young man replied that in his heart of hearts he knew it was the right decision, but still, he said, "I have been hoping that Hashem would send me a sign that it's the right thing to do."

My friend paused in his telling of the story, and when he continued I was astonished at his next words. The *rosh yeshivah* replied, "Don't worry, Hashem *will* send you a sign!"

With that assurance, the young man went ahead and booked his ticket. The night before he was due to fly he phoned his *rosh yeshivah* again.

"You said there would be a sign, but no sign has come. Perhaps

I should cancel my ticket after all."

The *rosh yeshivah* declared, "Don't worry. It's on its way!"

The morning of his departure the young man opened his mail. He had sent for a telephone calling card from AT&T so that it would be easy to phone home, and it arrived just in time for his departure. When he examined the card, he saw his name embossed on the front, and above it was the card number, 613248365.

As he looked again at the card something he had learned in yeshivah during the last summer started to stir in his mind. At the bottom of the card the number was printed again, only this time there appeared two spaces between the figures, splitting it up into three groups of digits — 613 248 365.

His sign had arrived, clear and unambiguous. There are 613 mitzvos, 248 positive commandments, and 365 prohibitions. The further away someone is, the louder the call will have to be to reach him!

My young friend from the Jewish youth organization came to my *shiur* the next day and heard answers to his questions that he was happy with. A while later my wife had the idea that he would be very suited to a certain young lady whom we also knew through this organization and its camps. They married and now have a beautiful young family.

Just when he was starting to slip away, Hashem called out to him. Today he is a *rav*, teaching other young Jews that the further away you are, the louder the call is likely to be. All you have to do is listen.

The Torah Is a Minimum

(Unpublished)

The winter holiday gave me the chance to spend a full two weeks with my family visiting one of my favorite communities. The first of those weeks I was to give a series of *shiurim*, and the last session was to be an "ask the rabbi" evening.

These events almost always throw up controversial questions, and this one was no different. A lady raised her hand. She wanted to know what I would say to a rabbi who said that it is a mitzvah to smuggle items through Israeli Customs without declaring them.

I stared at her, quite perplexed, and asked if she had actually heard a rabbi say such a thing or had merely heard that a rabbi had said such a thing. She assured me that she had been personally told this, so how would I react to such a statement?

The entire audience sensed that this was an important question, and a certain electricity filled the room.

In case you haven't come across this particular calumny before, it goes like this. *Frum* Jews in general and *yeshivah bachurim* in particular supposedly abuse Israeli Customs constantly. A *yeshivah bachur* may need to visit Israel for, say, a friend's wedding. Rumor has it that he'll go out and buy some fashionable item like a Walkman or whatever is the latest gimmick. He purchases this at a fraction of the price that it would cost in Israel. The young man is then supposed to conceal these items, and when he is safely in the Holy Land, he sells them for a tidy profit. In this way the proceeds might well cover the cost of his flight.

My first comment was to say that even though such activities are claimed to be common among *frum* Jews, in my seven years in yeshivah and four in *kollel*, I never came across anyone who actually did it.

My second response was to tell her of something Rav Matisyahu Salomon, *shlita*, once said when he addressed this subject in a *shiur* to the top boys in Gateshead Yeshivah. He said, "Whether or not the State of Israel is halachically allowed to levy taxes is a very complex issue in Jewish law, which I do not intend to go into now. But smuggling things through Customs without declaring them is teaching yourself to cheat and lie and swindle, and that is *never* permissible."

I concluded my answer to the question by sharing a suspicion of mine. "I suspect that since the founding of the State of Israel in 1948, there has been as many as one, two, or even three nonreligious Israelis who have also smuggled items through Israeli Customs without declaring them!"

The audience laughed, and my questioner smiled and nodded as the tension ebbed away, allowing the evening to finish on a happy note.

Two weeks after I returned home I found myself standing next to an old acquaintance from shul. He was visiting the UK from abroad and lived in the town I had just visited. My old friend apologized that he had missed my talks; he had been out of town at a conference. He then mentioned the incident of the lady and her question about smuggling things through Israeli Customs. Someone must have given him a pretty accurate report of the moment of tension. My friend asked me if what he had heard I had replied was

The Torah Is a Minimum

accurate. I told him that it was, and he said, "I see! Because I was the rabbi who told the lady that it was a mitzvah to smuggle things through Israeli Customs!" A smile spread across his face. "And with all due respect, I think I am right and you are wrong."

I spread an equally large smile across my face and told him, "Oh, that's fine, because with all due respect I think I am right and you are wrong!"

He gave me three justifications to prove his case. The first was that his father, who is a *talmid chacham*, had told him that this practice was a mitzvah. His second claim was that *gedolim* know that it goes on, and if they were against it they would have spoken out and condemned the practice. His third justification was extremely original.

He pointed out that the State of Israel levies taxes equally among all its citizens. "But," he claimed, "they don't redistribute the money equally. Secular institutions and organizations get a far higher proportion of the money than religious institutions."

He fixed his gaze on me and then concluded his ultimate justification. "Therefore, when you go through Customs in Israel and smuggle things in, you are not stealing! You are merely taking back the money the state has unjustly taken from you."

I responded that I had no comment on his father's statement. If my friend claimed his father said such a thing, I suppose I'd have to accept that he might have. His second point did allow me the possibility of a reply. I reminded him what Rav Matisyahu Salomon had told the top *shiur* in Gateshead Yeshivah and asked if he did not agree that this was an example of *gedolim* speaking out against such behavior.

My friend conceded that it was, and I moved on to my last argument. I asked him to remind me where he lived, and he told me.

"So tell me," I said. "Living in that great city in America, exactly what taxes do you have to pay to the Israeli government?"

My friend smiled sheepishly.

"Oh, and one last thing. When you go and sell your watches or Walkman, do you take the profits you've made to the nearest yeshivah or religious school and then say, like some Jewish Robin Hood, 'Here, take this money that the Israeli government has unfairly taken from you,' or do you put the money in your own pocket? If you put the money in your own pocket, then maybe the real motive for smuggling things through Customs is the same motive as everyone else, and that is to make *you* money."

My friend considered this for a moment and then laughed. "Perhaps I'd better think this through again!"

The Torah talks about this idea. The verse says, "Speak to the children of Israel and say to them, 'A man or a woman who separates himself to make a vow to become a *nazir* to Hashem. He must not drink wine or beverages distilled from wine.... All the days of his vow a razor must not pass over his head.... All the days of his vow he must not come near a dead body.... All the days of his vow, he will be holy to Hashem" (*Bemidbar* 6:1–8).

Rashi asks a simple question. "Why does the section of the Torah that deals with the laws of the *nazir* follow the section that deals with the laws regarding an adulteress? The juxtaposition is there to teach you that anyone who sees an adulteress in her disgrace should distance himself from wine because it leads to adultery."

Rashi makes it clear that the adulteress's disastrous mistake was caused because she became drunk.

(It is interesting to note that the protective enzyme that breaks down alcohol in the stomach, alcohol dehydrogenase, exists in significantly smaller amounts in women than in men. The results of this anomaly is that the average woman absorbs 30 percent more alcohol directly into her bloodstream than an average man drinking the same amount. Women consequently become drunk and subsequently more easily susceptible to the suggestions of their *yetzer hara* than men.)

The Torah Is a Minimum

Despite this, the Rambam cites the Gemara's conclusion in *Sotah* and writes: "Three things are prohibited to a *nazir*: contact with the dead, having his hair cut, and any product of the vine. Strong drink made from dates or figs or similar beverages, however, are permitted to a *nazir*" (*Hilchos Nazir*, ch. 5).

When I first read the words of the Rambam, I was baffled. A *nazir*, complete with long hair, could be lying in the gutter nursing an empty bottle of vodka, and he would not have infringed Jewish law in the slightest!

But Rashi's words stated that anyone who saw an adulteress in her disgrace "*should* distance himself from wine because it leads to adultery." As alcoholic as wine is, and the wine at the time of the Gemara was much stronger than it is today, whiskey, vodka, and rum are also very potent brews. Yet a *nazir* is at liberty to drink those. Surely that leaves him vulnerable to the very danger he is trying to avoid in the first place?

The solution to this paradox can be found in the words of the Ramban on *Kedoshim*. Those words are among his best known, and they explain what the Torah demands when it says, "You shall be holy because Hashem your God is holy."

The Ramban writes: "The Torah warns us against certain relationships and forbidden foods. At the same time, it permits other relationships and many foods. It is possible for a person to debase himself even with permitted relationships or a kosher diet and become a base person — with permission of the halachah!...

"That is why, when the Torah cites a list of things that are specifically forbidden, it will command us with a general statement that sums up the purpose of those prohibitions. The purpose behind the Torah's prohibitions is not only to avoid that which is specifically prohibited but also to minimize [have a balanced approach to] that which is permitted....

"This is the way of the Torah — to list specific forbidden activities and then to state the purpose of those specifics. In business laws the Torah specifies, 'Don't steal,' 'Don't misappropriate funds,' and 'Don't cheat.' Afterward it says, 'And you will do that which is *yashar v'tov*, straight and good.' "

The Ramban is saying that it is possible to be a businessman who doesn't steal or cheat and still behave badly in business.

My *rosh yeshivah*, Rav Leib Gurwicz, *zt"l*, writes about this *Ramban*, "The Ramban is pointing out that ultimately the Torah is trying to help us achieve the minimization of the permitted pleasures of this world. The Torah gives a list of prohibitions and then gives a statement that clarifies the purpose of those prohibitions.... The Ramban is saying that after the Torah has told us what is forbidden, it is essential to understand the purpose behind those proscriptions."

Rav Yerucham Levovitz, *zt"l*, illustrates this point by recalling that he often saw the army conscript the sort of person who spends most of his life either drinking or in bed recovering from the effects of drinking. After basic training, a strange transformation occurs. The same individual who displayed no self-control or self-pride his entire life becomes someone who is neat and efficient. His uniform is immaculate, and the shine on his boots is dazzling.

Amazingly, after he completes his service and returns to his civilian life, he returns to his former ways. Once again, he spends most of his existence either drinking or recovering from the effects of drinking. The reason is because the soldier, although he certainly followed the rules of the army, never internalized those rules nor allowed them to become a part of him.

Rav Yisrael Salanter often used to say that at the end of the entire Torah, before the entire Jewish people, it was necessary to express one statement. He said in Lithuanian, "*Ne bog dornei* — Don't be crazy! Understand what the Torah wants to produce in you by keeping the mitzvos."

This answers the paradox of the Torah banning only the produce of the vine. The Torah could hardly cite every alcoholic bever-

The Torah Is a Minimum

age and include them in the prohibitions of the *nazir*. But it doesn't have to. After stating the three areas that are prohibited to a *nazir*, contact with the dead, cutting hair, and the produce of the vine, the Torah concludes with the words, "All the days that he is a *nazir* he will be holy to Hashem." The purpose of the specific prohibitions is spelled out with those words. The idea of becoming a *nazir* is to come close to Hashem. Anyone who wants to achieve this will use the specific commandments to point him in the right direction.

Such a person will automatically realize that the Torah did not have to explicitly ban other alcoholic products. As Rav Levy of Zurich once expressed to me, "The Torah is a minimum, not a maximum."

It is this that I think my friend forgot when he counseled someone that they could smuggle items into Israel. Even if there were no halachic justification for a Jew, or even a Jewish state, to levy taxes on other Jews, a response where we train ourselves in dishonesty would never be allowed. And if there has been as many as one, two, or even three nonreligious Israelis who have also smuggled things through Israeli Customs without declaring them, that should not affect the behavior of those who are loyal to the Torah.

We have to recall that the Torah forbids stealing, misappropriation, and cheating in order for us to internalize what the Torah wants us to become — *yashar v'tov*, straight and good.

The Greatness of a Little Yud

(Hamodia)

A few years ago one of the boys who came to me for private lessons sat down to learn *parashas Pinchas*. After reading the second verse he asked a very simple question. "Why is the word *Pinchas* spelled with a little yud?"

I smiled at him and promptly replied, "A good question!" and started to cast my eye over the commentaries on the page, searching for an answer.

The obvious candidate to ask such a question is the Ba'al HaTurim, but he remained silent. I looked up at my student and smiled again. Another scan of the page found no one addressing the question. I congratulated him on the question again while secretly feeling embarrassed that I had never thought to ask it myself and told him I would find a solution by the next week.

Later that day another boy arrived for his lesson. His first question was "Why does *Pinchas* have a little yud?" When a third boy began his lesson with the same question, I realized that they were phoning each other up to pass on the news that I was stuck and didn't know the answer!

The Greatness of a Little Yud

Rav Zalman Sorotzkin, *zt"l*, provides a solution in an answer to a different question. Why did Pinchas merit a *bris shalom*, immortality, for his act of zealotry? Granted, Pinchas saved the Jewish people from a terrible plague by executing Zimri and Kozbi. Yet Moshe and Aharon had intervened and saved the people on numerous occasions. Why did they not receive the reward of a *bris shalom*?

Imagine reading a news article about a potential air disaster that was narrowly avoided. "Flight KY 613 was approaching its final destination of Los Angeles when the pilot was convulsed in agony, suffering from a perforated ulcer. The pilot took over the controls as the plane neared the airport. What happened next was almost a statistical impossibility. The copilot suddenly groaned and slumped over the controls. He had had a heart attack. The plane now had no one to fly it as they neared the runway. The senior stewardess made a desperate announcement over the loudspeaker explaining the situation and ending with the plea 'Can anyone aboard fly this jet?' Calmly, from row 12, a gray-haired man of about sixty stood up. He announced that he had retired as a pilot the year before, and he could fly the jet. He promptly moved to the cockpit and executed a perfect landing."

Well, it might make interesting reading, but imagine exactly the same story except that there is no ex-pilot on board. When the stewardess asks, "Can anyone fly this jet?" a businessman stands up and says, "I am willing to follow instructions from the control tower and try to land the plane." He moves to the front, and by meticulously following the instructions from an expert on the ground, he safely lands the jet. The second version would make the front page of every newspaper in the world, and the businessman would be an international hero.

Rav Zalman Sorotzkin says that Pinchas was a "little" Jew, and this is hinted at by the small yud. Until the incident with Zimri, he is mentioned only once in the Torah, when his birth is recorded.

Moshe and Aharon are the pilots of the Jewish people, safely delivering them to their various destinations. That is what they are both equipped and expected to do.

Pinchas could have chosen to do nothing. Who was he, after all, compared to all the other great Jews of the generation who chose not to intervene? Yet he did act, and he saved the people. It was this that gained Pinchas a *bris shalom* — a unique reward for a unique act.

The full story of Pinchas's courage and his motivation reveals just why he deserved this reward.

There is no mitzvah in the Torah that is repeated as much as the command to love a convert. It is repeated no fewer than thirty-six times. No other mitzvah comes close to being mentioned so much. Yet Rashi comments that Pinchas's full genealogy is recorded in the Torah because the heads of the tribes of the Jewish people ridiculed him and said, "Do you see? This man, a grandson of Yisro, who used to fatten cows for idolatrous sacrifice, has killed a prince of the Jewish people!"

His action was either halachically correct or not. What possible relevance does his background have, and how could they crudely ignore the mitzvah to love the convert?

Rav Yosef Salanter, *zt"l*, quotes the Rambam, who writes about the nature of the terrible sin committed by Zimri.

"Even though it does not merit capital punishment, there lies within the sin a loss that is not found among any other of the Torah's prohibited relationships. A man's son born from a forbidden relationship is still called his son in every respect and is still considered a Jew even if he is a *mamzer*. A son of a non-Jewish woman, though, is not his son, as the verse says, 'That they will remove your son from before Me.' This will cause attachment to idolatry, exactly that which Hashem has separated us from."

It is clear from the Rambam that Zimri's sin was a crime against the holiness of the Jewish people. Rav Yosef Salanter con-

The Greatness of a Little Yud

cludes, "That is why the halachah states that only a *kana'i*, a zealot, someone who, with every fiber of his being, is outraged against such an insult to the Jewish people and Hashem may execute a Zimri. Anyone who would not feel this level of outrage may not execute someone like Zimri, and if he did, the execution would instead be considered a murder!"

This was the reason the tribes pointed to Pinchas's background and lineage. They had not forgotten the Torah's demand that they must love a convert. Rather, they were convinced that someone who was the product of a Jewish father marrying someone who was born a gentile and who had antecedents who were idolaters could not feel that level of outrage. That was their complaint against Pinchas.

The Kli Yakar says that Pinchas was well aware that this would be the reaction of the tribes, but his prestige and respect was nothing compared to Hashem's honor.

Rav Yaakov Kamenetsky, *zt"l*, discusses a baffling incident in the Torah. Before his passing, Yaakov blessed his sons. In these blessings, Shimon and Levi were condemned for killing the inhabitants of Shechem. This was not because they did not deserve to die, but because Shimon and Levi executed them in anger. Rashi describes what Yaakov's solution was for these two brothers who were by nature *kana'im*, passionate zealots. Levi was to establish the holy tribe of the Jewish people, and Shimon was to become a tribe of educators. Two people accused of mass murder, and this was to be their rectification!

Yaakov realized that this passionate nature could provide the greatest benefits to the Jewish people if it could be harnessed within the boundaries of Torah. The greatest teachers are the ones who are passionate about the subject they teach, and "words that come from the heart enter the heart." Religious leaders, too, must bring passion to their position. Properly focused, Shimon and Levi's nature could enhance and guarantee the success of the Jewish people.

When Jewish history moved on, and the people started to experience the first bite of the Egyptian exile, the tribes began to leave the Torah environment of Jewish Goshen and mix with mainstream Egyptian society — all except one: Levi. Levi maintained their attachment to Torah and Torah values without interruption. Now, whenever their *kana'us* would reemerge, it was always within the parameters of the Torah. When they executed the guilty at the incident with the golden calf, it was only under the instruction of Moshe Rabbeinu.

But Shimon's *kana'us* did not remain completely harnessed to the Torah. It reemerged when his descendant Zimri paraded his non-Jewish princess before the people and declared to Moshe, "Is this permitted to me or not, and if not, who allowed you to marry your wife?" (Moshe's wife was Tzipporah, the daughter of Yisro.)

Moshe, in his distress, was uncertain how to proceed, and the verse reports, "Pinchas, the son of Elazar the son of Aharon HaKohen, saw and rose up from the congregation and took the spear in his hand."

Someone from the tribe of Levi, a true *kana'i*, punished Zimri's corrupted *kana'us*. And Rashi emphasizes how Pinchas acted as a true *kana'i* should by filling in a crucial detail that the Torah omits: " 'And Pinchas saw' — he saw the offense and remembered the halachah that Moshe forgot. He said to Moshe, 'I learned from you that this deed should be punished by a *kana'i*.' "

Pinchas did not act in anger, nor did he act independently. He went to the leader of the Jewish people, and only when he received Moshe's instruction to execute Zimri and Kozbi did he act. In so doing, he stopped a plague that had already killed twenty-four thousand Jews.

The lesson of Pinchas is that an ordinary Jew can find himself in a moment when his actions can avert Jewish disaster. Even a "little yud" can achieve greatness and ultimately a *bris shalom*. Such a *kana'i*, though, achieves all of this only because he maintains his passion within the parameters of the Torah. He does nothing without the endorsement of the leader of the generation. The other type of *kana'i*, who challenges and ignores the edicts of the *gedolim*, should be avoided like the plague he inevitably unleashes.

Selections on the Yamim Tovim

Rosh HaShanah

A Door That's Never Closed

(Hamodia, September 9)

A few years ago I was concluding a talk in front of a very large audience in London. After I had finished there were several people waiting to ask me questions or to express their appreciation. After everyone had left, one man remained behind. He approached and asked me if I lived in Manchester, and I confirmed that I did. He inquired which area in Manchester, and I told him. His next question was whether I knew a certain person who lived there, and I answered yes. "How is he getting on?" he asked. Next there tumbled a whole series of questions about this person from my inquisitor — what did he do for a living and how many children did he have and how old were they. I tried my best to answer, but since I didn't know the person very well, I couldn't be sure about some details. Then it was my turn to pose a question.

"How do you know him?"

My questioner looked at me intensely, and a very sad and pensive expression passed across his face. He hesitated, looked down at the floor, and very quietly replied, "He's my son."

I was taken aback and after a moment asked, "How is it that

you don't know how many grandchildren you have?"

I listened to his tale of a rebellious teenage son who had gone off the rails in a big way. The parents had tried every device they could think of to make their son see sense. They had tried bribery and threats and had gotten other people to talk to him, but nothing had worked. One night, in both frustration and desperation, the father had screamed at his son, "Get out! Get out and never come back!" And that's exactly what the boy had done. Fifteen years later the son had settled down and built his own family, but he had never come back or had any contact with his parents.

I listened with great sadness and told the father that although I didn't know his son well, I felt sure he would like to see his father again. The father shook his head firmly and replied, "It's too late now. Too much water has flowed under the bridge." Then an idea struck me. I suggested that if he gave me his address and phone number, I could send him regular reports on how his son and his family were getting along. The father liked this idea, and so we parted with me promising to keep in touch.

When I returned to Manchester, by coincidence I bumped into his son (you can always arrange coincidences). I told him I had just returned from London and had met someone there who was asking after him. He inquired who it was. I paused and said, "Your father."

He looked at me for a moment and then asked, "How is he getting on?"

It was obvious that the son was as concerned for the father as the father was for the son. I told him that I thought his father wanted to see him, and uncannily he replied in the identical manner as his father had. "I don't think so. Too much water has flowed under the bridge."

I tried to persuade him he was wrong and then tried a different approach. "By coincidence I am going back down to London in three days. Suppose I were to take you to see your father?" The son hesitated, but I was able to convince him to agree.

When I arrived home, I phoned the father and asked him if he would be at home on that Thursday at one o'clock. He probably assumed I intended to phone with a report and confirmed that he would be in. I told him that I was bringing his son to see him, and before he could reply I said goodbye and hung up.

The drive to London passed unusually quickly. We located the house right away, and I walked up to the door with my very nervous companion.

A very long time seemed to elapse before the door opened. The man who had had so many questions a few days before stood anxiously, looking at the face of the son he had not seen for fifteen years. I watched as tears welled up in his eyes and started to course down his cheeks. I looked at the son, and he, too, had tear-filled eyes. The son took one step toward his father, and the father rushed toward his son, and they folded each other in a hug. After a few moments they turned and walked into the house. I found myself wonderfully redundant and paused to wipe the tears from my own cheeks before smiling my goodbye and getting into my car for the drive back to Manchester. A few months later the son bought a house in London and moved there with his family to be near his father.

The Dubno Maggid asks a question on *birkas kohanim* (blessing of the priests). The *kohanim* face the congregation and say, "*Yevarechecha Hashem v'yishmerecha* — God will bless you and guard you." Surely they should face the *aron kodesh* (ark) when asking Hashem to bless and guard the people.

The Maggid answers with a parable about a son who had behaved so badly that his father turned his face from him. In shame, the boy fled the house. The young man sought refuge with a neighbor. When he told his story, the neighbor offered to mediate and reason with the father. The father listened as the neighbor pleaded with him to take the boy back and then said, "You are a fool. He's my son, and I love him with every ounce of my being. If you want to help the boy, go and explain to him what he's done wrong and how he should put it right. My door is always open. Help him correct his fault so that he can come back. I'm eagerly awaiting his return."

The *kohanim* do not have to turn to ask Hashem to give His blessings to *Klal Yisrael*. His door is always open to shower blessings on us. All we have to do is make ourselves worthy to receive them and walk toward the door.

One *erev Rosh HaShanah* I opened my *machzor* to insert an important piece of paper. Copying the practice of some *ba'alei mussar*, I had prepared a list of things for which I needed to do *teshuvah*. When I opened the *machzor*, I came upon a piece of paper from a previous year. I took it out and compared the two lists. They contained the same faults in almost identical order. This was hardly a coincidence; the *satan* had nearly achieved his goal. I felt disheartened and hypocritical.

It's a thought many people have told me crosses their minds on the *yom hadin*: "Aren't I trying to do *teshuvah* for the exact same things this year as I did last year and the year before? I slipped back into the same old faults then, so won't I do so all over again?"

The Alter of Slabodka, Rav Nosson Tzvi Finkel, *zt"l*, quotes the verse in *Bereishis*, "Hashem saw everything that He had created, and it was very good." The Midrash says, "This one was very good. The others were not." God had created other worlds before ours, and He had destroyed them because they were not "very good." How many worlds had Hashem created before this one? Nine hundred and seventy-four!

The obvious question is, how could the Creator ever make something that was less than perfect, that was not "very good"? And even if, God forbid, He had made failed worlds and then had to destroy them, why tell us about it? There were no survivors of earlier creations to point to the fact that they were flawed.

The Alter explains that the creation of our world after other,

A Door That's Never Closed

failed worlds was intentional. Hashem tells us about them so that we will realize that *binyan*, building, comes from *churban*, destruction. It is similar to an assumption and a conclusion in a *devar Torah*. One doesn't reach the correct conclusion without having toyed with one or several assumptions that are incorrect.

The lesson for us is that we are not expected to reach the conclusion until we have tried and failed — perhaps many times. We can fail as Jews no fewer than 974 times before we get it right. Hashem created that number of failed worlds and told us about it to encourage us not to let our lack of perfection prevent us from persevering toward our final goal.

The *rosh yeshivah* of Sunderland (in the north of England), Rabbi Shamai Zahn, *shlita*, often tells his *talmidim* not to become frustrated with what they see as their lack of progress. He asks them to imagine the sort of clocks that can sometimes still be found in train stations.

These machines are enormous and have huge hands. On some of the clocks the minute hand moves dramatically and abruptly from minute to minute. Stationary at five past the hour, it will suddenly fall to position itself at six minutes past. On other clocks, the minute hand moves slowly and imperceptibly so that it gradually arrives from five to six minutes past. "Some *bachurim*," he will say, "expect to see progress like the hands of the first clock — sudden, dramatic, and obvious. More usually, however, change comes about slowly and gradually."

We are not expected to get it right straightaway. It may take many Rosh HaShanahs before we compare lists and find that one of the items from last year is no longer on the new one. But as long as we are sincerely trying to do *teshuvah*, we should feel no hesitation about standing before the *aron kodesh* on Rosh HaShanah. He is, after all our Father. His door is always open, particularly to us, His children.

Rosh HaShanah

Hearing the Shofar's True Call

(The Jewish Tribune, October 5, 2000)

It is one of my sincerest regrets that on that day, seven years ago, no one took a picture of me. I was standing on the conductor's podium in the recording studio of the BBC Philharmonic Orchestra. In my hand I held a shofar. In front of me were the music stands and seats of the musicians. Some of the larger instruments, like the harp and double bass, stood there, too. But perhaps I'd better start at the beginning.

A few hours before I'd received a phone call from a producer I know at the BBC. The BBC had several planned radio programs on Jewish themes. My producer friend wanted me to listen to a CD recording of the sound of a shofar being blown. He wanted to check with me if it sounded all right. I listened as he played the recording to me over the phone. It was dreadful — or, rather, it wasn't.

The sound of the shofar should be just that — a call that evokes feelings of dread and fear. This shofar had obviously been played by a professional trumpet player. Each call, the *tekiah*, the *teruah*, and the *shevarim*, were perfectly produced. The notes were clear, sweet, and precise, and they had no feeling to them whatsoever. I told my friend that as nice as it sounded it was nothing at

Hearing the Shofar's True Call

all like a shofar should sound.

He expressed his alarm. The BBC needed an authentic shofar blast for an imminent broadcast, and he didn't know what to do. I suggested that I drive down to New Broadcasting House in Manchester and bring along my shofar.

That's how I found myself standing in an enormous hall where the BBC Philharmonic Orchestra normally records Beethoven and Schubert, facing empty orchestra seats and watching enormous microphones automatically descending from the ceiling to capture my solo performance.

On Rosh HaShanah, just before the blowing of the shofar in shul, I heard Dayan Gavriel Krausz, *shlita*, speak. He pointed out that the sound of the shofar should resemble a person crying. Rav Yonasan Eibeshutz said that on the day of Rosh HaShanah it's as if one is facing an enormous fire. Only a river of tears can extinguish the blaze. The true sound of the shofar is designed to unleash the tears of *Klal Yisrael*, and those, and only those, can extinguish the flames of Hashem's anger.

After *yom tov* there were phone calls to make and receive from our sons in various yeshivos. Gateshead was first, and we heard how the *yom hadin* had gone for two of our sons. Then came the call to Eretz Yisrael and the news that there had been trouble at the Kosel. I phoned a friend in Yerushalayim, and he e-mailed me pictures of the violence. They showed terrified women running from the Kosel as Arabs hurled missiles down on top of them. A little girl's face looked at the camera in total terror; she held her mother's hand as they ran. I was struck by how familiar that little girl's face was. I had seen it, or one very like it, in other pictures — older black-and-white pictures from over fifty years ago.

Dayan Krausz said that the dangers facing *Klal Yisrael* on this Rosh HaShanah were more intense than any other time in recent memory. There are two kinds of enemies: those from without and those from within. "Perhaps the greatest danger," he said, "is the

Dancing through Time

enemies from within." Then he went on to quote Chazal.

"The world's leaders are given less freedom of choice than most other people. They are merely puppets, and it is Hashem Who is pulling the strings. Neither Arafat, Hamas, the United States, or the government of Israel is deciding the course of events in Israel, only Hashem."

The course of events of the last year ran through my mind, and I recalled the two weeks I had spent teaching in Yerushalayim at around Tishah B'Av. I had never felt such an atmosphere of despair and uncertainty. The government was in tatters; the peace process was in tatters. The only thing Israelis expressed unity and certainty about was their disunity and uncertainty.

There was something else in that speech that struck an eerie chord. The *dayan* pointed to the second paragraph of the Shema, where Hashem states unequivocally that there is a direct correlation between the Jewish people's observance of the mitzvos and rainfall. Anyone who has ever studied tractate *Ta'anis* has read story after story of times when Hashem displayed His anger with *Klal Yisrael* by bringing a drought.

Just before *yom tov* our niece and nephew phoned from Yerushalayim, and my niece told my wife a fascinating and ominous thing. They live in Ramot Dalet, and from there she and her neighbors have observed a strange phenomenon. Banks of dark rain clouds have appeared in the sky, transforming a Jerusalem sky into a Manchester one. Slowly the clouds move toward them. The neighborhood becomes very excited, thinking that at last it is going to rain. The clouds are so heavy they have no choice except to rain. But these clouds, time after time, roll on past, and wherever they deposit their rain, it's certainly not Israel.

Hashem is making it transparently clear how He feels about *Klal Yisrael*, and not for a long time have our tears been so needed to extinguish the flames.

I once heard an intriguing parable from Rebbetzin Tziporah

Hearing the Shofar's True Call

Heller of Yerushalayim. A mother is at home waiting for her teenage daughter to come in. The mother knows the girl is standing in the street chatting with her friends. When the door finally opens at eleven-thirty, the mother looks at her watch and makes her distress very apparent.

"What sort of time do you call this to come home?"

The girl has no excuse, and the mother continues, "I told you to be home by ten o'clock. That was an hour and a half ago!" Her voice grows louder. "If you aren't back here tomorrow night by ten o'clock, *ten o'clock*, you'll find the door locked." By now she is really shouting. "Locked, do you hear me?"

The mother's anger, however, only underscores the fact that the last thing in the world the mother wants to do is lock her daughter out! The display of anger is really conveying, "I care about your safety. Please don't make me lock you out."

Hashem is making His voice heard very clearly. He is, however, our Father and our King. The last thing He wants is to have to carry out His threats. We are receiving a wake-up call, louder than any He has delivered to us for many a year. Our Rosh HaShanah promises not to repeat the mistakes of last year must be authentic and not just an expression of temporary regret. As Rav Dessler and his *talmid* Rav Chaim Friedlander put it, that means actively avoiding the places, circumstances, or people that led us to slip up last time. Changing ourselves means finding new ways to avoid falling back into our old ways.

This Yom Kippur the sound of our *tefillos* will have to emulate the true call of the shofar and be accompanied by our tears. It is those tears that will tell HaKadosh Baruch Hu that we've got the message. It is those tears that will extinguish the flames.

Yom Kippur

Forgiving the Unforgivable

(*The Jewish Tribune*, September 28, 2000)

Cincinnati's airport is, for some peculiar reason, situated in Kentucky. Sadly, I didn't manage to find out the reason while I was there. I was too busy waiting for a delayed flight to finally start boarding. As I strolled up and down, I passed a bookshop. In the window there was a poster that caught my eye. It said, "Read the most fascinating story ever told.... *The Jews' Gifts to the World.*" That was the title of a new book they were selling, *The Jews' Gifts to the World.*

I was intrigued. I went in and picked one up. Looking through the chapters revealed the sort of topics one would expect from such a title, and it didn't seem to contain any great surprises or revelations. Then I noticed what was written inside the front cover. It said that this book was the second in a series by the same author. The first one was called *How the Irish Saved Human Civilization*. I decided the story of *The Jews' Gifts to the World* could wait for another time.

My trip to America did reveal other fascinating stories about Jews. In New Jersey, a husband and his wife stayed behind after a *shiur* I gave to have a shmooze. She told me the tale of how her family had managed to leave Poland in 1936 and reach the safety of the United States. Her grandmother had been a *rebbetzin* who possessed a more than usual degree of *binah yeseirah*, understanding and intuition. She somehow felt that it was time to leave Poland.

The process of leaving required a visit to a Polish civil servant who had to stamp and approve the relevant papers. He was an anti-Semite and saw no reason that this Jewess and her family should be helped in any way. The *rebbetzin* stood in line holding her baby son in her arms. When her turn came, her application was rudely rejected, and she was sent away. The *rebbetzin* refused to give up. The next morning she returned. The whole process repeated itself day after day. The official came to like seeing her waiting in the queue; he enjoyed rejecting her application. As she joined the line, he would look up from his work and gaze at her for a fraction of a second, and the faintest of smiles would pass his lips.

In the second week the *rebbetzin* had an idea. Just before her turn came she gave her baby son a little pinch. The child erupted into furious and loud crying. Again she was greeted with rejection, but the next day she returned, and again, ten minutes before her turn came, the baby shook the room with his sobs. By the end of the week the decibels had reduced the civil servant's nerves to tatters, and when she arrived at his desk she found her forms filled in, stamped, and approved. And so a Jewish family sailed safely away from the tinderbox that was Jewish Europe, just ahead of the flames.

In Cincinnati a Jew who was a retired surgeon as well as a rabbi told me another tale. His story started in Antwerp, where he was born. The outbreak of the war saw his family fleeing to find temporary safety in what became Vichy France. His mother spoke perfect German, and on a train journey with her little boy she found herself in a compartment with an SS officer. He inquired what the child was called, and she replied that his name was Aryeh. The German scowled. "What sort of name is that?"

The mother didn't blink. "It comes from Aryan," she replied, and the Nazi smiled an approving and beneficent smile on little Aryeh.

Not every Jewish story, though, can be told, and not every one enjoys a happy ending. Rav Avraham Grodzensky, *zt"l*, points out that Hashem created the Day of Judgment, not to have a day when He finds us guilty but to have a day when He finds us not guilty! All of the classic works on *teshuvah* emphasize how eager Hashem is not only to receive our *teshuvah* but also to assist us in doing *teshuvah* in the first place.

In *Hilchos Teshuvah* the Rambam explains that although Hashem is willing and able to forgive us for things we have done against Him, he cannot forgive us for things we have done against other people. We must first try to put right whatever wrong we may have done, for example, returning money we may have stolen. Yet there is still more to do. He states that we must now ask them to forgive us. We must beg for this no fewer than three times. To show that we are both contrite and sincere we should even bring three of his friends with us as we plead. If after all that the person we offended does not forgive us, then, writes the Rambam, "*v'zeh shelo mochel hu hachotei* — the person who refuses to forgive, he, not you, is the sinner."

In the next halachah the Rambam goes on to say that it is part of a Jew's innate nature to forgive those who have hurt him. "It is forbidden," he writes, "for a Jew to be cruel and not forgive someone who is sincerely sorry."

But what if the story that leads to the request for forgiveness is so terrible and so unrepeatable that a Jew finds him or herself unable to forgive?

I once heard of a girl from America who had suffered terribly. Her mother was obviously badly in need of help, which she never received. The result was that her children suffered both appalling

Forgiving the Unforgivable

neglect and cruelty. Finally, together with her brothers and sisters, the girl was taken away and brought up by an aunt and uncle. Many years later, at the girl's wedding, someone thought it would be an act of *chesed* to bring the mother and daughter together. They had not had any contact for many years, and the *kallah* was asked if her mother could come in and sit beside her at the reception. The young woman considered the request for a few moments and answered yes.

Her mother came into the room and sat down beside the bride, but after only a few minutes the girl broke down into uncontrollable sobbing. The mother had to leave. The untold story of the girl's sufferings had been reawakened by her mother's presence, and she could not bear the memories that came flooding back.

It is obvious that this young woman had borne terrible experiences, which had cut deep scars into her very being. Was she guilty of the cruelty the Rambam speaks of that causes the person unable to forgive to be considered the sinner? Certainly not! If the motivations behind a person refusing to forgive are indeed cruelty and revenge, then the person becomes the offender. There are some people, though, whose stories are so terrible that their inability to forgive flows from a different source entirely.

In considering this article, I first discussed it with one of the *gedolei hador*, who told me that he agreed with my understanding of the Rambam. He was concerned, though, that upon reading this some people would use it as an excuse. Those who should and can forgive might use this to justify the fact that they choose not to forgive.

A good rule of thumb of what might be considered unforgivable is the sort of occurrence that literally becomes a story that cannot be repeated. It is the sort of tragedy that has such profound effects that the victim will probably need professional help to recover from it. Insults, theft, unpaid debts, and such do not fall under this category. No one would find it too painful or embarrassing to tell others that a certain Jew owes him money (in fact, the danger is that one might find it too easy to do just that). Those who struggle to forgive the unforgivable can be comforted to learn that they are not expected to do the impossible. They should, though, wish that they could bring themselves to do it.

David HaMelech says, "*Toras Hashem temimah...* — The ways of the Torah are perfect; they restore the soul. The testimony of Hashem is trustworthy and makes a simple person wise. The instructions of Hashem are straightforward, making the heart happy" (*Tehillim* 19:8–9). Hashem's instruction to forgive someone is ultimately advice that benefits the one who forgives more than the one who is forgiven. Forgiving someone allows us to let go of pain and move on. Not forgiving someone means that the original damage is kept alive and fresh, and in a sense it is reenacted every day. Even if a person can't see a way to forgive someone now, perhaps he will be able to forgive the person in the future.

I once felt a very great antipathy for a certain individual. I went to discuss my feelings with my *rav*, the Gateshead *rav*. This individual had done many terrible things to other people, and the fact that he seemed to get away with it scot-free caused me great distress. The *rav* smiled at me and uttered just a few words that helped me a great deal.

"I always find," he said, "that it helps if you can feel sorry for such people."

Those simple words helped then and have made other experiences so much easier to deal with. For those who cannot find it within themselves to forgive, or at least want to forgive, they should remember that they can discuss it with a *rav*. He might have a suggestion that will remove the weight that has been pulling them down. For the rest of us, whose stories can be told, we can actually guarantee ourselves a good judgment! Hashem is waiting to be asked for forgiveness in order forgive our offenses. We have to make sure we do the same to those who sincerely want us to forgive theirs.

Sukkos

Winning the War

(Hamodia, October 13, 2000)

A few months ago I spoke at a *Shabbaton* in South Africa. One of the participants was an Israeli whom I discovered was attending in order to help him on his way back to the sort of life from which he had once fled.

Over the weekend we sat down in a very plush hotel lounge in the sort of chairs that you sink into and that make you feel you'll never leave again. In this most comfortable of settings, he told me his story.

He came from a family where both sets of grandparents were German Jews who had suffered greatly in the Second World War. Their suffering had been passed on to their children, who would grow up and become this man's parents. Like a stone thrown into the Holocaust's sea of tears, the ripples spread out through time. He was brought up in the strictest atmosphere imaginable. The essential counterbalance of love was something that both his father and mother were simply unable to give.

Eventually he fled from his home. To solidify his rebellion and rejection of his parents, he joined the Israeli army. It was like jumping from the frying pan into the fire — Israel had just invaded Lebanon. As he told me his tale, two other Israelis sat listening. One had been a captain during the Six-Day War, and the other an officer during the Yom Kippur War.

The younger man pointed at them and said, "They will tell you that Lebanon, at least compared to their wars, was a piece of cake. That was not my experience."

He had served as a paramedic and proved to be very good at his job. Promotion after promotion led him to be an officer in charge of establishing field hospitals on or near the battlefield. It was his decision where the helicopter pad should be situated and where the operating tent should be. He decided who among the injured should be evacuated first.

Some of his stories described unbelievably terrible injuries and suffering. To my ears, it was hard to imagine anything worse in any war. The other two Israelis listened without surprise.

One day he was sent to a field hospital. When he arrived, he found his sister working there as a nurse. "It was strange," he said. "We were brought up to be unemotional and cold, yet when we met we hugged and cried for at least a half-hour. I hadn't spoken to my father for four years, but I told my sister that I loved my parents and understood that they had brought us up the best way they understood."

The rebellion was over. It was the first step on his journey home.

It is a peculiar paradox that war, which brings out the very worst in human beings, can also sometimes bring out the very best. The days of awe see this very theme appearing and repeating itself again and again.

The Torah portions that are read before Rosh HaShanah speak of laying siege to a city and psychological tactics that troops have to face on a battlefield. *Ki Seitzei* talks about taking a captive after a battle. The same theme carries itself into Tishrei and Sukkos. The *lulav* is likened to a sword waved triumphantly above our heads, proclaiming to all that we are confident that we have won the case recently heard against us in the Heavenly court. Chazal say that the ink of the writing of the verdicts that were written in the Heavenly book on Yom Kippur is not totally dry until after Sukkos. The battle is not quite over; victory can still be snatched from the jaws of defeat.

The first Manchester *rosh yeshivah*, Rav Tzvi Hirsh Ferber, *zt"l*, quotes the *gemara* in *Sukkah* which says that the waving of the *lulav* together with the *esrog*, *hadasim*, and *aravos* has a unique ability to confound the *satan*. He wonders why no other mitzvah can achieve this, and his answer takes us back to warfare.

In the ancient world, when nations went to war, they believed their gods went to war with them. While people clashed with their enemies on earth, their gods would fight with their enemy's gods on high. When a nation was defeated, it became apparent to them that not only were their enemies better fighters, but their enemies' gods were better and more powerful gods. They inevitably concluded that they should have been serving these other gods all along. That is why nations disappeared and vanished after conquest. They merged with and melted into the nation that had conquered them, content to become part of the new nation with the best gods.

Not so *Klal Yisrael*. The Jewish people knew that there are no other gods; there is only one Hashem. Over the millennia, when we have faced enemies, been defeated, and have fallen (at least temporarily), our reaction has always been different from the nations. We knew that there was no alternative but to repair the reasons that caused Hashem to withdraw His protection in the first place. This is hinted at when we prostrate on Yom Kippur and then pick ourselves up again and again. Hashem allows us to recover from our defeats and go on.

When we wave our *lulav* in six directions — north, south, east, west, up, and down — we are declaring to ourselves and to the world that Hashem is everywhere. There is only one Hashem, and we know that ultimately there is only one direction to travel in order to pick ourselves up — and that is back to Him. We say with reference to the past, "*Hodu laShem ki tov* — Praise Hashem, for He is good," and to the future, "*Ana Hashem hoshia na* — Please, Hashem, please save." We trust in Hashem completely. We know that there are no alternatives.

It is this statement of conviction after the whole *teshuvah* process that leads us to feel confident enough that we wave our *lulav* as the ultimate weapon of war, like a sword held high in triumph.

We have survived all our enemies and all our wars because of this unshakeable conviction. Even the *satan* has to retreat in the face of the *lulav* being waved as a banner of trust and connection to God. The Jewish people may forget Who really protects them for a little while and fall. But in Elul our own rebellions against Hashem start to collapse, and we take our first steps home again. By Sukkos those first steps have become huge strides, and we proudly let the world know that we have come to a festival of joy. It's a joy we demonstrate by waving our *lulavim* to the world. We have picked ourselves up again and come home to our Father.

Chanukah

Building with Mesiras Nefesh

(The Jewish Tribune, 2000)

An Israeli friend of mine once told me of an interesting article that appeared years ago in a secular Israeli newspaper. It had an imaginary a conversation between a nonreligious father and his son about Chanukah. The father had just told his little boy the Chanukah story, and the child began asking some questions.

"Were the Hasmoneans religious?"

The secular father was disturbed by the thought and immediately replied, "No, of course not. They were just like us."

The little boy said, "But you said they rededicated the Temple!"

The father conceded that indeed they had done that.

"So they must have been religious. Otherwise they wouldn't have bothered!"

The father became a bit uncomfortable. "Well, perhaps they were a bit religious."

"Did they keep kosher?" asked the son. The father agreed that they probably kept kosher.

"What about Shabbat?"

The father was quite sure about that. "No, I don't think that they kept Shabbat" came the reply.

"They must have if they were so religious that they wanted to dedicate the Temple and use only pure olive oil."

The father frowned and conceded that they must have kept Shabbos, too. Then the little boy said to his father, "Abba, we don't keep Shabbat or kashrut. We are not religious. If we had lived then, whose side would we have fought on, the Hasmoneans or the Greeks?"

When Yaakov had his dream and saw the angels ascending and descending a ladder that reached up to Heaven, the Ramban explains that these angels were the Heavenly representatives of the nations that would dominate and subjugate the Jewish people. Yaakov was being shown the future exiles of his descendants.

Of all the nations who would dominate the Jewish people, one was unique — Greece. The other nations conquered and exiled the Jewish people. Greece dominated the Jews in Eretz Yisrael.

This conquest was one of the spirit. Greece equaled beauty, and Hellenism was the *Zeitgeist*. Tens of thousands of Jews abandoned Judaism in favor of this enticing and fashionable lifestyle. It was later that the Greeks and their Jewish adherents took their antipathy of all things Jewish to its final conclusion by attempting to eradicate Judaism altogether.

Centuries later, when the Roman legions would march to destroy Judea and the Holy Temple, Greek cities within the Land of Israel fought on the side of the Romans. People who had once been Jews but for several generations saw themselves as Greeks now could avenge the Hasmoneans' victory. Chazal say of this, the final exile, *galus Edom*, that it would contain all the elements of all the previous exiles.

Not too long ago, my wife and I went to a family bar mitzvah in Yerushalayim. I was approached by someone from Manchester who was on the same flight to Israel. He held a book in his hand. "Here! You must read this," he said and gave me the book.

It was an account of what was happening in the State of Israel and in particular among Israel's secular Jews. I started to glance at

Building with Mesiras Nefesh

the book and found my eyes glued to the pages. I read in disbelief and profound depression.

There is a new movement, a new *Zeitgeist* in the modern state of Israel. It claims that the ideas and philosophy of Zionism, which shaped and created the state, are dead. New ideas have sprung up to replace them. This new movement is called "post-Zionism," and its adherents are called "post-Zionists."

As I read the book, I had the distinct impression that "the lunatics have taken over the asylum." These people see the struggle between the Israelis and the Palestinians as being one, and Israel's case is indefensible. The very concept of an Israel is anathema. The "*HaTikvah*" anthem is unacceptable. (This is not for the reasons that it is unacceptable to some religious Jews — because its "hope" and aspiration for Jews is merely to be a "free people in their land," with no mention of Torah, mitzvos, or even Hashem.) Post-Zionists reject "*HaTikvah*" because it uses the word *Jew*!

They argue that the words *nefesh Yehudi* exclude other peoples and that makes "*HaTikvah*" racist! So is the Israeli flag, because it features the Star of David. Post-Zionists want a crescent moon there, too, and perhaps a cross — after all, the State of Israel isn't just for Jews, is it? Another item on their wish list is the law of return. Could anything be more racist than that? It must be repealed!

Now if, as I did, you are starting to feel you have entered the surreal world of a nightmare where the lunatics have taken over the asylum, then you would be making a mistake. These ideas and much worse are being taught at all of Israel's universities. Allow me to give you a glimpse into one of the typical "wards" of post-Zionist academia.

A Tel Aviv University professor describes Israel as the "garbage heap of history" and "a regime that produces and distributes evil systematically." The reason for this is because Israel is a Jewish state. His solution: "We envision a state that will not be a Jewish nation state."

"*V'ein kol chadash tachas hashemesh* — There is nothing new under the sun," wrote Shlomo HaMelech. In ancient Greece the Jews who wanted to be Hellenists also envisioned just such a state.

Reb Simchah Zissel, *zt"l*, gives us the perfect antidote to the babble of the post-Zionists, and his words are summarized by Rav Eliyahu Dessler: "A person thinks he can replace what Hashem wants to happen with what he wants to occur. This is wrong. Who can challenge Hashem's plans?"

Pharaoh saw through astrology that a man would be born who would liberate the Jews, so he ordered all boys to be killed at birth. What did Hashem do? He had Pharaoh bring that boy up in his own palace.

Haman selected a day he thought auspicious for killing all the Jews and constructed a gallows on which he would personally hang Mordechai. But on that day the Jews killed their enemies, and Mordechai used the same gallows to hang Haman.

The same process occurred during Chanukah. The Greeks outlawed the teaching of Torah, circumcision, and Shabbos. They also banned the announcement of the day of Rosh Chodesh. The logic behind the first three is obvious. The Greeks wanted Jews to abandon Judaism and be just like them. Bris milah made Jews look different. Teaching Torah made Jews think differently. And a non-Jewish man of letters once commented, "More than the Jews have kept the Sabbath, the Sabbath has kept the Jews!" Its removal would be essential for the Greeks to achieve their goal.

The banning of the announcement of Rosh Chodesh, though, was a subtler device. Without knowing when the new moon was, the Jews could not celebrate their festivals. What did Hashem do? He made the Greeks the agents of bringing us a new Jewish holiday — Chanukah! All that was required was that we play our part.

The Bach explains what that part was. The rise of those who want to eradicate everything Jewish in the Land of Israel is possible only when *Klal Yisrael* become lax and uninspired in their perfor-

Building with Mesiras Nefesh

mance of that which makes us Jews: mitzvos. It required an act of self-sacrifice and commitment to reverse the process. That, in turn, allowed the Greeks to be defeated. The miracle of Chanukah was Hashem saluting and identifying the source of the Jewish people's victory. Flames rose up and illuminated the Temple once more.

At that family bar mitzvah my wife and I listened to a great-nephew make his first blessing over a *sefer Torah*: "*Asher bachar banu mikol ha'amim* — Who has chosen us from all of the other peoples."

Mattesdorf is full of religious Jews like that bar mitzvah boy's parents who have dedicated their lives to self-sacrifice and commitment to Torah and mitzvos. Towering over it, and, indeed, all of Yerushalayim, is another example of self-sacrifice and dedication to Torah and mitzvos, the new Belz shul. A visit there that Shabbos had me staring in wonderment. Everything is beautiful while still managing to be tasteful and unostentatious. At night it is illuminated and signals to Yerushalayim, and the entire world, that *Klal Yisrael* are growing in their commitment to Torah and mitzvos. Its light shines over homes in which rows after rows of well-used *sefarim* can be glimpsed.

As I walked from the Belz shul to the bar mitzvah *seudah*, I recalled the book I had read on the plane and my depression at discovering a new generation of Hellenists. Then I thought of this other Israel, and as I looked up at the beautiful Belz shul, I could feel that another building was about to be built. This other building will be illuminated by a Menorah that will be lit by a *kohen gadol*. It will signal the victory of those who remained loyal to the Torah and the final defeat of those philosophies that tried to separate Jews from Judaism. It can only be a moment away, and it will be built on the self-sacrifice of *Klal Yisrael*.

Chanukah

When "They" Become "Us"

(Hamodia)

The religious public relations organization Manof recently published a study. The study found that in the course of the last two years there has been a near tripling of the number of anti-religious Internet sites in Israel. There has also been a significant increase in acts of violence against religious Jews. In 1997 to 1998, eighty-six attacks on religious citizens and acts of vandalism against synagogues were reported.

Hamodia, Yated Neeman, and the UK's *Jewish Tribune*, among others, reported the "massive desecration of Shabbos" that took place when a huge turbine was transported along Israel's roads on the holy day. Far more disturbing even than the act itself was the fact that in some places the road was lined with Israelis clapping. That they were applauding *chillul Shabbos* was incidental. They were really applauding a victory of "them" over "us." It was "one in the eye" for the *"chareidim."* In the struggle between "us" and "them," they had won a battle.

Not too long ago an Israeli newspaper published a cartoon. It portrayed a *chareidi* child with one eye closed and the other staring down the barrel of a gun. The message was clear and very disturbing: "Beware, Israeli public. The *chareidim* are out to get you!"

The other day I was looking through a Jewish encyclopedia for a historical reference. I came upon the almost identical cartoon from an anti-Semitic publication called *Pluvium*, which flourished in St. Petersburg in around 1907. A caricature Jew with one eye closed was looking down the barrel of a gun. Same cartoon, same message. The only thing that was different was the identity of those playing the part of the anti-Semites.

Perhaps it was the fashionable boast of Israeli teenagers of the sixties and seventies who claimed that "I am not a Jew; I am an Israeli" that planted the seeds of today's ugly growth. No less a figure than Shulamit Aloni stated that the *chareidim* have taken the place of the Jew in Israeli society. It is no surprise (even though it will break our hearts) to hear an Israeli say, "When I see the ultra-Orthodox, I understand the Nazis" (so said artist Yigal Tomarkin in *Tel Aviv* magazine).

In *Bereishis* we read of the war between the four kings and the five. The Alshich comments on its significance to Avraham Avinu. Hashem was showing him a portent of the four exiles of the Jewish people. The first of the four kings, Amrafel, was Bavel. The last of the four, Sidol the king of Goyim, was Edom! How could Sidol be Edom if Edom hadn't been born yet? The Alshich explains that the angel of Edom, the angel who embodied the philosophy of Esav, was previously the angel of Sidol and his people.

The Alshich's words are frightening. He is saying that Esav's philosophy is mobile. It can be taken up by people other than Edom — even Jews.

The odd one out of the four exiles is Yavan, Greece. The Chanukah story takes place in the Land of Israel. The Greeks and their allies, who included many Jews who no longer saw themselves as anything but Greeks, launched an attack to eradicate Judaism in Eretz Yisrael. A campaign to replace Jewish values with the dominant non-Jewish ones could be waged by Jews against

Jews within Israel. *"Ein kol chadash tachas hashemesh* — Nothing is really new in the world."

Rav Eliyahu Dessler, *zt"l*, in his *Michtav MeEliyahu* (vol. 4, p. 42), points to a unique phenomenon of our times:

"There were always beliefs that were opposed to Torah, like the idolaters in their time or the followers of Greek philosophy. They opposed the Torah totally and fundamentally but never used the Torah itself to advance their arguments. In our time we've experienced something strange that never happened before. The Torah's enemies have taken hold of holiness itself to base their attacks on the Torah. Some use verses themselves to attack the authenticity of the Torah. Others absorb aspects of the Torah like Eretz Yisrael and *lashon hakodesh*."

How, wonders Rav Dessler, did such a change take place in our generation? He supplies a shocking answer. The *satan* gets his power solely from mitzvos that we do not do properly. The weakening of Torah learning in the later generations allowed heresy to be created from the Torah itself! Lack of sincerity in mitzvos powers the engine of the *satan's* attacks.

In a recent issue of *Hamodia* a cry from the heart appeared in the letters to the editor by Rav Chaim Miller, *shlita*, the deputy mayor of Yerushalayim. He appealed for help to alleviate the distress of Jewish girls who cannot find a seminary to take them.

"The situation is scandalous," he wrote. "In spite of the assertions — some legitimate — by seminary principals and supervising bodies, it is obvious that something is very wrong. The way to solve problems is not simply to disregard them. Problems are there to be dealt with, not to be ignored and allowed to fester. Moreover, in many cases the reason a girl was not accepted by any seminary is not because there is anything wrong with her, but because of some extremely far-fetched external situation."

It is certainly not a scandal exclusive to Eretz Yisrael. It is certainly not a scandal exclusive to seminaries. Wherever I have trav-

When "They" Become "Us"

eled in the Jewish world, there are educational institutions that are narrowing the criteria of acceptance more and more. Some schools have been content to reject children "not because there is anything wrong with them" and are undisturbed to know that those children are stuck at home or wandering the streets with nowhere to go.

While I was in America recently, I heard about one school that draws its children exclusively from *frum* families. Most of the parents have been lucky enough to have had a yeshivah or Bais Yaakov education. Recently the school differentiated between those whose fathers were in *kollel* and those who were not. This move was at the insistence of the *kollel* men themselves! "Us" and "them." Perhaps we will start to see where the *satan* gets the power to line up thousands of Israelis along a road to applaud *chillul Shabbos.*

Rav Shlomo Wolbe, *shlita*, wrote an essay in *Alei Shor* called "*Frumkeit.*" He says that *frumkeit* is a natural and instinctive feeling that we possess that makes us desire closeness to Hashem. Without this component in our nature, our *avodas Hashem* would be extremely difficult. Yet *frumkeit*, like all our "instinctive" reactions, is innately egoistic. "*Frumkeit* pushes a man to do only that which is good for him," says Rav Wolbe. Proper interactions with others, and even pure intentions in our service to Hashem, are "not sustained from *frumkeit.*"

"A man who builds his *Yiddishkeit* on that basis," Rav Wolbe says, "even if he imposes very many strictures upon his *Yiddishkeit*, will not become a really compassionate person, and he will never achieve the performance of mitzvos with pure intentions. This will be attained only if his sacrifice to God is based on Torah knowledge."

He secures his point with a quote from the Alter of Slabodka: "The verse says, '*V'ahavta l'rei'acha kamocha* — You shall love your neighbor as you love yourself.' You do not love yourself because it is a mitzvah. Your love for yourself is straightforward and spontaneous. That is how you are supposed to love your neighbor."

If *frumkeit* is the basis upon which you love your neighbor, then you are doing it as a mitzvah. You know you will eventually be rewarded, so ultimately you are doing it for yourself. It is not hard to look at ourselves and see the lack of pure intentions and the reasons for it. For those who are a little shortsighted, we have only to look at Rav Dessler's model and the terrible "us" and "them" mentality, which has become such a feature of Israeli life. We gave the *satan* the ability to create this fissure in the first place. Too many schools are content to accept only "our" types of children, and then they redefine and redraw the criteria of acceptance so that the definition of what "our" type of children is becomes narrower. Those who should be "us" are consigned to become "them."

When HaRav Shach, *zt"l*, spoke out against this scandal a few years ago, I heard someone in *chutz la'aretz* (who is a prime architect of "maximum exclusion") state that this ruling did not apply to *chutz la'aretz*.

It will take the unanimous voices of all of our *gedolim* inside and outside Eretz Yisrael to condemn what is being done to Jewish children who do not deserve such suffering. When we start to listen to their voices, we can be confident that we will be seeing Israelis transform themselves back into Jews. When "they" become "us," then we can feel confident that the end of the *galus* is only a few moments away.

Purim

Peering behind the Veil

(Hamodia, March 9, 2001)

One of the most amazing episodes of the Second World War was when some Jewish refugees found their way to safety in Japan, Germany's ally. They were temporarily settled in the city of Kyoto while their hosts decided their fate. Eventually they would be moved to Shanghai, where the great Mir Yeshivah would re-form and survive.

On one occasion, while their fate was still being decided by the Japanese, representatives of the refugees were summoned before a group of Japanese generals. They were kept waiting for some time, a considerable discourtesy in Japanese culture. When they were eventually brought before the soldiers, the table before them held a very sparse selection of food, another discourtesy; normally a lavish display would greet guests. The worried Jews stood before the table, and a translator conveyed the first question.

"Why do our allies the Germans hate you so much?"

There was a pause as the delegation struggled to find an answer that would convince and satisfy the Japanese. Among the group was the Amshinover Rebbe. He did not hesitate. "It is because we are Orientals!" he replied.

When this was translated for the generals, consternation broke out. The Asian nations had always been conquered and colonized by European empires. Europeans hating people because they were "Orientals" was something the Japanese could understand very well.

The Rebbe's answer was challenged, but the Amshinover continued, "Oh no, it is quite true. Check for yourself. A few years ago a Japanese consul in Berlin wanted to marry a German woman. The Nazis' race laws declared him a non-Aryan and therefore unacceptable. He was forbidden to do so."

The Jews was ushered outside and made to wait while phone calls to Tokyo were made that eventually confirmed the story. When the Jews were brought back in, the table was transformed. It was now crammed with every sort of fruit and delicacy. The generals had turned friendly, and Japanese monks engaged in religious discussions with the rabbis. The Japanese located a new home for their fellow "Orientals," and the Jewish refugees set sail for Shanghai.

When I was first told this story, the storyteller concluded, "It was the genius of the Amshinover that saved the Jews of Shanghai."

The Torah counts the sons of Leah who went down to Egypt. It arrives at a total of thirty-three. Rashi immediately points out that the arithmetic is wrong. If you count up the names mentioned, there are only thirty-two. The thirty-third person, he explains, was Moshe's mother, Yocheved. She was born just as the Jewish people were crossing the Egyptian border.

The Ibn Ezra rejects Rashi's explanation. The Jewish people were in Egypt for 210 years. Moshe was eighty years old when he led them to freedom. That would mean that Yocheved was 130 years old when she gave birth to Moshe!

"It would be astonishing that the Torah would not mention that Yocheved bore her son at such an age, when the Torah emphasizes that Sarah gave birth to Yitzchak when she was ninety years old."

The Ibn Ezra therefore concludes that the thirty-third person refers to Yaakov himself. The Ramban defends Rashi and does so with an amazing statement: "I will tell you a principle that is well established in the Torah. The miracles that occur that were heralded by a prophet or an angel are emphasized by the Torah. Miracles such as when a tzaddik is saved or a wicked person is punished that occur without any prediction or warning are not recorded in the Torah or Prophets."

According to the Ramban, the thirty-third person is Yocheved, and the Ibn Ezra's objection is resolved.

The Ramban's explanation opens up an intriguing window into human psychology. There is no difference between these two miracles. If anything, Yocheved's is more impressive than Sarah's. But since we are not warned about it beforehand, we do not see it as such. The reason, as Rav Yerucham Levovitz says in *Da'as Chochmah U'Mussar*, is simple: people don't look; people don't think!

It is a point Rashi makes at the end of *Noach*. There the Torah tells us that Terach, Avraham's father, was seventy years old when his son was born. The parashah ends with the verse "And it was that the days of Terach were 205 years, and Terach died in Charan." The next parashah starts with Hashem telling Avraham to move to Eretz Yisrael, and the Torah says he was seventy-five years old when he did so. By adding the two figures together, it is obvious that Avraham left his father in Charan and went to Eretz Yisrael when Terach was 145 years old. Intriguingly the Torah reports Terach's death first and only then reports that Avraham left to go to Israel. This is clearly an attempt to imply that Avraham left his father only after Terach died, which is not true. Rashi explains why:

"The Torah wrote events in a way that implied that Avraham left only after his father was already dead so that the truth would not be apparent to all and people would not say that Avraham was not scrupulous in honoring his father."

Of course, any child can add the seventy years of Terach at Avraham's birth together with the seventy-five years of Avraham's age when he left, and by subtracting that from Terach's total years he can see that Avraham left his father alone for sixty years. Obviously Rashi knows that. Rav Yerucham explains that the point Rashi makes is, if you want to draw a veil over the truth, it need only be the thinnest of veils, because people don't look; people don't think!

The miracle of the Purim story is so complex that it requires an entire megillah for it to be told. Other miracles, for example, the splitting of the Red Sea, are given only a few verses.

Chazal explain the Purim miracle as being a succession of miracles. The miracle of Vashti's refusal to appear before the king. The miracle of Esther being selected as the new queen. Mordechai overhearing the plan to kill Achashveirosh. The miracles of Purim, though, are miracles that occurred with the veil of nature drawn over them. The splitting of the Red Sea by comparison was supernatural; the veil was drawn aside. Still, it was only one miracle.

Rav Yerucham says, "Although nothing is difficult for Hashem, in a very real sense, a miracle concealed by nature is much greater than an open and supernatural miracle!"

He proves this with a *midrash*: "Rabbi Yehoshua ben Levi says: It is as difficult for Hashem to provide food for man as it was for Him to split the Red Sea." David HaMelech recalls what happened at the miracle of the splitting of the Red Sea and then says about Hashem, "Who gives food to every living thing." So we see that the splitting of the Red Sea is equated with the process of providing a person with food.

Yet another *midrash* goes further, saying that providing food is a greater miracle than the splitting of the sea. The splitting of the Red Sea was done by an angel. The providing of food is done directly by Hashem Himself, as it says, *"Posei'ach es yadecha u'masbia*

Peering behind the Veil

l'chol chai ratzon — You open Your hand and satisfy the desire of every living thing."

The festivals that were enacted in the exiles, Chanukah and Purim, occurred at times when Hashem was hidden from *Klal Yisrael*. The intrinsic nature of *galus* is the apparent absence of Hashem in the events that occur to the Jewish people. The challenge of these two festivals is *pirsumei nissim* — to consider the events that occur to us and peer behind the veil of nature.

When Esther reveals that she is a Jew and pleads for the lives of the Jewish people, she says, "*Ki ein hatzar shaveh b'nezek hamelech* — But our enemy [Haman] is not concerned with the damage that his plan will do to your coffers."

This argument turns the tide, and the king demands to know, "*Mi hu zeh v'eizeh hu asher malei libo la'asos kein* — Who and where is this individual whose heart has emboldened him to do this?" And Haman's downfall is complete.

Rav Yerucham elaborates on the brilliant point Esther was making. The Jews were hardworking and talented. They succeeded in business. Haman's plan to annihilate the Jews would cause the king harm, robbing him of tax revenues and ultimately impoverishing him.

Her argument was pure genius, and it struck the right chord. But it is not brilliant words or genius that saves the Jewish people in *galus*. It was not the undoubtable brilliance and genius of the Amshinover Rebbe that reversed the animosity of the Japanese who held so many Jewish lives in their hands.

Galus is the time when we have to look carefully behind the veil of nature to see and think about the truth that lies beyond. In this exile, at this time, when the Jewish people are suffering such difficulties, Purim provides us with a timely reminder that it will not be the "Clinton Plan" or a "Bush initiative" that will bring peace to Eretz Yisrael. It is Hashem, the Guardian of Israel in every *galus*.

Pesach

Saintly Women B'Chol Dor VaDor

(Hamodia, April 19, 2000)

The *sefarim* say that every Jew feels a special connection to a certain mitzvah, feeling in a very real sense that it is his mitzvah. My favorite mitzvah is that of the seder night, and Pesach is my favorite *yom tov*. Yet when I make this point in a women's *shiur*, the audience usually groans. I picture myself sitting and wearing my *kittel* at the very beautiful Pesach table my wife has prepared. They see the weeks of work that preceded and produced that seder table.

The Jewish people in Egypt presented a paradox. The Midrash relates that when they left Egypt an exclamation of indignation was heard in Heaven. The angel that represented Egypt complained, "My people are guilty of idolatry, but Israel is guilty as well."

The Alshich points to two reasons the Jewish people were reluctant to believe Moshe's claim that their exile was over. First, there was a tradition of prophecy reaching back to the *Avos* that they would be enslaved for four hundred years. This had been passed down through the generations. That meant they still had to complete another one hundred and ninety years. Second, they knew that Egypt was full of their own idols, which hindered their merits for redemption.

We also find, in tractate *Sotah*, that Rabbi Akiva states that the Jewish people achieved their freedom only in the merit of the saintly women of that generation. It was in reward for their courage that Hashem performed staggering miracles. When the Jewish women in Egypt would go to draw water, their containers always scooped up fish, too, and they would bring this essential food to their husbands as they struggled in the fields. When it was time for their babies to be born, they would go into the fields to give birth and say, "Almighty, I have played my part and brought these children into the world. You do Yours!" They could not return home with their infants because they knew the Egyptians would instantly throw them into the Nile. Instead they walked away, leaving their babies behind, trusting that Hashem would take care of them. And, indeed, Hashem Himself descended and cared for the babies and brought them up.

These women knew that a soul cannot get to Heaven unless it has come into this world first. Though it broke their hearts to leave their children behind, they knew that their actions would bring these souls their only opportunity for eternal life. When the men had given up hope, the women continued to insist that these tiny souls should make that journey into this world, which would guarantee them entrance into the next.

The Midrash says that when the Jews stood at the Red Sea and cried out, "This is my God, and I shall glorify Him," these were the voices of those same babies who been brought up by Hashem Himself. Their identification of Hashem publicly proclaimed the miracle that had happened to them so that the Jews would know about it and remember.

Theoretically miracles at such a level happen only for people who are themselves at the highest spiritual level. This does not fit with the description of a Jewish people who filled Egypt with their idols.

The Alshich points to the Torah's description of the Jewish people in Egypt and expresses amazement. The verse states, "And the children were fruitful and swarmed and multiplied and became strong very, very much." How could the Torah, which is so careful in its use of language and takes extra measures to make sure its expressions are positive and elevating — referring to impure animals as "*eino tahor*," not pure, for example — say about the children of Israel "*vayishretzu* — they swarmed"? Why does the Torah use a word that conjures up a far more negative image than the word *tamei*, impure?

The Alshich answers that there were really two types of Jews in Egypt and therefore two Pesach stories. One type, the majority, chose to become totally assimilated within Egyptian society. It was these people who the Torah says "swarmed." The second type were those who remained faithful to Hashem and the teachings of their fathers. They became "fruitful." One group filled Egypt with their idols, and the second group hung tenaciously to who and what they were.

But the saintly women of that time went even further. Rav Yitzchak Eizik Sher of Slabodka says their faith was strong and complete. It was they who set the example that inspired their husbands and the faithful Jews who were starting to weaken. When other women saw that the *nashim tzidkaniyos*, the righteous women, were prepared to carry on having children even in the cauldron that was Egypt, they were inspired to carry on, too.

Rav Dessler quotes Rav Tzvi Hirsch Broide, *zt"l*, who says that time is not a long line, as is often depicted in history books. Rather, time operates more like a spiral staircase. Looking up, you may see someone moving forward, but again and again he will return to the same spot he was at on a previous level. Thus Pesach is a chance not to commemorate what occurred at the Exodus but to relive it.

Is it possible that the phenomenon of the *nashim tzidkaniyos* of the Pesach story is also replayed through the millennia?

My *rosh yeshivah*, Rav Leib Gurwicz, *zt"l*, once told us a story of a woman's tragedy and her incredible courage. The Russian czars were tired of the Jews' stubborn refusal to abandon their faith. They had tried everything, from pogroms to excluding Jews from almost every type of employment, yet nothing caused the Jews to give up what they knew to be true. Finally one of the czars hit on the idea of kidnapping them as young children before they knew what was true. They would be brought up as Christians and then spend decades in the army. Assimilation by amnesia.

In one Jewish town a group of thugs arrived and surrounded the cheder. The teachers were expelled, and, with weapons in hand, the thugs ignored the heartrending pleas of fathers and mothers for their children to be released.

Eventually the wagons that would take the children away to their new lives arrived, and the children were forced to board. In the crush to get them aboard, one of the little boys was suffocated, and his tiny body was handed back to his weeping mother.

The sounds of a hundred families in mourning resounded throughout that night as the town wept for its lost children. Late in the evening a knock was heard on the doors of the homes that had lost a child. Outside stood one of the few children who had managed to escape. He had been sent by the mother whose child had died, and he held in his hands some cakes she had just baked. Her message was that they should take heart and not lose their hope. Her little boy had died knowing he was a Jew. Please God, theirs would, too.

A few years ago I heard a tale about a man learning in a *kollel*. He went to see one of the *gedolim* in Yerushalayim and said that he learned hard all week and it bothered him that his wife did not prepare the house on Friday to the standard that he thought was fitting for Shabbos. "She doesn't mop the floor tiles in the kitchen," he complained. He asked the *gadol* if he was right to be upset and demand that his wife have their home perfect for Shabbos.

His face registered relief and happiness when he was reassured by the *gadol* that he was one hundred percent correct to be upset that the house was not perfect for Shabbos, and he was further told to relate this in the *gadol*'s name to his wife.

The young man returned home to deliver the message. Two days later, on Friday, there was a knock at the door. The young man went to see who his unexpected caller was. He was astonished to see the same *gadol* whose advice he had sought standing outside.

"*Shalom aleichem*, Rebbe! How can I help you?"

The *gadol* replied, "Oh no, I've come to help you! Where is the mop and bucket? I came to clean the floor for your wife and help her prepare for Shabbos."

There has never been a time when the Jewish people have been blessed with so many yeshivos and other Torah institutions. There has never been a time when so many boys and so many young married men have had the merit to be able to sit and learn Hashem's Torah.

It would be a pity if we failed to relive and acknowledge all the crucial parts of the story of the Exodus. It would be truly sad if we didn't recall the message of Rav Tzvi Hirsch Broide that time consists of repeating patterns.

Women shouldn't be too tired to enjoy and participate in the seder. We men should offer all the help we can in our salute to those who made the Exodus possible in those days and Torah study possible in these.

Pesach

Struggling with Memory

(The Jewish Tribune)

Last November my daughter and I were traveling home on the motorway very near Manchester. There is something called "hydroplaning," which I knew nothing about at the beginning of the trip. I was about to discover all its intricacies.

There had been heavy rain, and we drove at the legal limit of seventy miles per hour. Ahead on the road I saw a pool of water. As we drove through it, the tires on one side of the car were making contact with the road, while the others were spinning on water. That's what's called hydroplaning! The car spun out of control and collided into the crash barrier four times. We demolished one hundred and twenty yards of the barrier before coming to a halt, completely blocking the fast lane.

The police arrived, and soon we were being driven away from the wreck of our car. The journey was full of thoughts of how easily there might not have been a happy ending and the *chesed* of Hashem in keeping us safe and unhurt. I came to a number of conclusions of how I could do more in my *avodah* to thank the Creator.

Five weeks later I was on a lecture tour in Gibraltar. My flight home would take off from Malaga Airport in Spain, which is about a two-hour drive from Gibraltar. I greeted my Spanish taxi driver and said, "*Como estas?*" He replied that he was fine. "*Muy bien!*" He asked the same of me and received the same answer.

We climbed into the car, and I asked him, "*Como se llama usted* — What is your name?"

"Manuel," he told me.

That was the end of my Spanish, but Manuel had got it into his mind that I was fluent. "*Los Ingleses son estupidos* — The English are stupid," he informed me. "*Pinochet es fantastico*" (he liked General Pinochet). There was a lot of other stuff about his mother-in-law, whom he seemed to dislike even more than the English.

Having established my credentials as a linguist, I found myself too embarrassed to admit that I hadn't a clue as to what he was saying, so I responded to Manuel's constant conversation by saying "*si*," with ever-increasing degrees of conviction. "*Si.*" "*Si!*" "*Si!!!*"

It began to rain. The flow of traffic sensibly slowed down to forty miles per hour. Not so Manuel, who continued at eighty while chattering like a bird. I desperately tried to recall the Spanish for "Slow down." I had seen a road sign with the word *velocidad*, which I guessed meant "speed," so I combined this with desperate hand signs, which were meant to indicate to the driver to slow down. Manuel looked at me, smiled, and indicated that he understood. "Heh! Heh! Heh!"

My heart sank as he sped on. I tried again, and he laughed some more, and then I saw it up ahead — a pool of water covering the entire road. Manuel did some more laughing and drove straight for the pool. The car hit the water, stopped for a microsecond, shuddered, and then shot out on the other side. I listened attentively for my heart to start beating again.

Manuel said, "Heh! Heh! Heh!"

There were six pools of water on that journey, and six more times I vividly and horribly relived my recent car crash. It needed no effort to find myself back in my own spinning car, it was so fresh in my memory.

Struggling with Memory

The Haggadah declares that it is a mitzvah to relive the Exodus from Egypt. Although the Gemara states that Hashem never asks us to do something that is impossible to do, it is very hard to see how this can be achieved. The Exodus happened three and a half thousand years ago!

Rav Yerucham Levovitz, *zt"l*, points to something that should be obvious and yet somehow isn't. When the Haggadah says, *"Chayav adam liros atzmo k'ilu hu yotzei miMitzrayim* — A person is obligated to see himself as though he is going out of Egypt," it does not say *"halailah hazeh* — on this night." It says you are obligated to see yourself as though you are going out all the time! This seems to lift the obligation totally beyond our abilities. Without the aids of a seder night, we are supposed to relive the Exodus constantly!

Rav Yechezkel Levenstein, *zt"l*, brings up a more insidious problem in achieving this mitzvah. It is not the obscurity and distance from the event that is the barrier. The very fact that we are too familiar with the story creates a problem.

Reb Simchah Zissel, *zt"l*, wonders how someone could read the story of those miracles and wonders that God performed for us without his faith being strengthened and transformed. Yet it is often so. Rav Yechezkel says the problem lies in *hergel*, the familiarity of the story. Having been taught about the Exodus from our earliest years, those simple images and interpretations inoculate us against discovering new depth and insights that could awaken the excitement that Reb Simchah Zissel says we should feel.

Rav Yechezkel experiments with learning some midrashim that reveal lesser known but exciting facets of the events. For example, there was a separate pathway for each tribe when the Red Sea split. The walls of water dividing each path were completely transparent so that each tribe could see the others and wouldn't worry about their welfare. Still, he says, despite these new insights the fire is not kindled. Faith is not strengthened.

Rav Yechezkel offers a solution that is very difficult to understand. He says that we must forget all that we were taught and knew until now about the redemption from Egypt. We must picture the events as though we had never heard them before.

It is a solution that I struggled with for three years, and, like a child given a jigsaw that is too advanced for his years, I did not know where to start.

Rav Eliyahu Dessler, *zt"l*, ignores the psychological barrier pointed out by Rav Yechezkel and insists that the problem of familiarity can be overcome. The more we learn and the deeper we make the learning, the more we must come to *hergel*'s opposite: *chiddush*! *Chiddush* causes the essential strengthening in *emunah* that the Haggadah requires.

These two approaches argued with each other in my mind, each contradicting the other. Rav Dessler believed *hergel* leads to *chiddush*, and Rav Yechezkel had proven that *hergel* suppresses *chiddush*.

A very good friend of mine sat *shivah* for his father a few weeks ago. I had been a boarder in his house when I first came to Manchester, and so I know the family well, or at least I thought I did. His father was elderly and struck me as a fine Jew, a *ba'al habayis*, a simple Jew. Of course, there really is no such thing as a simple Jew, but it was only at the *shivah* that I was dramatically reminded of it. It was there that I heard for the first time that the old gentleman I knew had been orphaned during the first World War. His parents were on a train, traveling through Galicia, when it was hit by a German shell. At the age of six a little boy was left alone in the world. He was sent to Germany, where a Jewish orphanage took care of him and brought him up.

As a young man he became an activist in his adopted community. He soon won their respect and trust. This was demonstrated as the last doors out of Europe were closing on the eve of World War II. He was put in charge of a trainload of children, a *Kindertransport*, the last to take precious and tender *neshamos* away from their parents to England and safety.

Struggling with Memory

When they arrived in Belgium, they were stopped by an anti-Semitic official who insisted that all of the children's papers be checked. This would mean they would miss the last boat to safety. Their young guardian pleaded with the official and offered a solution. He would stay behind and miss the ship while the papers were checked. If there was anything out of order, the English port could be telegraphed and the children returned. His presence would be the guarantee for their return — he would effectively be a hostage.

The official accepted the proposal, and the children boarded the ship. The anti-Semite began to go through the large pile of documents. After a while he looked up and considered the huge amount of work he had given himself and how much was still to process. "*Ach!*" he said. "Take them and go!" And so this Jew made it on the ship to England along with his precious charges.

When I heard this story, my eyes opened wide and I sat there in astonishment. I thought, *Wow! Was this young hero really the simple old Jew I knew?*

He had gone to his *Olam Haba* leaving hundreds of *neshamos* alive because of him. The gates of Heaven must have been thrown wide open upon his arrival.

That is what both Rav Levenstein and Rav Dessler mean. *Hergel* will both defeat *chiddush* and confound the strengthening of faith unless we are able to erase the simple and familiar understanding completely. We do that by pursuing a much deeper understanding of what happened, as Rav Dessler says. This means the *chiddushim* have to be so enormous that complacency is literally blown away and we are left thinking, *Wow! So that's the peshat! That's what happened.*

This is the Torah's demand, not just for Pesach but constantly. New discoveries in Torah are required at the deepest levels we can manage. When our learning produces "Wow!" then we have nothing to fear from *hergel*.

Sefiras HaOmer

Sorry, No Change

(Hamodia, May 18, 2001)

Not long ago I was sitting and chatting with two university students who had stayed behind to discuss the *shiur* I had just given. One of the students had become very close to me, and he sought my advice about the possibility of spending his summer in a yeshivah. I suggested a certain well-respected outreach yeshivah. The other student quickly intervened and suggested a different yeshivah. "If you go there," he said, "they will try to change you! The yeshivah I'm suggesting won't try to change you and will be quite happy for you to leave the way you arrived."

I know this other yeshivah, both by its reputation and its products, and I would have to agree that, sadly, the second student's analysis was totally correct. I decided, though, not to voice any criticism of this yeshivah or its approach but to respond to the complaint about the yeshivah I had suggested.

"I do not think they will try to change you," I said. "I do think that it's the sort of yeshivah that would expect its students to want to change themselves."

I was once approached by a young man who was teaching

Sorry, No Change

English in a religious Jewish school. He was constantly struggling to find textbooks that were suitable for his students. A colleague had recommended a certain book, but the teacher wasn't sure of the appropriateness of the final chapter. He asked me if I would look at it and advise him.

The book was a semi-autobiographical account of the author's early life. He was born in Stuttgart in a completely assimilated German Jewish family. When he was sixteen, he was sent to an exclusive German school, and there he struck up a friendship with a non-Jewish German boy. Twelve months later the friendship was over. The year was 1933.

In the course of the friendship, the Jewish author reports, his next-door neighbor experienced a terrible tragedy. A fire broke out, and two children were killed. This struck him as nothing had before. How could God let such a thing happen? His non-Jewish friend also could not understand it. He went on to discuss it with his priest, whose answer was unsatisfactory, and both boys rejected it. The author writes at the conclusion of this episode, "Once and for all I rejected all belief in a benevolent Mastermind."

How truly sad. A seventy-year-old man happily declares to the world that he never overcame the intellectual achievements of his sixteen-year-old mind. An entire lifetime had passed, and he still had not sought nor found an answer. A whole lifetime and still no change!

The journey the Jewish people would have to make after they left Egypt was far more than a geographic one. Their derelict spiritual state would have to be reversed and radically changed before they could successfully arrive at Mount Sinai. Throughout the millennia we have marked this time of transition through the counting of the omer. Chazal elaborate which particular deficiency was tackled and cured on each of the forty-nine days between Pesach and Shavuos. Every year we are invited to repeat this process of change in ourselves.

Dancing through Time

A picture emerges of a spiritual journey in which a hill was climbed stage by stage, day after day, until they arrived at the pinnacle, Mount Sinai, unrecognizable from the slave nation who left Egypt. Yet the Torah clearly states that the path to Mount Sinai was not the smooth one this picture suggests, with the Jewish people solely committed to spiritual growth. On the contrary, three days after the Exodus there was a rebellion.

"They traveled three days in the desert and did not find water. They came to Marah, and they were not able to drink water from Marah because it was bitter, which is why the place was called Marah. The people complained to Moshe, saying, 'What will we drink?' " (*Shemos* 15:23).

And this was not the only incidence of rebellion. There would be others before they received the Torah. So the forty-nine days that we think of as taking the Jewish people through forty-nine levels of spiritual growth did not exist. Some of those days were days of spiritual collapse!

In the first volume of *Alei Shor*, Rav Shlomo Wolbe, *shlita*, introduces an essay entitled "*Yemei Sinah Vimei Ahavah V'Hayei'ush*," which might best be translated as "Days of achievement and days of failure and despair."

He writes that anyone who has spent any time in a Torah institution engaged in serious Torah study knows that there were periods when they enjoyed tremendous success. And there were times when they experienced failure and nothing went right. There were weeks when it was easy to understand the lessons and when davening was something to look forward to. At these times, interpersonal relationships blossomed, and the graph of spiritual growth definitely pointed up. Other times saw no success. *Shiurim* were impenetrable. Davening was a process of mumbling words and no more. Interaction with others was a disaster. Of course, this process carries on through life even after we leave yeshivah or seminary.

Rav Wolbe quotes Rabbeinu Tam, who says this is the natural

state and that a period of spiritual success will inevitably retreat before a period of spiritual failure, which in turn will retreat as a new wave of spiritual success appears.

There is, though, a way of extending the ups and diminishing the downs. When a time of success arrives, one can use it to reach for new discoveries in Torah and new achievements in *Yiddishkeit*. This will have the effect of sustaining and elongating the upward momentum.

And Rav Wolbe reveals a heartening thought:

"Even when in the grip of the deepest trough one must not become disheartened or despair. It is possible that precisely through such times we can learn exactly what needs to be worked on and corrected within ourselves. Rabbi Tzadok HaKohen says that the very facets of our character that the *yetzer hara* attacks hardest are the same facets where an individual's key to greatness lies. Surely it is obvious that the *yetzer hara* will focus all of his attack where he sees the greatest potential in a person. The very same limb with which a person commits a sin can be used to perform a mitzvah."

The periods of greatest spiritual difficulty can become part of the process of the greatest spiritual success. They allow us to identify where our greatest weakness lies and encourage us to discover how it could become our greatest strength. The limb that did a sin becomes one that now does mitzvos.

The Alshich points out that when the Jewish people attacked Moshe three days after the Exodus and asked, "Why did you take us out of Egypt?" they revealed precisely where their chief flaw lay and what they still needed to work on. They lacked complete *emunah* in Hashem. Moshe did not take them out of Egypt; Hashem did. By taking their complaint to Moshe, they demonstrated that they were still not totally sure who had taken them out.

The Jewish people therefore did have forty-nine days of spiritual growth. They allowed their slips and lapses to become part of a process of identifying where their weakness lay and working to correct it. They might have slipped on this point again before the Torah was given, but eventually they would arrive at Mount Sinai and Hashem would tell Moshe, "Behold, I will come to you in a thick cloud in order that the people will hear when I speak to you, and also in you they will believe forever" (*Shemos* 19:9).

After forty-nine days of turning their downs into ups, they could now understand the nature of Moshe's prophetic relationship with Hashem and that Moshe did nothing and said nothing that did not come directly from Hashem. They had moved forward and changed themselves. They had removed their doubts and had their questions answered.

The young man who stayed behind after the *shiur* decided to spend the summer in a place where he was willing to allow himself both growth and change. The other young man was determined to go to a place where he would spend two months in order to become exactly the same as when he arrived.

So another Jewish soul has decided to set out on a journey on which he will face ups and downs, but in a place where he will be helped and shown how to change life's downs into ups.

Sefiras HaOmer

Putting Someone in Your Pocket

(Hamodia, April 2002)

The tragedy of the deaths of Rabbi Akiva's disciples is so immense that we mark it to this day. Had they lived out their lives, they could have conveyed Torah on such a scale that it could have transformed the history of the Jewish people. But if we have missed the inspiration of their lives, it is also a tragedy if we miss the significance of their deaths.

The Talmud tells the story: "He, Rabbi Akiva, had twelve thousand pairs of *talmidim*, and they all died during the same period, from Pesach to Shavuos. The reason was because they did not treat each other with *kavod*, respect" (*Yevamos* 62b).

The Gemara's account poses more questions than it answers. Why not say twenty-four thousand *talmidim*? Why "twelve thousand pairs"? And what does it mean that they did not show *kavod* to each other, and why did they deserve death for it? Also, why of all periods in the year did they die between Pesach and Shavuos? Why not between Rosh HaShanah and Yom Kippur?

The transformation that was required to turn the Jewish people from a nation of slaves into a people who could stand at Mount Sinai was immense. *Sefarim* say how a person's whole life is a journey to change just one aspect of his personality. To change six hundred thousand lives, and to do it in seven weeks, almost defeats our imagination. And yet it happened.

Rashi points to the verse in the Torah that proves that they had succeeded: "They camped in the desert, and *he* camped there, Yisrael opposite the mountain" (*Shemos* 19:2).

The Jewish people at Mount Sinai were as one person with one heart. It was this achievement that brought them the Torah. This unity, though, was more than just an absence of communal strife. There are six hundred thousand letters in the Torah according to the *Zohar*'s calculation. If one letter is missing from a *sefer Torah*, the whole *sefer Torah* is invalid. Had one Jew been missing from the nation that stood at Mount Sinai, that nation would have failed to function and no Jew would have received the Torah.

Rav Moshe Chaim Luzzato says something more about the six hundred thousand Jews who stood at Mount Sinai. Chazal tell us that there are no fewer than seventy answers to every question in the Torah. Rav Eliyahu Dessler illustrates this concept by imagining a person holding a piece of wood at someone's eye level. He keeps the wood at the same height and shows it to someone else who is much taller. If you were to ask each one what the piece of wood is like, one would reply, "Long and narrow." The other would say, "Broad and wide." Both are correct, though they totally contradict each other.

The Ramchal says that there are six hundred thousand ways of viewing the Torah because there were six hundred thousand Jews who received it. Each individual brought a unique perspective to the Torah and had a unique contribution. This echoes an incident reported in the Gemara, when Rabbi Yehudah HaNasi offered assistance to Torah scholars at a time of famine.

"Rebbi opened the storehouses at a time of famine and said, 'Those who study *Chumash*, those who study Mishnah or Gemara or halachah or *aggadah*, come and receive help' " (*Bava Basra* 8b).

Putting Someone in Your Pocket

Rebbi could have said, "Let *ba'alei Torah* come and receive help," but there are different types of *ba'alei Torah*.

The verse says, "These are the generations of Moshe and Aharon" (*Bemidbar* 3:1). Yet the Torah continues with only Aharon's descendants. Rashi explains that if you teach someone Torah it is considered as if you gave birth to them. Since Moshe taught Aharon's children, they were considered his children.

The famous kabbalist Rabbi Shlomo Alkebetz explains why: "A *rav* who teaches his *talmidim* conveys a part of his soul — in fact, he passes to them his very essence. If the *talmidim* are unified, the teachings and the character of those teachings achieve their fulfillment."

After my *rosh yeshivah*, Rav Leib Gurwicz, *zt"l*, passed away, one of the young rebbes of Gateshead Yeshivah decided to publish a collection of his teachings for the *sheloshim* (the thirtieth day after the person's passing, which marks a different stage of mourning).

He approached a number of *talmidim* and asked us to recall Rav Leib's Torah that had particularly made an impression on us. I was learning *Yoreh De'ah* at the time, but I had not discussed halachah much with Rav Leib, so I told him something I had heard from Rav Leib on a *Tosafos* in *Kiddushin*. Another *talmid* reported a new insight of Rav Leib's on halachah. Someone else may have reported a piece of *drush*, and another a lesson in *hashkafah*. By gathering each of the boys' memories of the Torah that stayed with them, a true sense of Rav Leib could be conveyed in the publication.

Rabbi Shlomo Alkebetz continues, "It is only if the *talmidim* are united that the teachings of the rebbe can continue, because it is obvious that each *talmid* captures only a specific area of the teachings of the rebbe. Each captures the area that matches his unique soul. Therefore only if all the *talmidim* come together can the teachings of the rebbe cross the generations."

Rabbi Akiva was known for one teaching above all others:

"*V'ahavta l'rei'acha kamocha* — You shall love your neighbor like yourself." This was reflected in the way he organized his *talmidim*: "Rabbi Akiva had twelve thousand pairs of *talmidim*" — not twenty-four thousand individuals, but *chavrusos*, pairs, *chaveirim*.

However, they did not give *kavod* to one another. The Maharsha says that the Gemara is referring to *kavod haTorah*. They did not respect or value each other's learning. Even today one can sometimes hear a boy in yeshivah say about another boy, "What does he know? I could put him in my pocket."

Someone who thinks like that, though, has failed to grasp an essential part — perhaps the essential part — of *Klal Yisrael*. If you fail to respect or value someone else's learning, not only are you saying that he does not shine in Torah, but you are essentially saying that you do not shine either. You may know more than someone else, but, as Rabbi Shlomo Alkebetz says, each *talmid* captures only a fraction of the rebbe. Your fraction may be a large one, but it requires all the fractions to complete the whole.

The *talmidim* of Rabbi Akiva died specifically between Pesach and Shavuos because this is the time more than any other that recalls the essential Jewish achievement of *"k'ish echad b'lev echad* — like one man with one heart." It was then that all the different Jews with their unique insights and contributions combined to start the Torah's journey from generation to generation. If they could not, or would not, realize this, they could not be the next link in the chain of the Torah's transmission.

Rav Aharon Kotler, *zt"l*, said that we recall the deaths of Rabbi Akiva's *talmidim* in order to recall the reason they died and uproot it from within ourselves. As Rabbi Yehudah HaNasi said, there are those who study *Chumash*, those who study Mishnah or Gemara or halachah or *aggadah*. There are many different types of Jews, and each one is essential for all the rest.

Shavuos

Finding the Right Place

(Unpublished)

It was a Pesach outing, and the place we had chosen to visit was about an hour and a half's drive. There were lots of good reasons for choosing this particular town. A large exhibition had been opened showing its early origins as a Viking settlement, and the tourist information office assured us that seeing it was a "must." There was also the Railway Museum and plenty of other things to keep day-trippers fully occupied.

There was also a good reason for not choosing this town. In 1086, William the Conqueror constructed a large mound on the banks of the River Ouse and built a wooden castle at the top. Just over one hundred years later, amid riots in York, a group of Jews took refuge in the tower, which was burned to the ground.

A gruesome legend exists among the locals about this incident. Apparently, the reddish vein running through the brickwork on the outside of the tower was "dyed" by the blood of the Jewish victims as they were mercilessly slaughtered. Actually, the Jews were compelled to kill themselves and died *al kiddush Hashem*, sanctifying Hashem's Name, rather than face the baying mob that awaited them outside the tower. Among the martyrs were *rabbanim* who wrote part of the Gemara's commentary of *Tosafos*.

We decided in the end we would go to York, and our car journey took us exactly to the spot where Clifford's Tower stands. We mounted the hill to the entrance and wandered around inside. To this day, there is a rabbinic ban on sleeping in York overnight, and a plaque declares that this was the place where the city's Jews died on that night in 1190. As I walked with my family around what is now a round stone tower, I remembered something I once heard from Rav Moshe Schwab, *zt"l*. "A place has to have a *mazal*! There are plenty of places where Jews settled, but their communities failed and disappeared. Maybe," he said, "the reason that Gateshead has succeeded is because it is not too far from York."

It might be in the merit of those *Ba'alei Tosafos* as well as their proximity that Gateshead became a capital of Torah.

The holy Alshich quotes an astonishing *midrash* that speaks of Moshe's attempts to save the Jewish people after they made the golden calf: "Almighty, the situation is like a father who had a very handsome son. The father bought him a shop in the middle of a busy market where he set him up in business selling perfume. The market was full of immoral non-Jewish girls. Youth played its part, the perfume played its part, and the place played its part. Eventually the young man went astray. The father is You, Hashem. The handsome young son is the Jewish people, and the place is Egypt. That is why the Jewish people came to make the golden calf."

Moshe's appeal was a claim that it was not their fault. The place is everything!

In the story of *Rus*, Elimelech, Machlon, and Kilyon die. The Alshich says that ultimately the reason was because they left the Land of Israel. The first verse of the megillah tells of the famine and that "a man and his family went to temporarily stay in the land of Moav." The second verse concludes with the words "And they came to the land of Moav, and they were there." The Alshich puz-

Finding the Right Place

zles over these words. If they came to the land of Moav, where else could they be?

The second verse tells us who the man and his family were. Of course, instead of writing "a man" in the first verse, it could have told us who he was right away. The Alshich explains that in fleeing the land at a time of famine Elimelech had not actually done anything wrong. In fact, Hashem had sent the famine precisely to provoke the Jewish people to leave.

Initially they went from place to place, not putting down roots anywhere. This is hinted at in the first verse, when it says that they came to "stay in the fields of Moav." The word *fields* in Hebrew is a euphemism for a city. The "man" stayed in the "cities." The plural form indicates that he never stayed long in one place so as not to become too attached to that place and subsequently less attached to the Land of Israel.

But by the end of the second verse it reports that they "came to the fields of Moav and they *were* there." Now they put down roots. For someone as great as Elimelech to cut himself off from the holiest place on earth was an unforgivable sin. His identity is not revealed in the first verse, where his motives were correct. When the second verse discloses that he had changed his intention to return, it no longer conceals who he was.

The consequences for someone on his spiritual level were immediate. The next verse says, "And Elimelech died."

Once, when my wife and I were first married, we were waiting at Ben-Gurion Airport for a plane to London. The flight was delayed by four hours, and we found ourselves sitting opposite a lady with a young child. My wife and she began to chat, and it turned out that she was the daughter-in-law of one of my rebbes, Rav Alter Halpern, *zt"l*, who was the *rosh kollel* of Schneider's Kollel in London.

She told us that when she and her husband married they had settled in Israel. After a few years, their financial situation was such that they could not stay. They decided to come back to London, find a job, and buy a house. After a while, when they had saved enough and their property had appreciated sufficiently in value, they would return and buy an apartment outright. This would mean that they could live in Israel and would never have to think of leaving again. She told us that the plan was working well and then added an interesting comment. "The house we have is a mess. It needs all sorts of improvements. My husband wants to go ahead and carry out the work, but I won't let him do it."

I asked her why not, and she replied, "Because then it will stop being a house and become a home!"

Elimelech chose the wrong place to make his home, and for a Jew that is a mistake. The place is everything.

When Na'ami decided to return to Eretz Yisrael, and Orpah returned to her old life, Rus explained why she had decided to stay with Na'ami. "Rus said, 'Do not press me to leave you and go away from you. Where you go, I will go. Where you sleep, I will sleep. Your people will be my people, and your God will be my God. Where you die, I will die, and there I will be buried...'" (*Rus* 1:15).

Rav Yitzchak Eizik Sher, zt"l, the *rosh yeshivah* of Slabodka, questions these words. He says that surely they reveal what Rus's ultimate motive was for wanting to become a Jew. Rus loved Na'ami and couldn't bear to be parted from her!

The Gemara (*Yevamos* 24) lists motivations that invalidate a potential convert. One of these is if they want to become Jewish precisely because of a Jew. The motive behind a conversion has to be because a candidate wants a relationship with Hashem, not with one of His people.

Rav Yitzchak Eizik answers his question by explaining that Rus's attachment to Na'ami was not motivated by the pleasure of being close to a unique human being and a saint. It was because she realized that only by clinging to such people could she learn how to attach herself to Hashem.

Finding the Right Place

Tzaddikim are by definition individuals who have succeeded in becoming close to the *Ribbono shel Olam*. The way they walk is an expression of that relationship. The Torah expects us to speak about Torah even as we walk along the streets, as it says, "*u'velechtecha vaderech* — when you walk along the road [speak words of Torah]." Sleeping, too, involves preparation, and often a tzaddik reviews his performance as a Jew that day before saying the Shema and *HaMapil* prayers. Rus wanted to learn all of this, and that is why she wanted to stay close to Na'ami — because it would allow her to become close to Hashem.

The city of Liverpool once had a *rav*, Rav Plitnick, *zt"l*, who was known as a tzaddik. A non-Jewish man in Liverpool wanted to convert, and he approached Rav Plitnick.

The universal practice in England is that all conversions are carried out by the London Beth Din. The man eventually started to learn with the rabbi and occasionally would be summoned to London so his progress could be assessed.

On these occasions the *beis din* went much further than the halachah demands in "pushing away a convert." They actually mocked and ridiculed him. But eventually the man was converted and joined the Jewish people.

After his conversion the London Beth Din again summoned him to appear before them. This was highly unusual. When he stood before the judges, they said to him, "We are a court and as such do not have to explain our actions. In your case, though, we felt we had to make an exception. You are aware that we treated you very badly." The Jew obviously agreed, but whether he vocalized his agreement I never knew. The judges said, "You see, you are a *talmid* of Rabbi Plitnick, and Rabbi Plitnick is a tzaddik. We wanted you to realize that not all Jews, and not even all religious Jews, are tzaddikim."

The only way a Jew can build that relationship is by seeking out a place that has *mazal* and where he or she can find tzaddikim and learn from them. Ultimately, though, a Jew has to seek a relationship with Hashem.

Elimelech's mistake was to leave a place — *the* place — where tzaddikim are to be found. Rus's brilliance was in realizing that she could succeed only by going to this place where she could find tzaddikim to emulate. One went down and the other up.

The sixth chapter of *Avos* tells the story of Rabbi Yosei ben Kisma: "Once I was walking along the road when I came upon a man, and he greeted me with '*Shalom,*' and I replied to him, '*Shalom.*' He said to me, 'Rebbe where do you come from?' I replied to him, 'From a city great in rabbis and scribes.' He said to me, 'Rebbe, if you agree to move to [our city], I will give you thousands and thousands of gold dinars and jewels and pearls.' I replied, 'Even if you were to give me all the gold in the world, I wouldn't stay anywhere except in a place of Torah.' "

Rav Chaim of Volozhin says that the man whom Rabbi Yosei ben Kisma met was Eliyahu HaNavi. He had come to tempt Rabbi Yosei with this offer because Rabbi Yosei was "walking along the road." He had left his city of Torah, and that process itself could be the start of a longer journey to a different place without *mazal* and without Torah. This is precisely what happened to Elimelech. But, unlike Elimelech, Rabbi Yosei ben Kisma saw the danger and immediately resolved to return to his city.

As Rav Moshe Schwab pointed out, a place needs *mazal*. *Mazal* for *Klal Yisrael* is generated when they stay firmly rooted in places where they can learn from tzaddikim how to come close to Hashem.

Tishah B'Av

Even Still

(Hamodia)

At least twice a year a Jew's memories turn to an event whose memory haunts and pains us still. Secular Jews created a specific day for the collective memory. They called it "*Yom HaSho'ah*," Holocaust Day. Religious Jews saw a clear link between this catastrophe and all the other catastrophes of Jewish history. Tishah B'Av acquired a new set of lamentations.

I am writing this article the day after I addressed a synagogue congregation in London. Since my topic was "Why Do Bad Things Happen to Good People?" questions about the Holocaust became inevitable. The questioner was not a religious Jew, and he was baffled by those who were. "The majority of Jews who were killed in the Holocaust were religious," he said. "How is it that they are still religious?"

He was correct. The center of the chassidic and yeshivah world burned fiercely. Still, they survived the flames and rebuilt and renewed themselves. It is not only how we remember that is different from our secular brothers and sisters, but what we choose to recall that is different.

When the Jewish people approach the month of Av, we come to the source of the first link in the chain of those Jewish catastrophes. Tishah B'Av is when the spies brought back their report, which condemned the Land of Israel. In so doing, they caused the

Jewish people to shed so many tears that if they could have been gathered together they would have formed a sea.

The Ramban wonders why the Torah tells us in *Mattos-Masei* of the forty-two journeys of *Klal Yisrael*. He quotes *Moreh Nevuchim*, whose words strike an eerie familiarity in our own days.

Those Jews who lived through the events of the Exodus could testify to a catalogue of miracles. In the future, though, people would claim that it never happened. Perhaps the Jews spent time in populated areas of the desert where they could have obtained food from Arabs. Perhaps the Jews had wandered to oases where there were plentiful supplies of water. The Torah therefore pinpoints their camping sites, desolate places totally unable to supply them with anything.

The Ramban goes on to explain that the Torah's recording of the Jewish people's journeys could not be in order to demonstrate the Jewish people's faithfulness to the instructions of Hashem. That point was already demonstrated in *Beha'aloscha*, when the verse testifies, "According to the word of Hashem they traveled, and according to the word of Hashem they camped."

On this verse the Ramban says something that explains how it is that religious Jews have kept moving from place to place and on journey to journey despite the difficulties they faced.

"Even if the cloud tarried somewhere for a long time," says the Ramban, "and that place was very unpleasant in the eyes of the Jewish people, although they longed very much to move away from there, even then they did not budge from Hashem's command.... Sometimes they had just unpacked their wagons and set up homes and started to settle down when the cloud moved off. They had to undo all of their work and repack. Even still, they followed."

Rav Eliyahu Dessler questions why Hashem did that to them. It seems as though He was mocking them. He answers that for the Jewish people to move on through history they would have to be conditioned to realize that sometimes, for reasons we might not be

Even Still

able to see, things would get tough and the road would become very rocky.

It is that phrase, "even still," which troubles our secular brothers and sisters. How can we carry on with our loyalty to Torah and mitzvos? How can we even continue being loyal to Hashem — even still?

The answer is that we have absolute faith that even if we can't see the journey's end we will get there. And when we look back along the road we have traveled, we will understand, not only the stopping places with names like New York, London, and Prague, but even the ones called Treblinka and Auschwitz.

During the 1930s the trickle of Jews fleeing Germany turned into a flood. The United Kingdom opened its doors to those who possessed a useful skill that the country could use. Refugees were known by the pejorative "refu-Jews." When war broke out, thousands of such Jewish souls became officially categorized as "enemy aliens." The government had them temporarily shipped off to the Isle of Man, off England's west coast. Eventually it was decided to send them to Australia.

England was losing thousands of tons of its merchant fleet every week to German U-boat packs, and vessels and sailors were very precious. A ship was eventually found to bring the refugees to Australia. It was called the *Dunera*.

Finding a crew proved more difficult. Someone came up with an unusual idea. England's prisons contained many sailors. Some of them had committed terrible crimes, and their sentences were very long. If they would volunteer to crew the *Dunera*, they might receive a pardon. This was promptly arranged, and those poor Jewish souls, many of whom had lost wives and children, set sail for Australia.

Two days into the voyage the crew went berserk and robbed their passengers of everything they possessed. Watches and jewelry were ripped from terrified hands. Suitcases were ransacked and valuables stolen, and the rest was thrown into the sea. Those poor souls, who had already suffered so much, were left with nothing in the world other than the clothes on their backs.

One can easily imagine the anguish and frustration they must have felt as they stood at the foot of the gangplank, having finally arrived in Australia. After all that has happened to us, why did Hashem have to allow that, too?

It took many years for that question to be answered. Someone was browsing in a bookstore when he discovered the journal of a U-boat captain. The submariner recounted that one day he was sailing underwater in the Atlantic when he ordered the periscope raised. As he gazed through the eyepiece, he saw a British merchant ship on the horizon. It was the *Dunera*.

Swiveling the periscope 360 degrees, he discovered no escorting warships. A plump and easy target. He ordered a torpedo fired at the ship, but after a few seconds there was no sound of an explosion. The torpedo must have missed.

He raised the periscope a second time to take new bearings, and indeed the ship was sailing along, ignorant of the fact that it was being attacked. Then the captain became confused. Floating in the water was lots of debris. He could see suitcases bobbing up and down. That is what he often saw after he had hit a ship. He ordered the U-boat to the surface, and some of his crew grabbed some of the floating luggage. This was taken below and opened.

The Nazi sailors were horrified to see what was inside. Among assorted clothes were books — German books! German Jews read German books, Goethe and Kant and others. The German captain, though, came to a different conclusion. This ship was carrying German prisoners of war! The captain radioed back to the German admiralty to relay what he had discovered and received an order to escort the *Dunera* on its journey to Australia. It should also signal to other Axis submarines not to attack.

I told this story in a *shiur* in yeshivah recently, and one of my

Even Still

talmidim told me his grandfather had been on the *Dunera*. It was the culmination of a flight from Germany to England and then imprisonment. Despite the fact that he neither wanted to be there nor understood why he was there, he carried on as a Jew must — even still. A long time would have to pass before he could see that what looked like the final straw — the final indignity of losing his last precious possessions — was exactly what Hashem had designed to save his life. Eventually Hashem would allow him to see and understand that this had been part of the plan.

Chazal say that when Mashiach comes Tishah B'Av will be the greatest *yom tov* of all. It seems impossible for us to envision this day, which marks so much suffering, transformed into a time of rejoicing. But it seemed just as impossible to the Jews who stepped off the *Dunera* to see that voyage as anything but a tragedy. Once the truth was known, though, an ordeal that could only have produced painful and bitter memories would now be one that would produce a knowing smile and perhaps a tear of gratitude.

As the Jewish people approach the very last leg of our journey, we can be proud that we were willing to follow where Hashem led us, even still. We can also be confident that very soon we will come to the journey's end, and the bitterest of memories will be replaced by tears of gratitude.

Glossary

Acharei Mos — A portion of the Torah found in Leviticus, ch. 16–18.

Adar — The sixth month of the Jewish year.

aggadah — Non-halachic material in the Talmud.

agunah (pl.: *agunos*) — A woman whose husband has left her without a halachically valid divorce contract.

akeidas Yitzchak — The binding of Isaac on the altar, one of the ten trials of his father, Abraham.

al kiddush Hashem — For the sanctification of God's Name.

aliyah — Literally, "ascent"; immigration to the Land of Israel.

aravos — Willow branches; one of the four species waved on the festival of Sukkos.

aron kodesh — Holy ark, where the Torah scroll is kept in synagogue.

askan (pl.: *askanim*) — Community activist.

Av — The eleventh month of the Jewish year.

Avodah Zarah — Tractate of the Talmud.

avodas Hashem — Service of God.

Avos — The patriarchs, Abraham, Isaac, and Jacob.

ba'alei mussar — Masters of the ethical teachings of the Torah.

ba'al habayis (pl.: *ba'alei batim*) — Householder; layman.

ba'al teshuvah — Penitent; Jew who has returned to observant Judaism.

bachur (pl.: *bachurim*) — Young man, usually referring to a boy who is learning in YESHIVAH.

bar mitzvah — Jewish male who reaches the age of thirteen, when he becomes responsible for his actions and obligated to fulfill the commandments of the Torah as an adult; celebration for this occasion.

bas — Daughter.

bas mitzvah — Jewish female who reaches the age of twelve, when she becomes responsible for her actions and obligated to fulfill the commandments of the Torah as an adult; celebration for this occasion.

bashert — Soulmate.

batim — Cases in which the TEFILLIN parchments are kept.

Bava Basra — Tractate of the Talmud.

Bava Kama — Tractate of the Talmud.

Bava Metzia — Tractate of the Talmud.

b'chol dor vador — "In every generation," a well-known phrase from the Passover HAGGADAH.

Bechukosai — Torah portion found in Leviticus, ch. 25–27.

Beha'aloscha — Torah portion found in Numbers, ch. 8–12.

beis din — Jewish court of law.

Beis HaMikdash — Holy Temple in Jerusalem.

beis midrash — Study hall where Torah is learned.

Bemidbar — Numbers; portion of the Torah found in Numbers, ch. 1–4.

berachah — Blessing.

Berachos — Tractate of the Talmud.

Bereishis — Genesis; portion of the Torah found in Genesis, ch. 1–6.

bimah — Platform or dais; the raised platform from which the Torah is read in synagogue.

birkas kohanim — Blessing of the priests.

Glossary

bnei Torah — Literally, "sons of Torah"; learned, observant Jews.

bris milah — Circumcision.

Chanukah — Festival of Lights, when we commemorate the Hasmoneans' victory over the Greeks.

chareidi (pl.: *chareidim*) — Religious Orthodox Jew.

chasan — Bridegroom.

Chashmonaim — Hasmoneans.

chassid (pl.: *chassidim*) — A follower of CHASSIDUS.

chassidic — Relating to CHASSIDUS.

Chassidus — Movement founded in Poland around 1750 in opposition to ritual laxity and lack of feeling in the service of Hashem.

chaveirim — Friends.

Chayei Sarah — Torah portion found in Genesis, ch. 23–25.

Chazal — Acronym for "*chachomim zichronam livrachah* — our Sages of blessed memory," referring to the Talmudic Sages.

chazzan — Cantor.

cheder — Religious boys' elementary school.

chesed — Kind-heartedness; giving to others.

chevrah kaddisha — Burial society.

chiddush (pl.: *chiddushim*) — New insight in Torah.

chillul Hashem — Profanation of God's Name.

Chumash — Pentateuch; the five books of the Torah.

chutz la'aretz — Any place outside the Land of Israel.

da'as Torah — Knowledge of Torah.

daven — Pray.

dayan (pl.: *dayanim*) — Judge.

derech — Way; approach.

Devarim — Deuteronomy; portion of the Torah found in Deuteronomy, ch. 1–3.

divrei Torah — Words of Torah.

drashah — Speech.

drush — Homiletic exposition.

Edom — Descendants of Esau.

emunah — Faith.

Eretz Yisrael — Land of Israel.

erev — Eve.

esrog — Citron; one of the four species on which a special blessing is made on the festival of SUKKOS.

frum — Religious.

frumkeit — Religiosity.

gadol (pl.: *gedolim*) — Great man; leader of the Jewish people.

gadol hador (pl.: *gedolei hador*) — Leader of the generation; a great man.

galus — Exile.

Gemara — Talmud, usually referring to the Babylonian Talmud, written in the third through sixth centuries.

Ha'azinu — Torah portion found in Deuteronomy, ch. 32.

hachnasas orchim — Hospitality.

hadasim — Myrtle branches; one of the four species waved on the festival of SUKKOS.

Haggadah — Book containing the service for the night of Passover.

HaKadosh Baruch Hu — The Holy One, blessed is He; God.

halachah — Jewish law.

Har Sinai — Mount Sinai, where the Torah was given to the Jewish people.

Glossary

Hashem — Literally, "the Name"; God.

hashkafah — Torah outlook and values.

Haskalah — Enlightenment.

im yirtzeh Hashem — If God wills it.

kallah — Bride.

kareis — Divine punishment that brings childlessness, early death, and being cut off from God.

kashrus — Dietary laws.

Kedoshim — Torah portion found in Leviticus, ch. 19–21.

kedushah — Sanctity; holiness.

Ki Sissa — Torah portion found in Exodus, ch. 30–35.

kiddush — Food served on Shabbos day, before lunch, usually in synagogue, either in celebration of a mitzvah such as an engagement or to commemorate the death of a loved one, and KIDDUSH is recited.

Kiddush — Blessing said over wine at the beginning of Sabbath and festival meals.

Kiddushin — Tractate of the Talmud.

kiruv rechokim — Outreach.

kittel — White robe-like garment worn on YOM KIPPUR and at the Passover SEDER.

Klal Yisrael — The Jewish people.

Kli Yakar — Rabbi Shlomo Efraim of Luntshitz, a foremost commentator on the CHUMASH (1550–1619).

Koheles — Ecclesiastes.

kohen (pl.: *kohanim*) — Priests, descended from Aaron, brother of Moses.

kohen gadol — High priest.

kollel — Group of married men who learn Torah together, following the same approach or system, usually receiving some sort of payment.

Kosel — The Western Wall in Jerusalem, the only remnant of the Holy Temple.

lashon hakodesh — Literally, "the holy tongue"; language in which the Torah is written made up of the letters of the Hebrew alphabet.

levayah — Funeral.

lulav (pl.: *lulavim*) — Palm branch; one of the four species waved on the festival of SUKKOS; commonly used to refer to three of the four species.

ma'ariv — Evening prayer service.

machzor — Holiday prayer book.

maggid — Itinerant lecturer.

Maharal — Acronym for Rabbi Yehudah Loewe of Prague. He lived in the sixteenth century.

Makkos — Tractate of the Talmud.

mashgiach — Supervisor; the spiritual dean of a YESHIVAH.

Mashiach — The Messiah.

mattan Torah — The giving of the Torah on Mount Sinai.

Mattos-Masei — Torah portions found in Numbers, ch. 30–36.

mazal (pl.: *mazalos*) — Fortune; constellation.

mechanchim — Educators.

mechitzah — Partition separating women and men's sections in synagogue.

megillah — One of the five scrolls found in Writings, read at certain times of the Jewish year — Song of Songs, Ruth, Lamentations, Ecclesiastes, and Esther.

Glossary

Megillah — Tractate of the Talmud.

Menorah — Seven-branched candelabra that was kindled in the Temple.

middah (pl.: *middos*) — Character trait.

Midrash — Collection of homiletic interpretations of the Scriptures by the Sages of the MISHNAH.

mikveh — Ritual bath.

minchah — Afternoon prayer service.

minyan (pl.: *minyanim*) — Quorum; communal prayer.

Mishkan — Tabernacle.

Mishlei — Proverbs.

Mishnah — First codification of the Oral Torah, compiled by Rabbi Yehudah HaNasi and the TANNAIM in the third century C.E.

Mishpatim — Portion of the Torah found in Exodus, ch. 21–25.

Mitzrayim — Egypt.

mitzvah (pl.: *mitzvos*) — Commandment.

Moreh Nevuchim — Guide for the Perplexed, a philosophical treatise written by Maimonides.

motza'ei Shabbos — Saturday night.

mussar seder — Designated hour of a YESHIVAH student's schedule to study ethics.

nachas — Pleasure; usually the pleasure felt at seeing a child or student's achievements.

Naso — Torah portion found in Numbers, ch. 4–8.

nazir — Nazirite; someone who has taken a vow to abstain from wine and getting his hair cut.

nebbech — Pitiful.

Nedarim — Tractate of Talmud.

neshamah (pl.: *neshamos*) — Soul.

Noach — Torah portion found in Genesis.

Olam Haba — World to Come.

parashah (pl.: *parshiyos*) — Torah portion from the Pentateuch.

Pesach — Passover, when we commemorate the Exodus from Egypt.

peshat — Straightforward interpretation; plain meaning.

peyos — Sidelocks.

pidyon haben — Redemption of the firstborn.

Pinchas — Torah portion found in Numbers, ch. 22–29.

poskim — Rabbinic authorities on Jewish law.

Purim — Holiday on which we commemorate our victory over Haman in Persia in the time of Mordechai and Esther.

rabbanim — Rabbis.

Rambam — Maimonides; Rabbi Moses the son of Maimon (1135–1204), one of Judaism's leading Torah authorities and philosophers.

Ramban — Nachmanides; Rabbi Moses the son of Nachman (1194–1270), one of the leading commentators on the Torah and Talmud.

Ramchal — Rabbi Moshe Chaim Luzzato, author of such works as *Mesilas Yesharim* and one of the foremost mystical thinkers.

rasha (pl.: *reshaim*) — Wicked person.

Rashi — Rabbi Shlomo Yitzchaki, one of the foremost commentators on the Torah and Talmud (1040–1105).

rav — Rabbi.

rebbe — Male teacher of Torah subjects.

Rebbe — Leader of a CHASSIDIC sect.

Glossary

rebbetzin — Wife of a rabbi.

Ribbono shel Olam — Master of the universe; God.

Rosh Chodesh — The New Moon; the first day of a Hebrew month.

Rosh HaShanah — The Jewish New Year, when the Jewish people are judged for their actions over the past year.

rosh kollel — Head of a KOLLEL.

rosh yeshivah (pl.: *roshei yeshivah*) — Head of a YESHIVAH.

Rus — Ruth.

Saba — Grandfather

Sanhedrin — The seventy-one member legislative body that had jurisdiction over all religious matters in the Land of Israel during the Second Temple period.

seder — Ritual meal held on the first night (and on the second night outside Israel) of Passover.

Sefardic — Jew of Spanish or Middle Eastern descent.

sefer (pl.: *sefarim*) — Book; holy book.

sefer Torah — Torah scroll.

sefiras ha'omer — Period between PESACH and SHAVUOS when we count the days leading to Shavuos and mourn the passing of the twenty-four thousand disciples of the Talmudic Sage Rabbi Akiva.

seudah — Meal; meal eaten in celebration of the fulfillment of a MITZVAH.

seudah shelishis — Third meal eaten on the Sabbath.

Shabbaton — Weekend get-together devoted to spiritual inspiration.

Shabbos — Sabbath.

shacharis — Morning prayer service.

shalom zachor — Celebration of a newborn son on the first Friday night after his birth.

Shavuos — Festival when we commemorate the giving of the Torah.

Shechinah — Divine Presence.

shechitah — Ritual slaughter.

Shelach — Torah portion found in Numbers, ch. 13–15.

Shema — Prayer in which one affirms one's faith and God's unity.

Shemini — Torah portion found in Leviticus, ch. 9–11.

Shemoneh Esreh — Literally, "eighteen"; central prayer recited three times daily.

Shemos — Exodus; Torah portion found in Exodus, ch. 1–5.

sheva berachos — Literally, "seven blessings"; the seven blessings added to the Grace after Meals recited in the presence of the bride and groom at their wedding and during the seven days following; the festive meals at which these blessings are recited.

shidduch (pl.: *shidduchim*) — Date; person one is dating.

shiur (pl. *shiurim*) — Torah lecture.

shivah — Seven days of mourning after a mother, father, or child has passed away.

shlita — Acronym for "*sheyichyeh l'chaim tovim va'aruchim amen* — may he live a good, long life"; often said after mention of a TZADDIK's name.

shmuess — Talk given by a REBBE in YESHIVAH, usually on ethics or Torah values.

shofar — Ram's horn blown during High Holiday services.

shul — Synagogue.

Shulchan Aruch — Code of Jewish Law.

Shushan — Capital city of ancient Persia, featured in the Story of PURIM.

siddur — Prayer book.

Glossary

simchah — Joy; celebration.

siyum — Celebration of the completion of a portion of the Written or Oral Torah.

Sotah — Tractate of the Talmud.

Sukkos — Festival of Tabernacles, when we sit in huts with roofs of branches to commemorate how God protected us in the desert after we left Egypt by providing booths to dwell in.

taharas hamishpachah — Laws of family purity.

tallis (pl.: *talleisim*) — Prayer shawl.

talmid (pl.: *talmidim*) — Student of Torah.

talmid chacham (pl.: *talmidei chachomim*) — Torah scholar.

Talmud Torah — Jewish elementary boys' school.

Tanna (pl.: *Tannaim*) — Mishnaic Sage.

tav — Last letter of the Hebrew alphabet.

tefillah (pl.: *tefillos*) — Prayer.

tefillin — Phylacteries.

tekiah, shevarim, teruah — Three different types of blasts sounded with the SHOFAR on ROSH HASHANAH, the first a long continuous blast, the second three short blasts, the third nine staccato blasts.

teshuvah — Repentance.

tichel — Head scarf worn by a married woman.

Tishah B'Av — Fast of the Ninth of Av, when we mourn the destruction of the two Temples and the other tragedies that befell the Jewish people.

Tishrei — The first month of the Jewish year.

Tosafos — One of the foremost commentaries on the Talmud.

treif — Non-kosher.

tumah — Impure.

tzaddik (pl.: *tzaddikim*) — Righteous man.

tzidkus — Righteousness.

tznius — Modesty.

Va'eschanan — Torah portion found in Deuteronomy, ch. 4–7.

Vayakhel — Torah portion found in Exodus, ch. 35–38.

Vayechi — Torah portion found in Genesis, ch. 47–50.

Vayeira — Torah portion found in Genesis, ch. 18–22.

Vayeishev — Torah portion found in Genesis, ch. 37–40.

Vayigash — Torah portion found in Genesis, ch. 44–47.

Vayikra — Leviticus; Torah portion found in Leviticus, ch. 1–5.

Vayishlach — Torah portion found in Genesis, ch. 32–36.

vidui — The confession recited on YOM KIPPUR and before one's death, in which one admits his sins in order to repent.

Yechezkel — Ezekiel.

yemach shemo — May his name be erased.

Yerushalayim — Jerusalem.

yeshivah (pl.: *yeshivos*) — Torah institution.

yetzer hara — Evil inclination.

yetzias Mitzrayim — Exodus from Egypt.

Yevamos — Tractate of the Talmud.

Yid — Jew.

Yiddishkeit — Judaism.

Yirmeyahu — Jeremiah.

yom hadin — Day of judgment, usually referring to ROSH HASHANAH.

Yom Kippur — Day of Atonement, when we fast and spend all day in prayer, pleading with God to forgive our sins and give us a

Glossary

good verdict for the coming year.

Yoreh Deah — Section of the SHULCHAN ARUCH that includes the laws of KASHRUS and TAHARAS HAMISHPACHAH.

yud — Tenth letter of the Hebrew alphabet.

zeidy — Grandfather.

Zohar — The primary text of Kabbalah, compiled by the Talmudic Sage Rabbi Shimon bar Yochai and his disciples.

zt"l — Acronym for *zecher tzaddik livrachah* — may the memory of this righteous person be blessed.

Photo: Mike Poloway

RABBI YEHUDAH YONAH RUBINSTEIN is probably the most sought after Jewish speaker in the UK. He regularly lectures in the United States, Gibraltar, South Africa, Israel, and Belgium. He is a broadcaster on the BBC and writes for *Hamodia* and *The Jewish Tribune*.

His educational activities span teaching in a *yeshivah gedolah* and a seminary for girls, as well as outreach. He received his rabbinical ordination from Gateshead Yeshivah.

thank you

Thank you so much for supporting the Simplicity Project launch! I am so grateful for all of your love and support and could not have done this without you.

xox Corie

Share the book on social media and be sure to tag me @corieclark and use the hashtag #simplicityproject
Tell your friends to grab their own copy at simplicityprojectbook.com
Submit a review to shop@corieclark.com